A DREAMSPEAKER CRU

VOLUME 6

The West Coast of Vancouver Island

INCLUDING BUNSBY ISLANDS & THE BROKEN GROUP

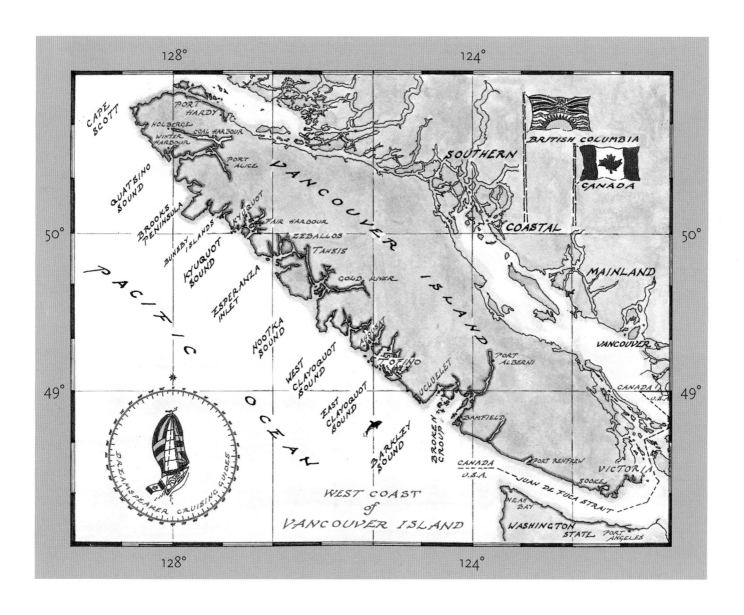

ANNE & LAURENCE YEADON-JONES

HARBOUR PUBLISHING

FEATURED DESTINATIONS

TABLE OF CONTENTS

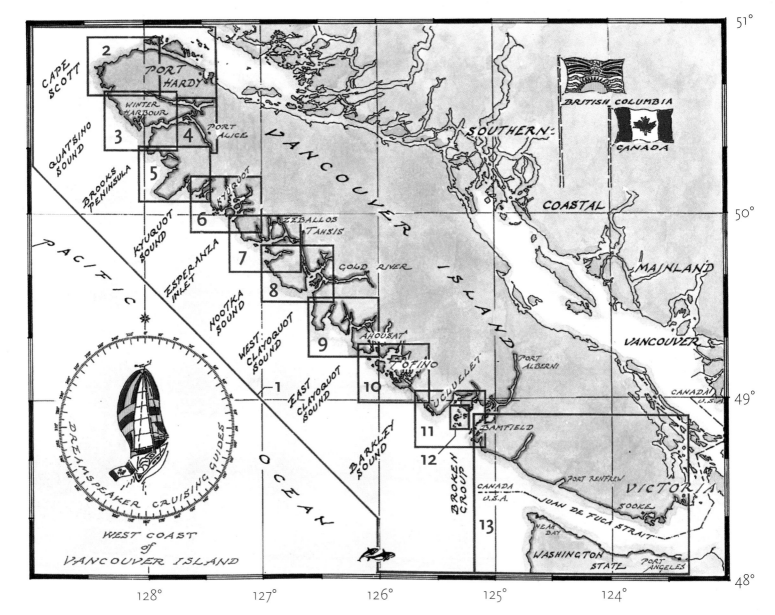

Dreamspeaker at anchor off Benson Island, Broken Group.

Grateful Appreciation to our Industry Support

Broadband Express; Marine Wireless Broadband Network: www.bbxpress.net
Corilair; Coastal Floatplane Service based in Campbell River: www.corilair.com
Canon Canada Ltd; Camera and Lenses: www.canon.com
Canadian Hydrographic Service (CHS); Charts and Nautical Publications:
www.charts.gc.ca
Cooper Boating Centre; Yacht Charter and Recreational Boating School:
www.cooperboating.com
HUB International Insurance Brokers; Specialist Marine Insurance Services: www.tos.boat@
hubinternational.com
Henshaw Inflatables Ltd; *Dreamspeaker's* Tender *Tink*, a Tinker Folding Rib: www.henshaw.co.uk
Leitch & McBride; Custom Sailmakers - North Vancouver: sbsdnw@aol.com
Sidney, Vancouver Island: msails@telus.net
Mustang Survival Ltd.; Marine Safety Apparel and PFD's:
www.mustangsurvival.com
Nautical Data International; Electronic Charts: www.digitalocean.ca
Nobeltec; Navigation Software by Jeppesen Marine: www.nobeltec.com

Acknowledgements

Bruce Jackman, Port McNeill Marine and Auto Parts Plus, for helping us progress beyond Port Hardy.
DFO-Small Craft Harbours and Port Alberni Port Authority, for their valuable assistance.
Marion and Rob, MY Office, for their steady support and quality service.
The West Coast communities, for their friendship and valuable local information.
Katrina and Neil, caretakers at Cougar Annie's Garden, Boat Basin Foundation.
The team at Harbour Publishing, Elsie and Steve Hulsizer, and Duart Snow.
Our family and friends, for their conviction that we would reach our intended destination.

Harbour Publishing Co. Ltd.
P.O. Box 219, Madeira Park, BC V0N 2H0
www.harbourpublishing.com

Edited by Duart Snow
Typeset by Martin Nichols
Printed and bound in China

THE CANADA COUNCIL FOR THE ARTS SINCE 1957 | LE CONSEIL DES ARTS DU CANADA DEPUIS 1957

BRITISH COLUMBIA ARTS COUNCIL
Supported by the Province of British Columbia

Harbour Publishing acknowledges financial support from the Government of Canada through the Book Publishing Industry Development Program and the Canada Council for the Arts, and from the Province of British Columbia through the British Columbia Arts Council and the Book Publisher's Tax Credit through the Ministry of Provincial Revenue.

Library and Archives Canada Cataloguing in Publication

Yeadon-Jones, Anne
    A Dreamspeaker cruising guide / Anne & Laurence Yeadon-Jones.—New, rev. 2nd ed.

Includes bibliographical references and index.
Contents: v. 1. The Gulf Islands and Vancouver Island, from Sooke to Nanaimo - v. 2.
    Desolation Sound & the Discovery Islands - v. 3. Vancouver, Howe Sound & the
    Sunshine Coast - v. 4. The San Juan Islands - v. 5. The Broughtons and Vancouver
    Island, Kelsey Bay to Port Hardy - v. 6. The west coast of Vancouver Island.
ISBN-10: 1-55017-402-9 (v. 1).–ISBN-13: 978-1-55017-402-1 (v. 1 : pbk.).–
ISBN-10: 1-55017-404-5 (v. 2).–ISBN-13: 978-1-55017-404-5 (v. 2 : pbk.).–
ISBN-10: 1-55017-397-9 (v. 3 : pbk.).–ISBN-13: 978-1-55017-397-0 (v. 3 : pbk.).–
ISBN-10: 1-55017-406-1 (v. 5 : pbk.).–ISBN-13: 978-1-55017-406-9 (v. 5 : pbk.).–
ISBN-13: 978-1-55017-445-8 (v. 6)

    1. Boats and boating–British Columbia–Guidebooks. 2. Boats and boating–
Washington (State)–San Juan Islands–Guidebooks. 3. British Columbia–
Guidebooks. 4. San Juan Islands (Wash.)–Guidebooks. I. Yeadon-Jones, Laurence II. Title.
FC3845.P2A3 2006   797.1'09711   C2005-907723-9

WE WOULD LIKE TO HEAR FROM YOU!

We hope you enjoy using Volume 6 of *A Dreamspeaker Cruising Guide*. We welcome your comment, suggestions, corrections and any ideas about what you would like to see in future editions of the guide. Please drop us a line at the address above (c/o Dreamspeaker) or send an e-mail via the authors' website, dreamspeaker.ca.

Caution: This book is meant to provide experienced boaters with cruising information about the waters covered. The suggestions offered are not all-inclusive and, due to the possibility of differences of interpretation, oversights and factual errors, none of the information contained in this book is warranted to be accurate or appropriate for any purpose other than the pursuit of great adventuring and memorable voyages. A Dreamspeaker Cruising Guide should be viewed as a guide only and not as a substitute for official government charts, tide and current tables, coast pilots, sailing directions and local notices to boaters.

FOREWORD

Welcome to the West Coast! As Anne and Laurence Yeadon-Jones point out in their Introduction to this volume of their *Dreamspeaker Cruising Guide* series, perhaps no stretch of Canada's Pacific coastline offers more challenges and thrills per nautical mile than the outer coast of Vancouver Island. Here, ocean swells, swiftly changing weather and strong winds, fog, and rock-studded shorelines test mariners' skills and self-reliance. But the rewards include myriad uncrowded anchorages, almost endless possibilities for getting "lost" in a place of one's own, and a sense of accomplishment big enough to last a lifetime.

Anne and Laurence bring the relaxed, intimate style of the *Dreamspeaker* guides to this rugged place, and make it seem a little less forbidding, a little less intimidating—an adventure within reach of the average cruiser. They aim to make us feel that, with preparation and care, we're capable of meeting the challenges and returning home safely…with some good stories, of course. The strength of the *Dreamspeaker* guides has always been their colourful illustrations of anchorages, harbours and shoreline features. Exquisitely detailed, with a hint of humour, they transport you to some inviting nook or cove in a way no chart or photo can. The entries for each region and destination open with clear, concise outlines of local piloting, anchoring and weather essentials, while the friendly, informative narrative sketches the character of each destination: local history, wildlife and attractions, and local knowledge about finding everything from groceries and ice cream to spectacular views and sunsets.

Whether you are planning your first cruise to the West Coast, choosing tonight's anchorage, or just imagining a voyage to this big, wild place, *Dreamspeaker Vol. 6* will bring your destination—or your dream—a little closer.

Duart Snow,
Past Editor
Pacific Yachting

To *Dreamspeaker, Tink,* the "Motley Crew," our publishers,
family, friends and the coastal communities who have all
made this series of guides possible.

The call of the West Coast—a sea lion issues a challenge to all.

Chapter 1

WEST COAST OF VANCOUVER ISLAND: AN INTRODUCTION

"Communications," fuel and provisions are accessible on the West Coast.

Chapter 1
WEST COAST OF VANCOUVER ISLAND

CUSTOMS

Canada Customs Ports of Entry

(1-888-226-7277 toll-free seven days a week, 24 hours a day).
Campbell River, Ucluelet, Victoria

Note: Bamfield is not a customs port of entry.

US Customs Ports of Entry
Port Angeles (360-457-4311)

Note: Neah Bay is not a customs port of entry, but boaters with valid I-68 forms or Nexus cards may phone in from here.

NO-SEWAGE-DISCHARGE AREAS

Currently there are no designated No-Sewage-Discharge Areas on the west coast of Vancouver Island. However, check pleasure craft sewage regulations annually. According to a BC Ministry of Environment website (www.env.gov.bc.ca/epd/epdpa/mpp/boat_sewage.html), Barkley Sound and Lemmens Inlet have been nominated by the province as no-discharge areas and are under federal review. Sewage pump-out stations are available in Tofino at 4th Street Wharf and Island West Fishing Resort.

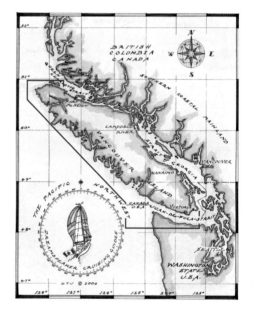

North to South: The chapters in this volume are linked from N to S, cruising with the prevailing summer NW winds and currents.

South to North: For cruisers travelling from S to N or who only have time to visit Barkley Sound and the Broken Group, Volume 6 works equally well. Start with Chapter 13—Juan de Fuca Strait and work forward from there.

Note: Customs regulations change frequently so it is wise to check with Canadian and US Customs on this point before planning your trip.

Vancouver Island, the largest island on the western edge of North America extends 500 km (300 miles) from top to toe and forms an integral part of British Columbia. Its mountainous backbone creates a natural breakwater to the Inside Passage, sheltering some of the world's finest cruising grounds.

Vancouver Island's western shoreline is usually referred to simply as the West Coast. With its rugged, rock-studded shoreline, relentlessly crashing ocean swells, miles of sandy beaches, variety of wildlife, and countless coves and bays, this coast presents one of the Pacific Northwest's most challenging and thrilling adventures. Magical, awe-inspiring, wild, forbidding and downright dangerous—the West Coast can be all of these. Cruising here demands a keen respect for the open Pacific Ocean, extra-diligent navigation, and care in timing tides and weather. Waiting for safe "weather windows" is critical to avoiding local hazards such as strong winds and fog, especially when rounding Cape Scott on Vancouver Island's northern tip, Cape Cook on the Brooks Peninsula, Estevan Point on Hesquiat Peninsula, and the long run of Juan de Fuca Strait. However, the distances between protected inlets are relatively short, allowing cruisers to spend each evening in a sheltered cove or bay, even if the wind is blowing hard outside.

This coastline is conveniently carved into five principal sounds, each with its own flavour and culture. Starting from the north, Quatsino Sound includes the communities of Winter Harbour, Coal Harbour and Port Alice. The Brooks Peninsula south of Quatsino was traditionally the dividing line between the Kwakwaka'wakw First Nations in the north and the Nuu-chah-nulth in the south. The area immediately south of the Brooks Peninsula includes the Bunsby Islands in Checleset Bay and the sheer fjords of Kyuquot Sound. Between Kyuquot Sound and Nootka Sound lie the busy commercial inlets of Esperanza, Zeballos and Tahsis.

In historic Nootka Sound, home of the Nuu-chah-nulth, British and Spanish explorers vied for control of the land and trade with the natives.

Internationally recognized Clayoquot Sound—the quintessential West Coast destination—offers sheltered waterways and tranquil inlets bordered by forested mountains, as well as Hot Springs Cove and bustling Tofino.

More open to the ocean than the sounds and inlets farther north, Barkley Sound is divided by Imperial Eagle Channel into the Broken Group of islands, islets, rocks and reefs, and the smaller Deer Group. Conveniently situated to the west is the lovely town of Ucluelet, and to the east, the welcoming village of Bamfield.

KEY DESTINATIONS–NORTH TO SOUTH—SERVICES

KEY   F. Fuel   M. Moorage   P. Provisions   Ms. Medical Services   Po. Post Office   C. Customs

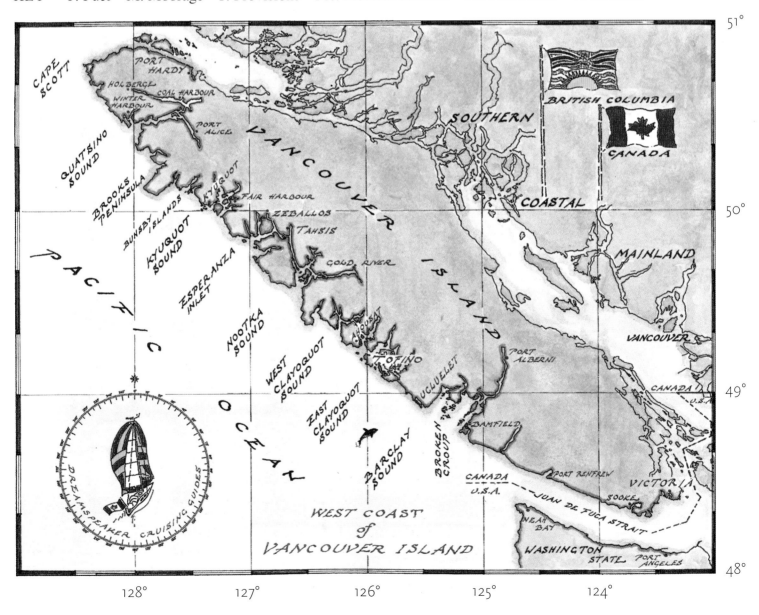

WEATHER, WIND, WAVES & FOG

An understanding of weather and its patterns is key to safe cruising on the west coast of Vancouver Island.

At the beginning of each chapter we list the VHF weather channels, the areas covered and reporting stations to listen for. In this volume, courtesy of Environment Canada, we illustrate a portion of the West Coast weather map that is pertinent to the west coast of Vancouver Island.

Weather and safe seafaring go hand in hand.

FORECAST TIMES

04.00, 10.30, 16.00 and 21.30. These times remain the same throughout the year.

WIND SPEEDS

These are given in knots and are the average winds expected over the open water.

Light Winds 0–10 knots

Moderate Winds 11–21 knots

Strong Winds 22–33 knots

Gale Force Winds 34–47 knots

Storm Force Winds 48–65 knots

Hurricane Winds 64 knots plus

CAUTIONARY NOTE

Both tide and current can be used to a boater's advantage, to speed up a passage. It is also important to appreciate how current interacts with wind—wind opposing current can create exceptionally rough seas.

W eather on the west coast of Vancouver Island differs significantly from the more moderate conditions of the Inside Passage and lower coastal mainland. The weather is a fundamental factor to be considered in planning of a voyage along this exposed coastline.

One major difference is the speed of changes in weather—monitoring forecasts and condition reports regularly between scheduled forecast times is essential in transiting safely to a protected anchorage when bad weather prevails. Environment Canada transmits weather from Tofino several times each day on Navtex. Navtex may be received where VHF weather forecasts cannot.

The Pacific high-pressure system by its presence—or absence—dictates the prevailing summer weather conditions on the West Coast.

If present, the Pacific High anchors itself off northern Vancouver Island, between Cape Scott and Cape St. James, and brings northwesterly winds, blue skies, and excellent sailing conditions. But don't be fooled—these northwesterlies can reach gale force as they blow unimpeded down the coast.

If the High is absent, SE to SW winds will march into the void, bringing overcast skies and the worst-case scenario, gale-force, or even storm-force winds and torrential rain. Then it's time to be snug in an anchorage with a good supply of books.

WAVES

The westerly ocean swell, always present in summer months, is not dangerous in itself and one soon grows accustomed to its motion. But when the swell becomes a wave with the potential to break, then it can be dangerous. Landing a dinghy or kayak on an exposed beach with a swell running can be a tricky task. However, for the cruising boater, it is the interaction of wind against current that can create sea conditions that pose a real threat.

An ebbing current against a NW wind at Nahwitti Bar is best avoided (see 2.1 Nahwitti Bar page 20). A strong afternoon westerly blowing against an ebbing current in Juan de Fuca Strait can give real meaning to rough seas: the short, steep chop makes for an uncomfortable, possibly dangerous ride in a small craft. In Scott Channel, a flooding current against a northwesterly wind—or an ebbing current against a southerly wind—will produce similar results. Plan ahead to avoid these situations.

FOG

On the West Coast fog forms regularly in the summer months. It tends to sit low in the sounds and hug the coast. During our research, we found that fog would burn off by midday as the wind strengthened. But offshore fog banks can drift onshore at any time and with remarkable speed—so be prepared with a backup plan. Fog is more prevalent south of Estevan Point.

WHEN TO GO

The weather window on the west coast of Vancouver Island can extend from late May to mid-September. Locals often refer to the month of August as "Fogust," but apart from fog, August often has the best weather record. The time to go will differ for every boater; your aim should be to allow adequate time to enjoy your planned destinations.

TIDES AND CURRENTS

This guide references the official *Canadian Tide and Current Tables—Volumes 5 and 6.*

TIDES

At the beginning of each chapter we indicate the tidal reference and secondary ports that lie within the chapter boundaries.

CURRENTS

At the beginning of each chapter we indicate if there are current reference stations and secondary stations within the chapter boundaries.

The West Coast does not have tidal rapids similar to those of the Inside Passage, but it is still imperative to understand tide and its height at any time—as well as the current, its direction, velocity and time of slack water.

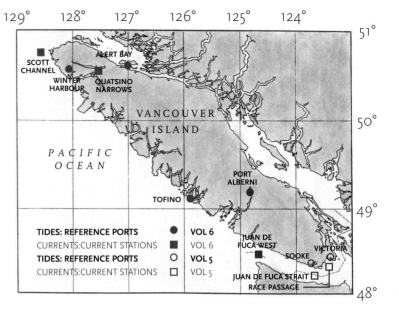

TIDES: REFERENCE PORTS	●	VOL 6
CURRENTS:CURRENT STATIONS	■	VOL 6
TIDES: REFERENCE PORTS	○	VOL 5
CURRENTS:CURRENT STATIONS	□	VOL 5

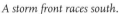

A storm front races south.

Morning calm.

Sunset after the rain.

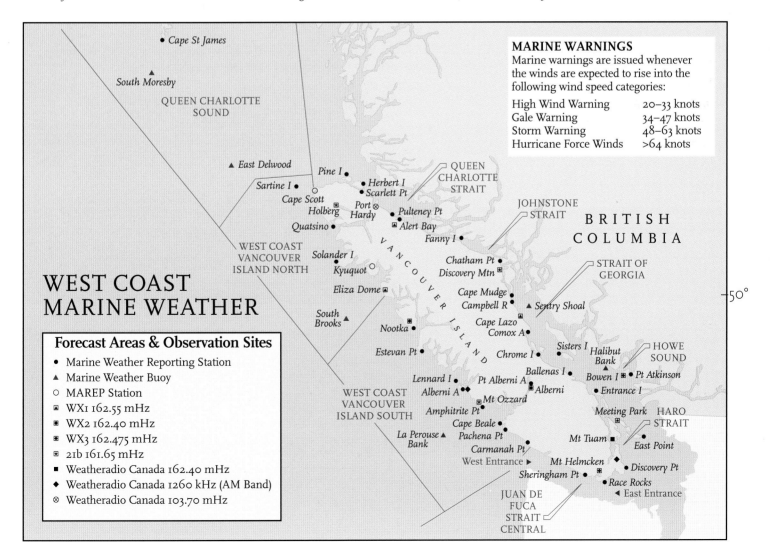

MARINE WARNINGS
Marine warnings are issued whenever the winds are expected to rise into the following wind speed categories:

High Wind Warning	20–33 knots
Gale Warning	34–47 knots
Storm Warning	48–63 knots
Hurricane Force Winds	>64 knots

WEST COAST MARINE WEATHER

Forecast Areas & Observation Sites

- ● Marine Weather Reporting Station
- ▲ Marine Weather Buoy
- ○ MAREP Station
- ▣ WX1 162.55 mHz
- ▨ WX2 162.40 mHz
- ▧ WX3 162.475 mHz
- ▤ 21b 161.65 mHz
- ■ Weatheradio Canada 162.40 mHz
- ◆ Weatheradio Canada 1260 kHz (AM Band)
- ⊗ Weatheradio Canada 103.70 mHz

CHAPTERS, CHARTS AND PUBLICATIONS

CHAPTERS

Chapters 2–11 are of equal area: 22 nautical miles W to E by 18 nautical miles N to S. They are centred around the major capes, peninsulas and sounds, with a balance of destinations within each chapter, including at least one provisioning and fuelling stop (except Chapters 2, 5 and 12) and a selection of beach or picnic stops to enjoy en route before anchoring for the night. The distance to transit a chapter is approximately 30 nautical miles.

Because of the density of destinations, our map of Chapter 12—Broken Group, Pacific Rim National Park mirrors Chart 3670 of the Broken Group.

Chapter 13—Juan de Fuca Strait covers the strategic ports, bays and harbours that provide shelter on this often challenging stretch of water.

CHARTS

We have designed this cruising guide to work in conjunction with Canadian Hydrographic Service (CHS) charts; above each destination we have referenced the appropriate chart or charts required. The majority of charts for the west coast of Vancouver Island display metric depths; however, a few are still in fathoms and will eventually be phased out.

For their safety, all operators of ships and boats are required to have official, up-to-date paper charts and publications on board that cover the area where they are navigating. These charts can be referenced from the CHS *Pacific Coast Catalogue*, available from any chart dealer free of charge—visit www.charts.gc.ca

ELECTRONIC CHARTS AND SOFTWARE

Electronic charts are either Raster or Vector scans of CHS charts. They may be viewed independently on your computer or with the appropriate navigational software as an onboard aid to navigation. We recommend the following:

Electronic Charts by Nautical Data International (NDI) www.digitalocean.ca 1-800-563-0634.

Navigational Software by Nobeltec www.nobeltec.com, 1-800-946-2877.

SMALL SCALE CHARTS

3602   Approaches to Juan De Fuca Strait
3603   Ucluelet Inlet to Nooka Sound
3604   Nootka Sound to Quatsino Sound
3605   Quatsino Sound to Queen Charlotte Strait- Inset Scott Channel
3606   Juan De Fuca Strait
3624   Cape Cook to Cape Scott—Inset Sea Otter Cove
3679   Quatsino Sound

LARGE SCALE CHARTS

3410   Sooke Inlet to Parry Bay
3412   Victoria Harbour
3440   Race Rocks to D'Arcy Island
3548   Queen Charlotte Strait
3549   Queen Charlotte Strait, Western Portion—Inset Bull Harbour
3646   Plans—Barkley Sound
3647   Port San Juan and Nitinat Narrows
3651   Scouler Entrance and Kyuquot
3668   Alberni Inlet—Inset Port Alberni & Robbers Passage
3670   Broken Group
3671   Barkley sound
3673   Clayoquot Sound, Tofino Inlet to Millar Channel
3674   Clayoquot Sound, Millar Channel to Estevan Point Inset Hayden Passage—Hot Springs Cove—Marktosis
3675   Nootka Sound—Inset Gold River & Princesa Channel
3676   Esperanza Inlet—Inset Tahsis
3680   Brooks Bay
3681   Plans—Quatsino Sound
3682   Kyuquot Sound
3683   Chesleset Bay
3685   Tofino
3686   Approaches to Winter Harbour

The charts listed will cover the entire area included in *A Dreamspeaker Cruising Guide—Volume 6*.

PUBLICATIONS

OFFICIAL PUBLICATIONS

Canadian Tide and Current Tables, Volumes 5 and 6: Current annual edition.

Symbols and Abbreviations, Terms—Chart 1, as used on Canadian Charts.

Pacific Coast List of Lights, Buoys and Fog Signals

Sailing Directions—British Columbia Coast (South Portion): Current edition

The Canadian Aids to Navigation System: Marine Navigation Services Directorate

Note: For further reading consult Selected Reading (page 190)

APPROACH

WAYPOINTS are latitude and longitude positions based on NAD 83 datum and presented in degrees, minutes and hundredths of a minute. They are located in deep water in a position from which the illustrated features on the maps will be readily discernable in daylight.

EMERGENCY PROCEDURES

EMERGENCY PROCEDURES

THE CANADIAN COAST GUARD is a multitask organization whose primary role of search and rescue is supported by the following roles: maintaining the Aids to Navigation, operating the Office of Safe Boating and, in association with Environment Canada, the Marine Weather Forecast. For a copy of the Safe Boating Guide, call 1-800-267-6687 or download from Transport Canada at http://www.tc.gc.ca/marine-safety/tp/tp511/menu.htm. For search and rescue call:

TELEPHONE: **1-800-567-5111**
CELLULAR: ***311**
VHF CHANNEL: **16**

An operational VHF on board is essential—an additional portable handheld is advised; VHF distress signals can aid in rescue and recovery.

EMERGENCY RADIO PROCEDURES

MAYDAY: For immediate danger to life or vessel.

PAN-PAN: For urgency but no immediate danger to life or vessel.

For MAYDAY or PAN-PAN transmit the following on **VHF Channel 16** or **2182 kHz**.

1. MAYDAY, MAYDAY, MAYDAY (or PAN-PAN, PAN-PAN, PAN-PAN), this is (vessel name and radio call sign).

2. State your position and the nature of the distress.

3. State the number of people on board, and describe the vessel (length, make/type, colour, power or sail and registration number).

Note: If the distress is not life-threatening, the coast guard will put out a general call to boaters in your area for assistance. A tow at sea by a commercial operator can be expensive. HUB International TOS Limited provides marine towing insurance as part of their Platinum Bluewater Contract— 1-877-986-5265 or www.hubinternational.com

HOW TO USE THIS GUIDE

This sample layout identifies the various features of this cruising guide that will help you to reach your destination safely and well informed.

Chapter & featured destination reference
Chapter legend
Destination locator
Approach waypoint Latitude & Longitude
Tips on best approach & anchorages
Cautionary note

☀Asterisk indicates approximate position of approach waypoint
Depth contour (approximate position). Depths reduced to lowest normal tide (zero tide)
Sepia area indicates shoreline that covers and uncovers with the tide
Solid black line indicates HW mark
Green area indicates land above HW mark
Blue area indicates shallower water
White area indicates deeper water that is safe for navigation
Broken red line indicates safe approach course
Ambient photograph

HW: high water
LW: low water
All depths are indicated in metres.

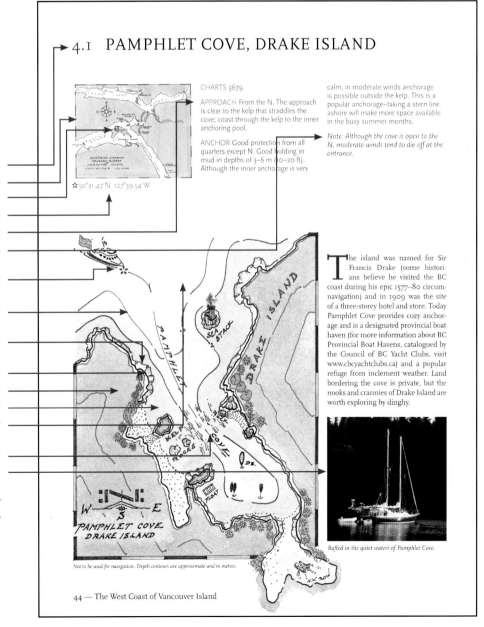

4.1 PAMPHLET COVE, DRAKE ISLAND

CHARTS 3679.

APPROACH From the N. The approach is clear to the kelp that straddles the cove; coast through the kelp to the inner anchoring pool.

ANCHOR Good protection from all quarters except N. Good holding in mud in depths of 3–6 m (10–20 ft). Although the inner anchorage is very calm, in moderate winds anchorage is possible outside the kelp. This is a popular anchorage–taking a stern line ashore will make more space available in the busy summer months.

Note: Although the cove is open to the N, moderate winds tend to die off at the entrance.

☀50°31.47'N 127°39.54'W

The island was named for Sir Francis Drake (some historians believe he visited the BC coast during his epic 1577–80 circumnavigation) and in 1909 was the site of a three-storey hotel and store. Today Pamphlet Cove provides cozy anchorage and is a designated provincial boat haven (for more information about BC Provincial Boat Havens, catalogued by the Council of BC Yacht Clubs, visit www.cbcyachtclubs.ca) and a popular refuge from inclement weather. Land bordering the cove is private, but the nooks and crannies of Drake Island are worth exploring by dinghy.

Rafted in the quiet waters of Pamphlet Cove.

Not to be used for navigation. Depth contours are approximate and in metres.

44 — The West Coast of Vancouver Island

PORT HARDY—HARDY BAY AND GOLETAS CHANNEL TO HOPE ISLAND

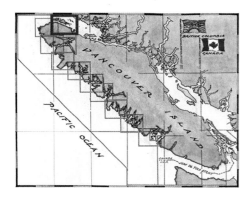

Chainsaw art in Carrot Park fronts Seagate Wharf.

Comprehensive provisioning is possible in downtown Port Hardy.

A sailboat passes a coast guard cutter in Shushartie Bay.

Port Hardy is the last major community on the NE coast of Vancouver Island and is considered by most cruising boaters as the gateway to the west coast of Vancouver Island. Here you will find a comprehensive service and provisioning centre, the southern terminal for the Vancouver Island–Prince Rupert ferry and an airport for convenient crew changes or meeting friends and family.

We found Seagate Wharf in downtown Port Hardy a convenient spot to tie up and walk the half-block to Glen-Way Foods, a well-stocked and locally owned grocery store that will deliver to the dock. The area around Market, Rupert and Granville streets has every type of shop or service a boater might need; pop into the Visitor Info Centre on Market Street and pick up a downtown map, which will direct you to the post office, hospital, pharmacy, gift stores, art galleries, museum, hardware and marine stores, a BC Liquor Store and even a traditional barber shop.

Restaurants in this area are highly recommended for their choice of fresh fish and seafood and will often turn your catch into a gourmet meal. Alternatively, pick up a live crab at Hardy Boys Smoked Fish and let the chef at Malone's Oceanside Bistro cook it to perfection for you. To end the evening, enjoy a leisurely stroll along the waterfront sea walk, which is amber-lit at night and connects to the green lawns of Carrot Park.

The Inner Basin offers moorage at the public wharfs and at the Quarterdeck Inn and Marina Resort, which offers all the necessities: fuel, clean shower and laundry facilities, a well-stocked marine store, and a pub and restaurant. The hearty pub grub made for a very pleasant stay while we worked on our engine and made *Dreamspeaker* shipshape.

With long-awaited NW winds in the forecast, we left Port Hardy after a three-day stay and motored the 25 nautical miles through Goletas Channel to Bull Harbour on Hope Island. The current in the channel reaches 3 knots so it is wise to take advantage of the west-going ebb before the NW wind picks up; Goletas Channel can become very choppy when wind opposes current.

As we neared the entrance to Bull Harbour (2.2) we felt a gentle ocean swell on our bow and a sense of excitement in the breeze. We found more than twenty boats at anchor and keenly felt the anticipation of a big adventure.

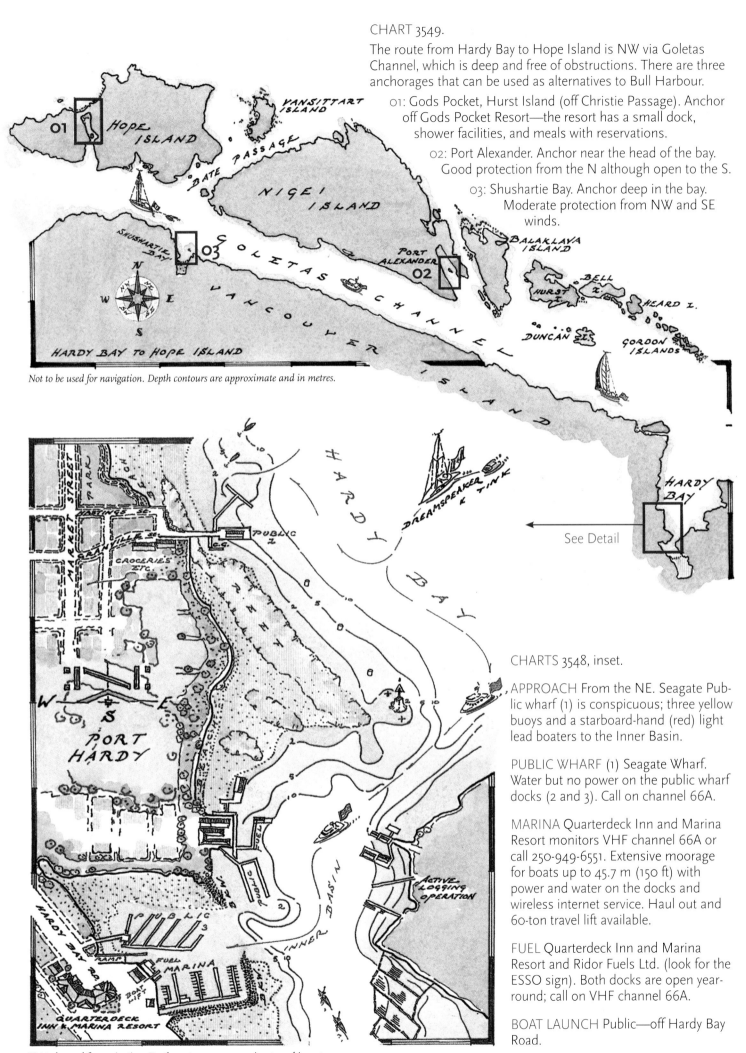

CHART 3549.

The route from Hardy Bay to Hope Island is NW via Goletas Channel, which is deep and free of obstructions. There are three anchorages that can be used as alternatives to Bull Harbour.

01: Gods Pocket, Hurst Island (off Christie Passage). Anchor off Gods Pocket Resort—the resort has a small dock, shower facilities, and meals with reservations.

02: Port Alexander. Anchor near the head of the bay. Good protection from the N although open to the S.

03: Shushartie Bay. Anchor deep in the bay. Moderate protection from NW and SE winds.

Not to be used for navigation. Depth contours are approximate and in metres.

CHARTS 3548, inset.

APPROACH From the NE. Seagate Public wharf (1) is conspicuous; three yellow buoys and a starboard-hand (red) light lead boaters to the Inner Basin.

PUBLIC WHARF (1) Seagate Wharf. Water but no power on the public wharf docks (2 and 3). Call on channel 66A.

MARINA Quarterdeck Inn and Marina Resort monitors VHF channel 66A or call 250-949-6551. Extensive moorage for boats up to 45.7 m (150 ft) with power and water on the docks and wireless internet service. Haul out and 60-ton travel lift available.

FUEL Quarterdeck Inn and Marina Resort and Ridor Fuels Ltd. (look for the ESSO sign). Both docks are open year-round; call on VHF channel 66A.

BOAT LAUNCH Public—off Hardy Bay Road.

Not to be used for navigation. Depth contours are approximate and in metres.

Chapter 2
CAPE SCOTT

Beyond Cape Scott's rocky shoreline lie fine sandy beaches, sea stacks and safe anchorages. Russ Heinl photo.

Chapter 2
CAPE SCOTT

TIDES

Volume 6, Canadian Tide and Current Tables

Reference Port: Alert Bay

Secondary Port: Shushartie Bay (for Bull Harbour)

Reference Port: Tofino

Secondary Port: Cape Scott

CURRENTS

Current Station: Scott Channel

Secondary Station: Nahwitti Bar

Note: The current turns to ebb at HW minus 20 minutes on Alert Bay.

WEATHER

Weather Channel VHF WX3 Calvert Island. 21B Holberg. WX2 Eliza Dome

Area: Queen Charlotte Strait—listen for Pine Island reporting station

Area: West Coast Vancouver Island North—listen for Cape Scott Lighthouse and Sartine Island reporting station

Note: The weather changes rapidly in this area, and conditions can develop from flat calm to gale-force winds in under an hour.

Approaching Cape Scott—Anne keeps her hat on.

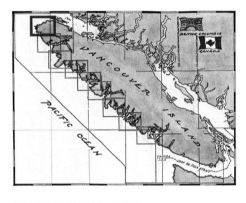

CAUTIONARY NOTES

Nahwitti Bar: Currents reach 5.5 knots across the bar. A crossing should not be attempted when current opposes swell or wind conditions because swell breaks across the bar.

Scott Channel: Currents reach 3 knots in the channel. Wind opposing current produces short, steep seas.

Sea Otter Cove: Under moderate to strong SW swell and sea conditions, waves break across the entrance.

Note: Scott Channel is best negotiated at slack water or with the ebb current if travelling south.

Bull Harbour is a strategically situated anchorage, and a convenient staging point for boaters waiting for good weather to cross Nahwitti Bar and round Cape Scott. It also offers an opportunity to meet other adventurers who might want to "buddy boat" part or all of the way south.

The longer route past Cape Scott is approximately 55 nautical miles to Quatsino Sound and the anchorage in North Harbour or moorage in Winter Harbour (Chapter 3). The shorter route to Sea Otter Cove (covered in this chapter) is 32 nautical miles from Bull Harbour. In settled weather you may also have the opportunity to explore Guise and Hanson bays en route.

The morning after our arrival many boaters left early to cross Nahwitti Bar by the direct route at HW slack and take full advantage of the six-hour ebb current that would carry them around Cape Sutil, west to Cape Scott and south through Scott Channel to Quatsino Sound. We left two hours later because we planned to round Cape Scott at LW slack. The ebb current was running, and to avoid the possibility of rough water over Nahwitti Bar we followed the inside route between Tatnall Reefs and the Vancouver Island shoreline.

Cape Sutil to Cape Scott is 15 nautical miles and rocks extend seaward up to 1 nautical mile. Most boaters round Cape Scott well offshore; we followed the 20-metre (66-ft) depth contour at LW. Legendary Cape Scott is low-lying and presents a dramatic shoreline with waves crashing and foaming over the islets and jagged off-lying rocks. We were elated after rounding the cape—we felt we were leaving civilization behind on a new journey of discovery.

Cape Scott Provincial Park and its fine sandy beaches are difficult to reach from the northern Vancouver Island shore, and are best accessed from the anchorages in Guise Bay and San Josef Bay. We anchored overnight in Guise Bay, where the northerly wind kept us relatively steady in a lazy swell that entered the bay.

On the Pacific Coast a westerly swell is always running. If the swell is light, Hansen Bay, with its pioneering history, would make a good LW lunch stop before you continue south to the safe, summer anchorage of Sea Otter Cove. We were getting used to swell surging and breaking over the rocks and reefs, and had been warned that this would be the case on the approach to the marked channel to the cove.

A stop in San Josef Bay with its sea stacks, rock formations, caves and soft-sand beaches is worth a visit.

FEATURED DESTINATIONS

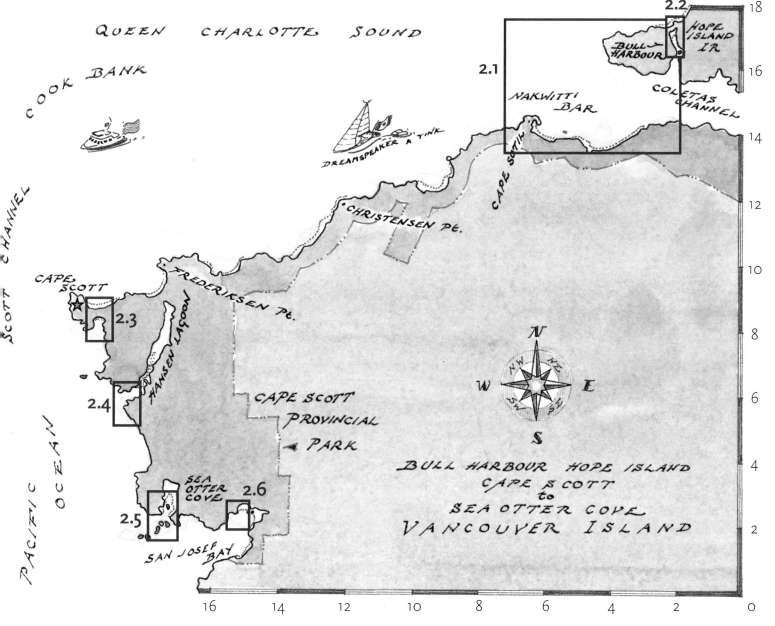

Not to be used for navigation. Depth contours are approximate and in metres.

2.1 NAHWITTI BAR

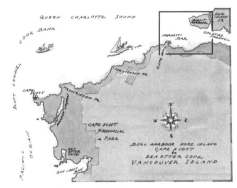

✿ 50°53.85'N 127°56.17'W

ANCHOR Temporary anchorage lies east of Cape Sutil. Tuck well in. Depths of 4–6m (13–19 ft) in mud and sand.

CHARTS 3549.

A small craft has two possible routes NW across Nahwitti Bar:

(1) DIRECT ROUTE: Cross the bar at HW slack as the current turns to ebb (minus 20 minutes HW Alert Bay). The ebb current will assist you all the way to and around Cape Scott.

(2) INDIRECT ROUTE: Cross the bar inside Tatnall Reefs, timing your passage to round Cape Scott before the turn to flood in Scott Channel.

Note: This option allows a later departure from Bull Harbour. The kelp on Tatnall Reefs will dampen the swells and the ebb current will assist you all the way to Cape Scott.

The evening before the big day—Bull Harbour, Hope Island.

Nahwitti Bar is the gateway to a grand adventure. Assessing the weather and sea conditions and timing the current are critical to crossing the bar safely. The bar is best crossed at slack water. The duration of HW slack is 12 minutes and LW slack 17 minutes. Secondary current station Nahwitti Bar, referenced on Alert Bay minus 20 minutes. A crossing should not be attempted when current opposes swell or wind conditions as swell breaks across the bar.

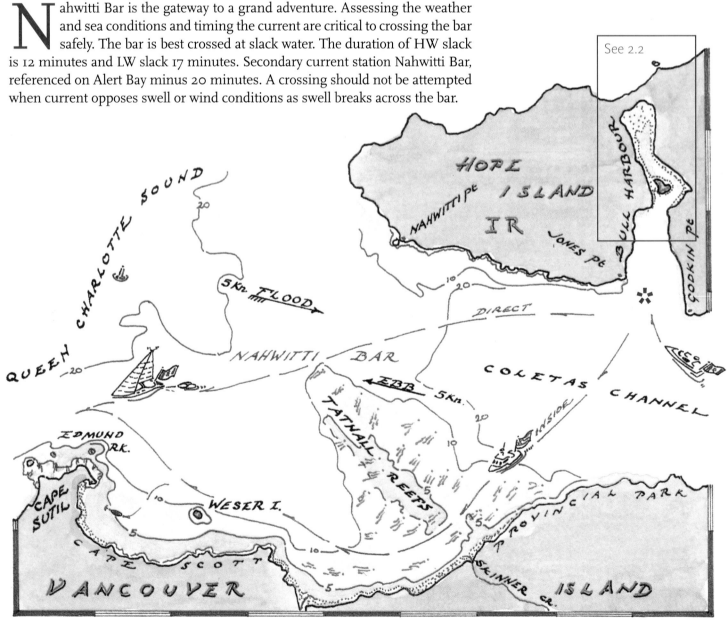

Not to be used for navigation. Depth contours are approximate and in metres.

CHARTS 3549 (inset).

APPROACH Between Godkin Point and Jones Point. The outer limit of the harbour is shown on the chart and the above waypoint lies on this line. The approach through "The Narrows" and east of Norman Island is clear.

ANCHOR The harbour offers good, all-round protection. There is swinging room for numerous boats in depths of 4–6 m (13–19 ft) with good holding in mud.

MARINA Hope Island is a Tlatlasikwala First Nations Reserve. The community has an extensive private wharf and welcomes transient boaters. Call on VHF Channel 6 or tie up and wait for a member of the community to pop by. The welcome sign states that "Moorage, anchorage and other fees are in effect."

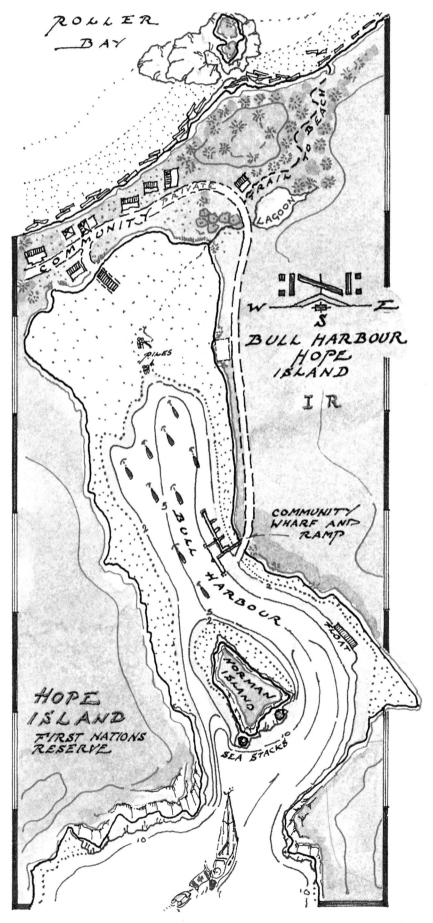

Hope Island or Xwamdashe is one of the Tlatlasikwala First Nation's six reserves. The village of Humtaspi was established in Bull Harbour in 1850. Named in the mid-1800s for the numerous seal lion bulls that guarded the Hope Island shoreline, this tranquil harbour lies in a pastoral setting with the neat community of Humtaspi at its head. The commodious anchorage offers all-weather protection and is a convenient stopover for boaters waiting to cross the Nahwitti Bar and round Cape Scott. When we visited, many expectant boaters were completing last-minute chores before departing the following day.

Don't pack your dinghy on board before taking a pleasant half-hour hike from the private dock (a small fee may be in effect as this is reserve land) to dramatic Roller Bay and its sweeping sandy beach; there is a well-marked and maintained trail beside a lagoon. From here the roar of crashing waves will lead you through cool, mossy forest to a spectacular crescent beach lined with sun-bleached driftwood limbs and a thrilling assortment of ocean-rolled rocks and pebbles. The community of Humtaspi beyond the lagoon requests that visitors respect their privacy.

Note: A moderate to strong northwesterly wind will whistle across the low-lying portion of land and into the harbour, often making conditions inside the anchorage seem worse than outside.

Not to be used for navigation.
Depth contours are approximate and in metres.

2.3 GUISE BAY

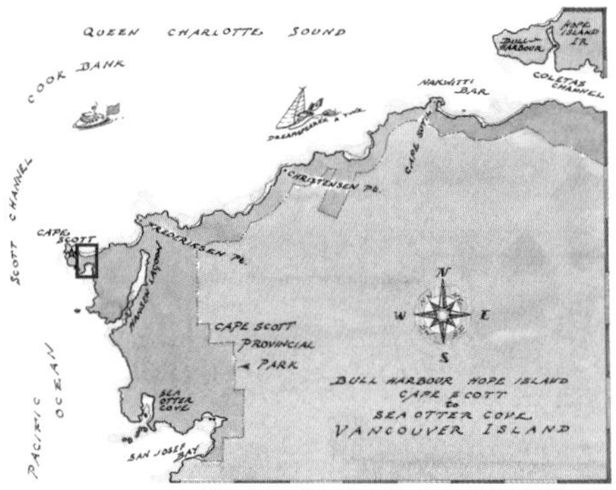

✲ (A) 50°45.81'N 128°25.17'W

CHARTS 3605 (metric) inset, Scott Channel. 3624 (fathoms).

APPROACH (A) From the W where a kelp-lined channel lies between the rocks. (B) From the S between the rocks and the Vancouver Island shore.

ANCHOR This temporary anchorage affords good protection from northerly winds in the NW portion of the bay. Open to the S and W. Anchor in depths of 4–6 m (13–19 ft) with good holding in sand.

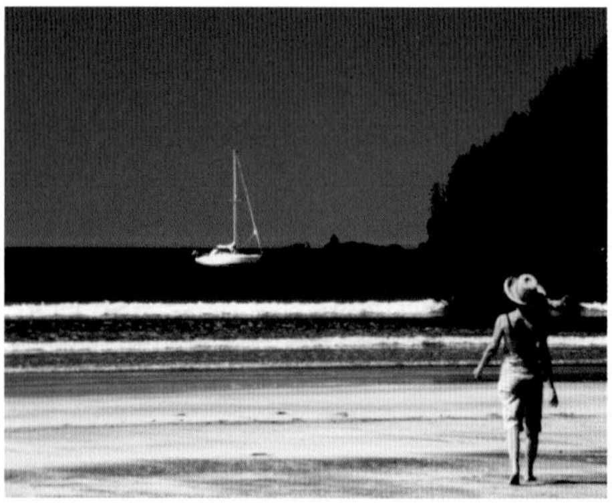

Rewards include uncrowded anchorages.

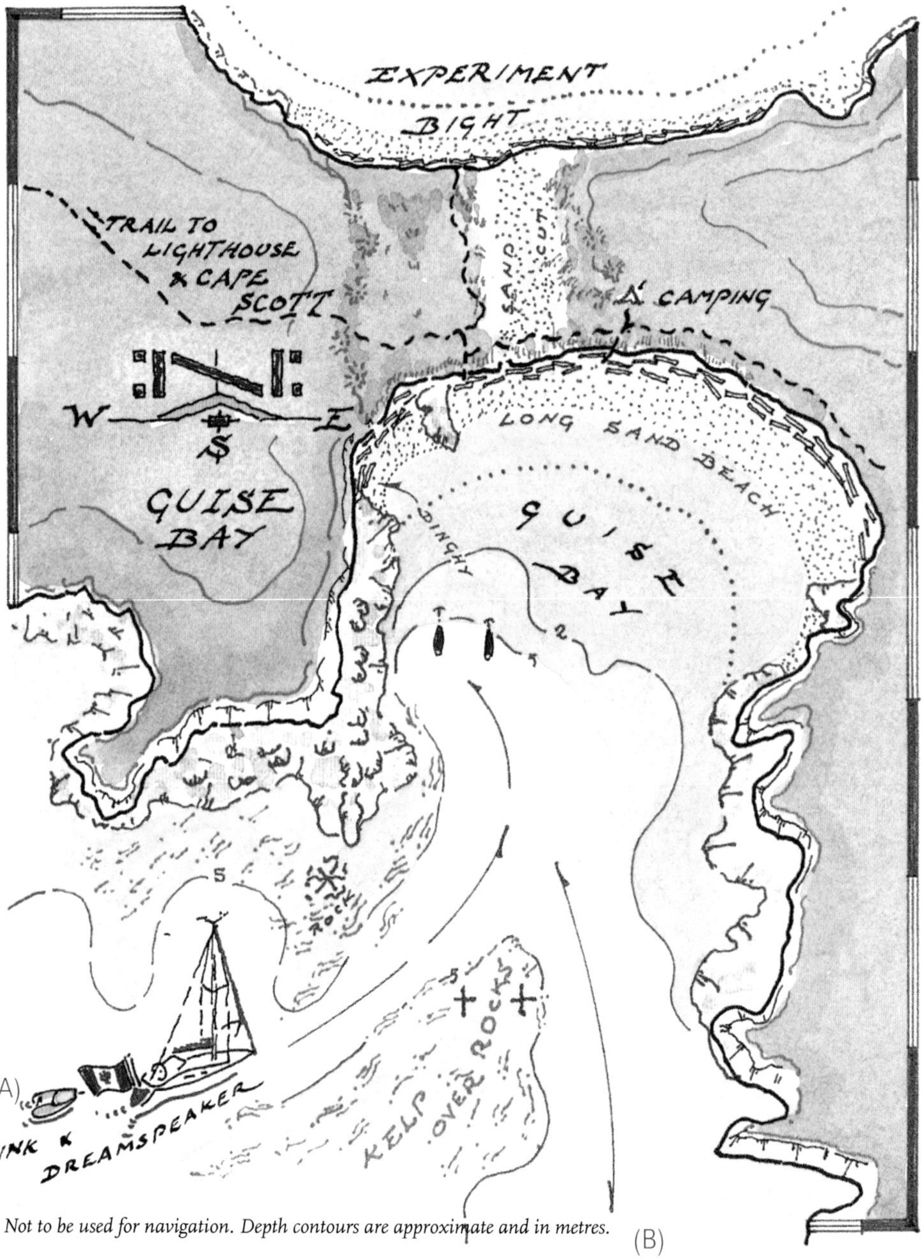

Not to be used for navigation. Depth contours are approximate and in metres.

(B)

Cape Scott became a provincial park in 1973 and protects over 15,000 hectares (37,000 acres) along the shore of northern Vancouver Island. The park trail ends at the manned lighthouse where you can picnic on the grounds, enjoy views to Cox Island and sign the guest book.

Recognized as a First Nations burial site, the wide sandy and grassy neck connects Guise Bay to Experiment Bight in the north. The bight was once the site of a native village called Gwegwakawalis, which translates as "whales on the beach." Both bays have sweeping, white-sand beaches lined with driftwood and colourful flotsam stacked above the HW line—both invite a barefoot run along the surf line. The driftwood stakes and hardy plant species that cover the grassy neck were introduced by Danish settlers to stabilize the shifting sand and provide pasture for their cattle. (Author Lester Peterson spent his childhood in the colony and wrote *The Cape Scott Story*–see Selected Reading page 190.

Note: Swell is constant in the bay. If you take your dinghy ashore, be aware that the deceptively small-looking waves are very powerful if mistimed, and can easily flip both boat and contents in a flash. Ensure that anything precious is in a waterproof pack and glasses are strapped on!

Anne watches the break at the lagoon entrance.

CHARTS 3624.

APPROACH From the W at LW. The small bay serves as a pleasant lunch stop in light westerly wind and swells.

ANCHOR Off the beach in 4–6 m (13–19 ft) with good holding in sand.

Note: The bar to the lagoon is marked by swells breaking over the shallows.

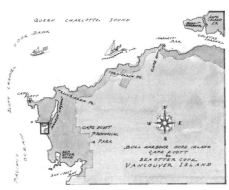

❖ 50°44.00'N 128°23.37'W

While you enjoy a leisurely lunch in the cockpit, reflect on the history of this peaceful bay and lagoon when it was home to Danish pioneers in the late 1800s. By 1914 the cape had a population of nearly 1,000 people with a school, post office and church. But by 1918 only a few families remained, thanks to broken promises, poor transportation, and lack of a protected harbour.

Where humans fail, wildlife often survives. The saltwater marsh and tidal mud flats of Hansen Lagoon, with rich intertidal life and a bountiful supply of food and shelter, is a favoured stop for a variety of migrating birds, including great blue herons and trumpeter swans.

Not to be used for navigation. Depth contours are approximate and in metres.

2.5 SEA OTTER COVE

✽ (A) 50°39.82'N 128°20.95'W

CHARTS 3624 (fathoms) inset.

APPROACH

(A) From the SE—the landslide on Mt. St. Patrick is conspicuous. The narrow entrance channel, marked by a white light with a solar panel, has a least depth of 6 m (19 ft) and lies E of the Helen Islands. Inside the light the waters are shallow and murky—navigate with caution and enter the anchorage between the marked islet (starboard) and the islet to the NW with a rock at its southern tip. The rock dries at LW.

(B) An alternative, unmarked channel with some rocks and shallow patches can be approached from the west in moderate NW conditions.

ANCHOR N or S of the mooring buoys. Holding is good in mud and sand in depths of 2–4.5 m (7–15 ft). Depth of water around the buoys ranges from 3 to 5 m (10–16 ft) with the westernmost buoy offering the least depth.

The *Sea Otter,* commanded by Capt. James Hanna, visited the cove in 1786 and left its name. Once you have successfully navigated the narrow entrance and marked shallows, it's a relief to drop anchor in this popular cove or pick up one of the mooring buoys anchored to the rocks by heavy chain. For a little exercise, take a HW row to the head of St. Patrick Creek, where a 2-km (1.3-mile) trail (not advisable after a few days of rain) leads to the white-sand beach at Lowrie Bay.

Note: A surge enters the cove during southerly storms making it less than comfortable.

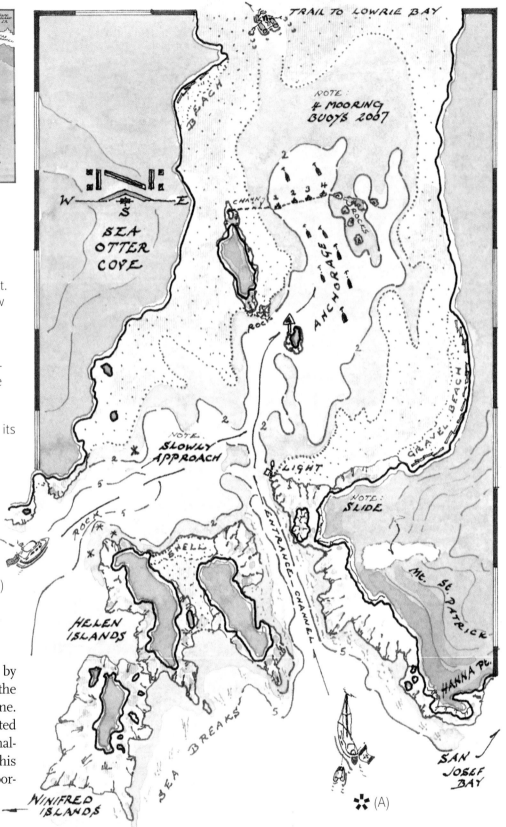

Not to be used for navigation. Depth contours are approximate and in metres.

Three boats raft to a hurricane-strength buoy in Sea Otter Cove after rounding Cape Scott.

A magical West Coast beach—all to ourselves.

CHARTS 3624.

APPROACH At LW in northerly wind and light swell conditions. The bottom shallows very gently.

ANCHOR In the NW corner where the swell and breaking waves on shore are smallest. Good holding in sand in depths of 3–5 m (10–16 ft) but exposed to the SW.

Note: Chart 3624 marks a rock in the SW corner of the bay, as indicated on our map.

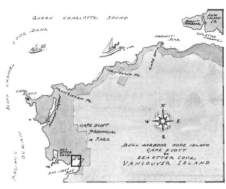

✻ 50°39.50'N 128°19.00'W

S ea stacks, rock formations and caves divide the "little" and "large" soft-sand beaches at the head of enchanting San Josef Bay. Happily, we arrived on a sunny, blue-sky day and, after dropping anchor, rowed *Tink* and our picnic to shore with care, as even the smallest wave can flip a dinghy or kayak. The larger of the beaches is perfect for a barefoot hop, skip and jump along the water's edge, and letting the fine sand squelch through your toes while you search for treasures. Some evidence remains of the Danish settlers who, in the early 1900s, built a number of homesteads, a store and a church on property surrounding San Josef Bay.

Note: The 2.5-km (1.6-mile) trail from the Cape Scott trailhead makes for a good hike. The 10-km (6-mile) trail to Sea Otter Cove is not maintained and is for serious hikers only!

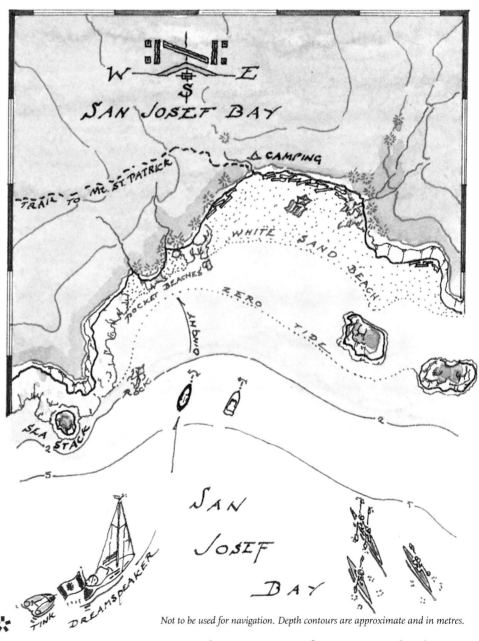

Not to be used for navigation. Depth contours are approximate and in metres.

The lighthouse atop Kains Island marks the entrance to Quatsino Sound.

Chapter 3
QUATSINO SOUND

Chapter 3
QUATSINO SOUND

TIDES

Volume 6, Canadian Tide and Current Tables

Reference Port: Winter Harbour

Secondary Port: Hunt Islets, Kwokwesta Creek

CURRENTS

No current stations cover this area. The flooding tide produces an east-flowing current in Quatsino Sound.

WEATHER

Weather Channel VHF WX1 Eliza Dome.

Areas: West Coast Vancouver Island North—listen for Quatsino Lighthouse for weather at the entrance to Quatsino Sound, and South Brooks weather buoy for offshore conditions.

Note: Topographical features in the sound affect wind and weather conditions. Winds tend to build during the day and funnel along the direction of the sound and inlets.

A sea otter in North Harbour—cute and furry with a voracious appetite.

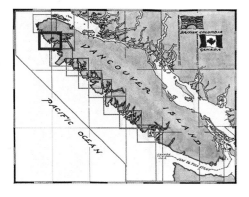

CAUTIONARY NOTES

When rounding Kains Island, leave Robson Rock to the east. Careful navigation is required when exploring the eastern shoreline of the entrance to Quatsino Sound, between Cliffe Point and Kwakiutl Point. A minefield of rocks and reefs extends well offshore here.

Quatsino Sound, the northernmost of Vancouver Island's five principal sounds (Inner Quatsino Sound is covered in Chapter 4), offers many sheltered inlets and an interesting number of communities to visit. The sound has experienced some major clear-cut logging and the introduction of fish farms, so we have concentrated on areas where little or no evidence of this activity is visible once visitors have anchored or tied to a dock.

The passage S from San Josef Bay to Quatsino Lighthouse at the entrance to the sound passes 20 nautical miles of rugged coastline, with no protection in either Rafi Cove or Grant Bay. The latter bay's inviting sandy beach can be visited by motorized dinghy or kayak, or on a hike from Browning Inlet (see 3.1). Commanding Quatsino Lighthouse sits atop Kains Island to guide boaters into Quatsino Sound and Forward Inlet, the first sheltered waters south of Cape Scott.

To the NE of Matthews Island lie the popular all-weather anchorages of North Harbour and Browning Inlet; in North Harbour we saw our first raft of sea otters.

At the head of Forward Inlet, beyond Greenwood Point, the small community of Winter Harbour is an important stop for boaters heading south—here you will find fuel, provisions, a BC Liquor Store, and a chance to stretch your legs on the wooden boardwalk.

A trip east into Quatsino Sound will take you to Koprino Harbour and the small, sheltered anchorage in East Cove, south of a protective grassy isthmus. On Quatsino Sound's southern shoreline, tucked inside the shelter of the Koskimo Islands, is a cozy two-boat anchorage where you can relax in the cockpit and watch sea otters feed. Alternatively, anchor off Mahatta Creek and row or paddle the lower creek to a small pool and waterfall.

On the eastern shore of Quatsino Sound's entrance lies Gooding Cove, which is well protected in southeast winds, with good holding. The cove has a sandy, driftwood-strewn beach and a logging road for hiking, although bear sightings have been reported to be plentiful here.

Many boaters choose to round Brooks Peninsula after exploring the entrance to Quatsino Sound, but we encourage you to take a little time to enjoy Inner Quatsino Sound and Holberg, Rupert and Neroutsos inlets.

FEATURED DESTINATIONS

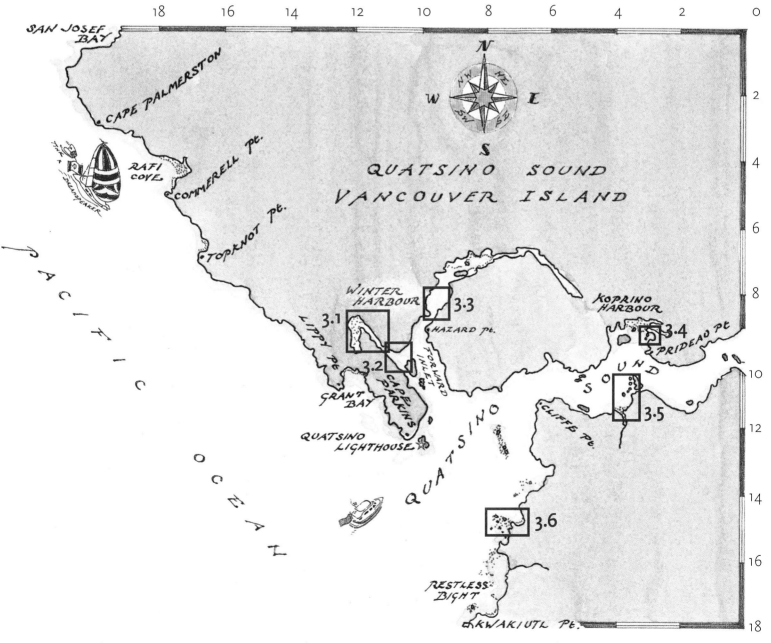

Not to be used for navigation. Depth contours are approximate and in metres.

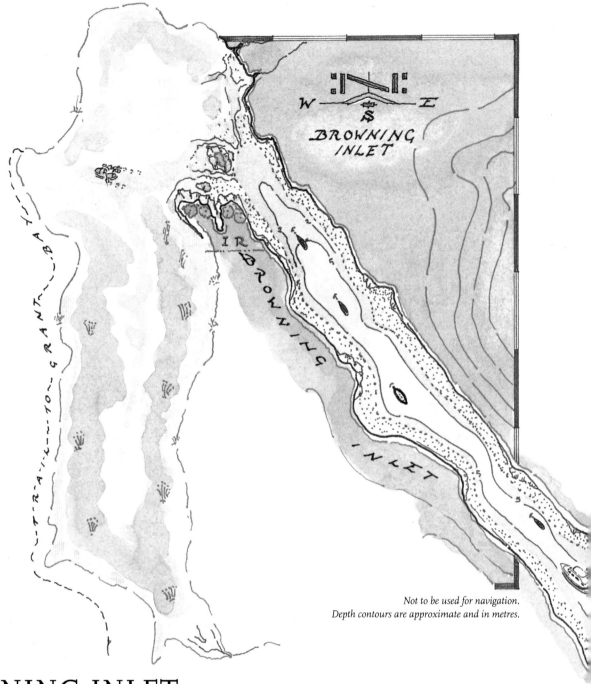

Not to be used for navigation.
Depth contours are approximate and in metres.

3.1 BROWNING INLET

Current and wind vie to hold boats steady in
Browning Inlet.

CHARTS 3686.

APPROACH From North Harbour—
clear the rock and gravel outcrop on the
eastern shoreline. Stay in centre channel.

ANCHOR Just off the centre channel.
Moderate northerly and southerly winds
tend to funnel through the channel,
although not uncomfortably. Anchor in
5–8 m (16–26 ft) with good holding in
mud.

In this quiet, narrow anchorage, trees on either side conceal the shoreside
logging; there is a drying mud flat at its head where the mountainside has
recently been logged. A trail from here leads to the sandy beach at Grant Bay,
a pleasant half-hour hike. Pack a picnic and enjoy a day at the beach.

At dusk, while we enjoyed the inlet's tranquility from the cockpit, a black bear
cub ambled along the shoreline foraging for food, bald eagle parents took turns
feeding their squawking young, and sea otters crunched on their daily quota
of seafood. We woke at dawn to the cheerful sound of chirping birds before we
moved on to Koprino Harbour.

NORTH HARBOUR 3.2

CHARTS 3686.

APPROACH From the NE out of Forward Inlet. The passage in is clear. The starboard-hand buoys (red) off Matthews Island mark a shoal and rocks.

ANCHOR In prevailing northerly winds protected anchorage can be found along the northern shore, while in southerly winds sheltered anchorage is possible in the lee of Matthews Island. Good holding in sand and mud in 5–8 m (16–26 ft).

Note: The starboard-hand buoys (red) off Matthews Island mark a shoal and rocks.

✳ 50°29.38N 128°02.60W

Not to be used for navigation. Depth contours are approximate and in metres.

Quatsino Light guides boaters into Quatsino Sound and Forward Inlet, the first truly sheltered waters south of Cape Scott. North Harbour is a popular anchorage for visitors who have provisioned and topped up fuel and water in Winter Harbour, and choose not to be tied to a dock.

Anchoring off Matthews Island is a delight; it holds the setting sun longest and gave us the opportunity to meet a charming community of female sea otters rafted in the midst of the kelp with their young, feeding and floating on their backs around the marked rock. The harbour provides significant habitat for a wide variety of seabirds, including trumpeter swans, and is an important area for geoduck and abalone (thus the otters!).

Western Boy snug in North Harbour.

The West Coast of Vancouver Island — 33

3.3 WINTER HARBOUR

✳ 50°30.60'N 128°01.50'W

The community of Winter Harbour lines the shore from Greenwood Point.

Visitors moor at the public wharf.

The protected fishing village of Winter Harbour was so named in the 1800s, became Queenstown in 1890 and Leeson Harbour in 1930, then reverted to its original name in 1947. It was known as Oyagamla to the four Kwakwaka'wakw tribes that used the site as their winter village. Lee Leeson pre-empted the surrounding land in 1891, and built a crab and clam cannery and a trading post that became a popular meeting place for whaling ships and local First Nations. Today Winter Harbour is evolving from a commercial fishing hub to serve the sport fishery and ecotourism; the salmon and halibut fishing in nearshore waters is world-class.

Winter Harbour is an important stopping-off point for recreational boaters heading south, and its one-stop shopping allows them to stock up the wine cellar, provision, and take on water (check for boil water advisory notices) and fuel.

The waterfront village is connected by a traditional wooden boardwalk which, thanks to regular maintenance, remains to give the small community a strong sense of history. The Winter Harbour General Store sells "everything from bolts to bananas," including fresh produce and frozen seafood, chicken and meat. The liquor store has a good selection of popular wines and beer.

The Botel Park Trail leads from the store through old-growth rainforest to a rocky beach that overlooks the Pacific Ocean. Pack lunch or supper to sandy Picnic Beach south of Hazard Point, where sunset views can be spectacular.

Note: The post office is open Monday, Wednesday and Friday 9 am-1 pm. The general store will also hold mail for visitors—c/o Outpost at Winter Harbour, General Delivery, Winter Harbour BC Canada V0N 3L0.

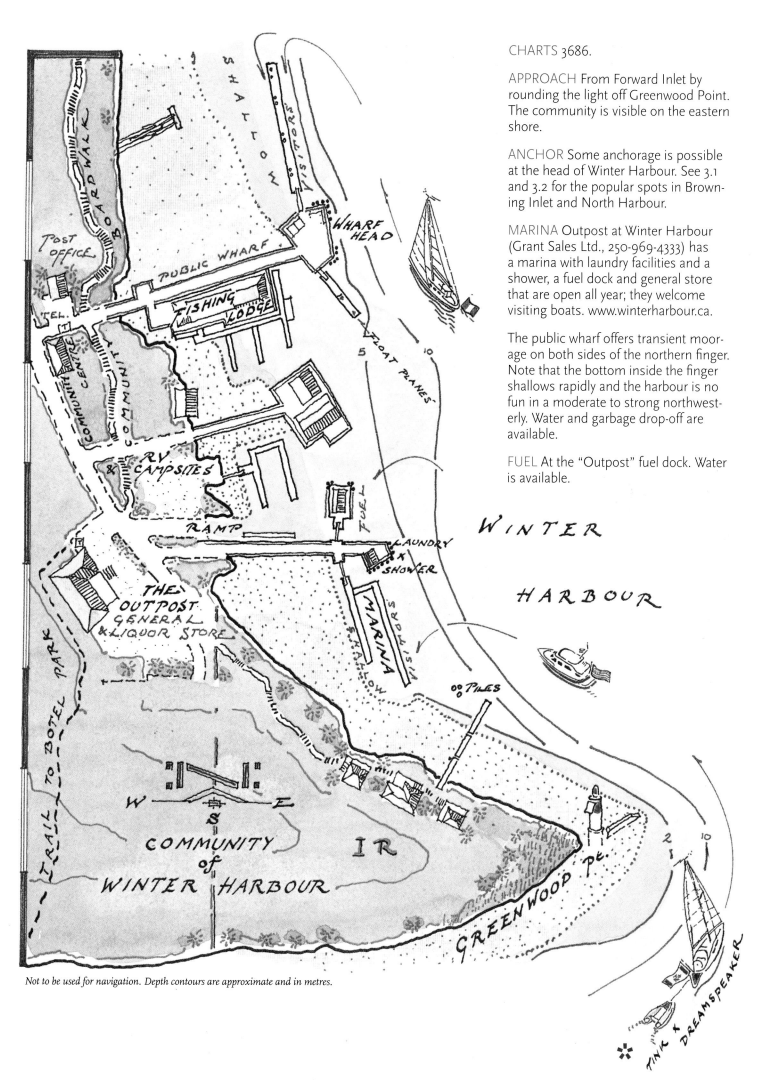

CHARTS 3686.

APPROACH From Forward Inlet by rounding the light off Greenwood Point. The community is visible on the eastern shore.

ANCHOR Some anchorage is possible at the head of Winter Harbour. See 3.1 and 3.2 for the popular spots in Browning Inlet and North Harbour.

MARINA Outpost at Winter Harbour (Grant Sales Ltd., 250-969-4333) has a marina with laundry facilities and a shower, a fuel dock and general store that are open all year; they welcome visiting boats. www.winterharbour.ca.

The public wharf offers transient moorage on both sides of the northern finger. Note that the bottom inside the finger shallows rapidly and the harbour is no fun in a moderate to strong northwesterly. Water and garbage drop-off are available.

FUEL At the "Outpost" fuel dock. Water is available.

Not to be used for navigation. Depth contours are approximate and in metres.

3.4 EAST COVE, KOPRINO HARBOUR

CHARTS 3679.

APPROACH From the W. East Cove lies in the NE portion of Koprino Harbour. Leave the islets to the W. Kelp marks the shallows off the southern inlet. Enter between the edge of the kelp and the rock.

ANCHOR Good all-round protection. Tuck in NE of the islets. Good holding in sand and mud in 3–5 m (10–16 ft).

Note: Do not be deceived by the protection inside the harbour—winds on the outside increase as they funnel up the Koprino River Valley.

✣50°29.86'N 127°50.59'W

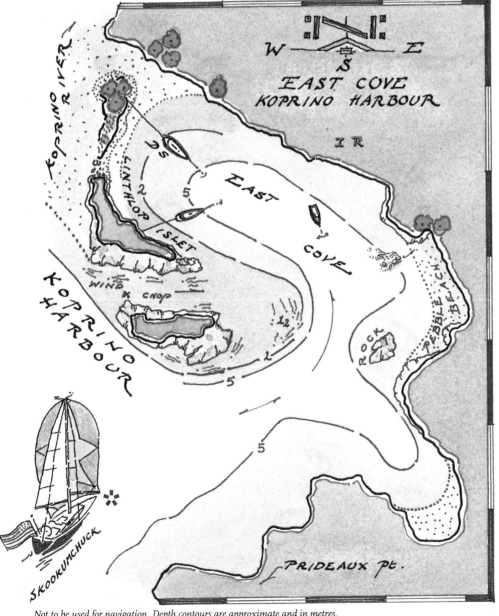

Not to be used for navigation. Depth contours are approximate and in metres.

Friends recommended East Cove as a "special spot," and we weren't disappointed. We sailed in from Koprino Harbour and anchored in a small, sheltered pool south of the grassy isthmus. There is good protection here from the wind and swell, especially at LW. The enchanting isthmus and midden, with their stunted, wind-swept trees, support a variety of soft grasses, sea asparagus and wildflowers. It's fun to explore the pebble and shell beach in the southeast corner of the cove and observe the schools of darting silver fish and bell-shaped moon jellies in the shallows. The surrounding lands are Indian Reserve and part of Quatsino Provincial Park.

Anne rows Tink to the pebble beach.

KOSKIMO ISLANDS AND MAHATTA CREEK 3.5

CHARTS 3679.

APPROACH From the W. (A) Enter the "Basin" between the two small islands as indicated. (B) Enter the Mahatta Creek anchorage as indicated. Watch for the extended shallows. There is a narrow "pass" into the anchorage basin from the E with a rock in it. Because of kelp and a lack of depth we do not recommend this approach.

ANCHOR

(A) In the "Basin" with a stern line ashore. All-round protection in all but strong westerly winds, with good holding in depths of 8–12 m (26–40 ft).

(B) To the E of the creek with good protection from the SE. Good holding in sand and gravel in depths of 5–10 m (16–33 ft).

✳ 50°28.04'N 127°51.95'W

Tucked inside the shelter of the Koskimo Islands lies a cozy two-boat anchorage where visitors can relax in the cockpit and watch sea otters feed and play, or hunt for shells on the pocket beach. The islands also offer breeding ground for sea urchin, abalone and sea cucumber.

An alternative spot, popular with locals, is east of Mahatta Creek, which we are told is navigable by dinghy and outboard at HW to a lovely pool and falls. The pebble beach east of the anchorage allows for a good leg stretch and a spot of beachcombing.

CAUTIONARY NOTE

Pass to the south of Koskimo Islands is navigable with caution on a rising tide. Kelp-lined and only viable for small craft.

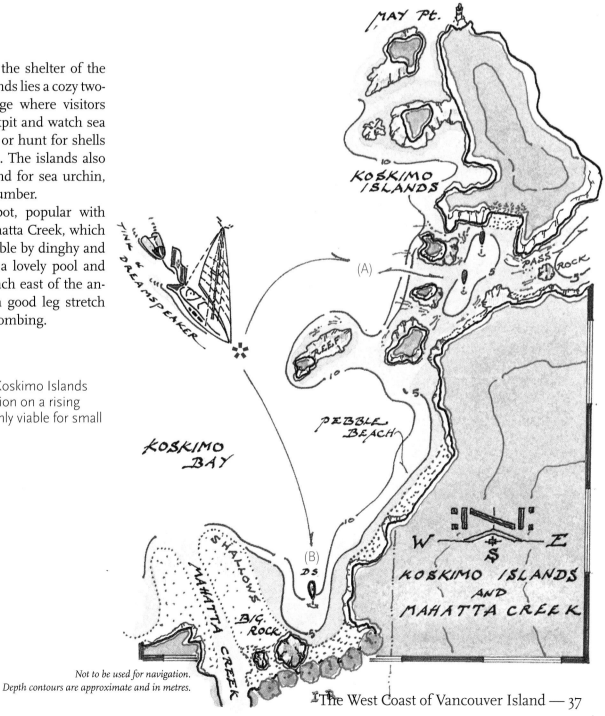

Not to be used for navigation.
Depth contours are approximate and in metres.

A bald eagle stares us down.

CHARTS 3679, 3686.

APPROACH From the NW in settled weather or SE winds. Favour the eastern shoreline.

ANCHOR In the SW portion of the cove. Good protection from SE wind and swell that is dampened by a barrier of kelp to the W. Good holding in 4–8 m (13–26 ft) in gravel and sand.

✳ 50°24.60'N 127°57.45'W

We could only stay a few hours in what looked like an inviting anchorage with a sandy beach backed by driftwood. But with the winds beginning to back to the west, the swell began to make this cove very uncomfortable. The crew of *Western Boy* (our neighbours) had stayed overnight in southeast conditions and reported that the anchorage was well protected with good holding. There is a logging road for hiking; however bear sightings have been plentiful.

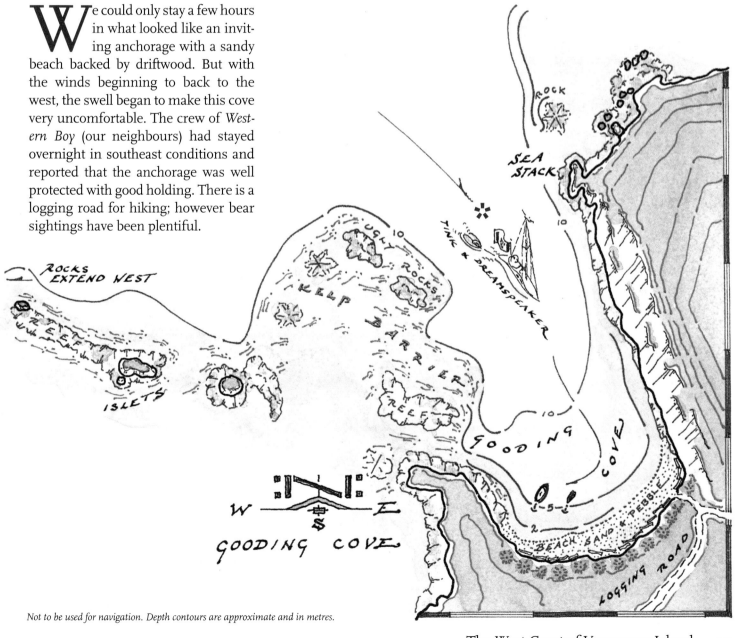

Not to be used for navigation. Depth contours are approximate and in metres.

Chapter 4
INNER
QUATSINO SOUND

In Quatsino Narrows, a West Coast cruiser heads south.

Chapter 4
INNER QUATSINO SOUND

TIDES

Volume 6, Canadian Tide and Current Tables

Reference Port: Winter Harbour

Secondary Port: Bergh Cove (Eastern Quatsino Sound), Coal Harbour (Rupert Inlet and Holberg Inlet), Port Alice (Neroutsos Inlet)

CURRENTS

Current Station: Quatsino Narrows

WEATHER

Weather Channel VHF WX1 Eliza Dome. 21B Holberg.

Areas: West Coast Vancouver Island North—listen for Quatsino Lighthouse for weather at the entrance to Quatsino Sound and Holberg for the inner sound and inlets.

Note: Deep in the sound and inlets the area's topography affects wind and weather conditions. Winds tend to build during the day and funnel along the direction of the sound and inlets.

Whale jawbone, Coal Harbour, Holberg Inlet.

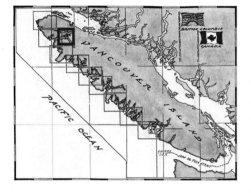

CAUTIONARY NOTES

The flooding tide produces an east-flowing current in Quatsino Sound, whereas Holberg, Rupert and Neroutsos inlets will experience an up-inlet current. The current direction is reversed by the ebbing tide. Current in Quatsino Narrows will reach 9 knots, tabulated at the current station at Quatsino Narrows. The narrows are best transited at slack water with the turn of the current in your favour.

East of Brockton Island in Inner Quatsino Sound, the Pacific swell diminishes and a variety of interesting anchorages and communities draw visitors into the inlets of Holberg, Rupert and Neroutsos. Tucked into the middle section of northern Drake Island, Pamphlet Cove is a cozy anchorage with protection from all quarters except the N. In Hecate Cove, the "lower cove" offers good protection from SE winds and is a convenient spot to wait for favourable current in Quatsino Narrows.

The channel through Quatsino Narrows is approximately 3 km (2 miles) in length and about 270 metres (900 ft) in width, with currents that can reach 8 knots. The most turbulent waters are near Makwazniht Island, on the NE side of the narrows. Twice each day the tidal waters of Rupert and Holberg inlets have to squeeze into and out of the narrows—so timing is critical. Transiting at slack water is recommended, and you can enjoy the forested sheer cliffs rising on either side. Watch for a burial cave on the western shore; the narrows are also prime sea otter habitat.

The community of Coal Harbour in Holberg Inlet has expanded the public wharf and added a much-needed fuel dock, making this a more attractive stop for the visiting boater. Local attractions also include a massive whale jawbone, and ice cream from Lucky Louie's Café.

West of Coal Harbour, at the entrance to Rupert Inlet, the curious cruiser will find a pristine anchorage with a superb view: Varney Bay, the Marble River estuary and magnificent Marble Canyon offer a haven for migrating birds and boaters.

Back outside the narrows and down to the SE, the community of Port Alice perches on the side of a mountain with a magnificent view of Neroutsos Inlet and the west shore mountains. Port Alice is a friendly spot to spend a few days: you can provision, fill with fuel, throw in the laundry, and enjoy one of the best hot showers since Port Hardy.

On your way out of Quatsino Sound, you will find two anchorages on Buchholz Channel: popular Julian Cove, which will accommodate a large boat; and Smith Cove, a peaceful hideaway encircled by forest that provides almost landlocked protection.

Note: The small wharf in Bergh Cove, NE of Drake Island, is used primarily by the Native community. The wharf at Jeune Landing, N of Port Alice, is used by the coast guard and local boats.

FEATURED DESTINATIONS

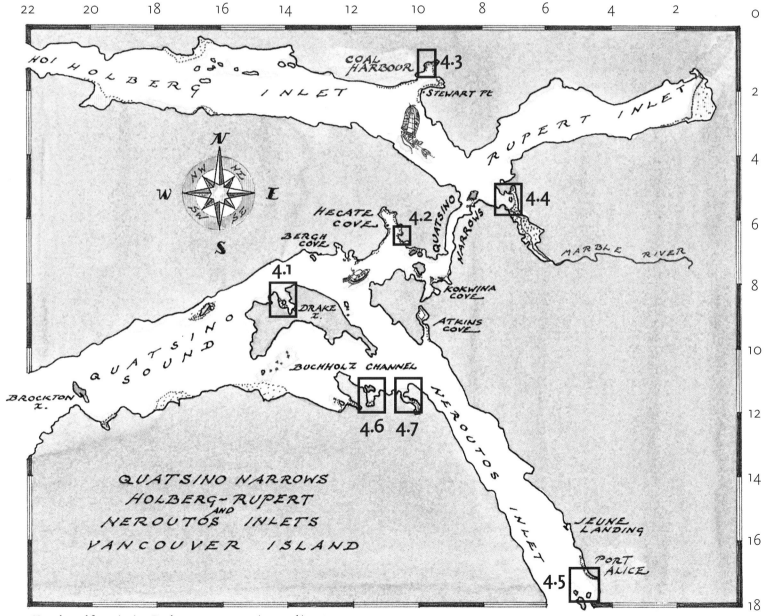

Not to be used for navigation. Depth contours are approximate and in metres.

CHARTS 3679.

APPROACH From the N. The approach is clear to the kelp that straddles the cove; coast through the kelp to the inner anchoring pool.

ANCHOR Good protection from all quarters except N. Good holding in mud in depths of 3–6 m (10–20 ft). Although the inner anchorage is very calm, in moderate winds anchorage is possible outside the kelp. This is a popular anchorage–taking a stern line ashore will make more space available in the busy summer months.

Note: Although the cove is open to the N, moderate winds tend to die off at the entrance.

✿ 50°31.47'N 127°39.54'W

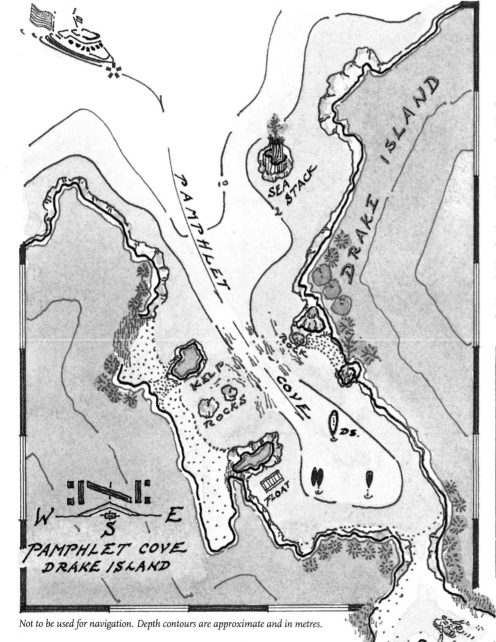

Not to be used for navigation. Depth contours are approximate and in metres.

The island was named for Sir Francis Drake (some historians believe he visited the BC coast during his epic 1577–80 circumnavigation) and in 1909 was the site of a three-storey hotel and store. Today Pamphlet Cove provides cozy anchorage and is a designated provincial boat haven (for more information about BC Provincial Boat Havens, catalogued by the Council of BC Yacht Clubs, visit www.cbcyachtclubs.ca) and a popular refuge from inclement weather. Land bordering the cove is private, but the nooks and crannies of Drake Island are worth exploring by dinghy.

Rafted in the quiet waters of Pamphlet Cove.

CHARTS 3679. 3681 (detail Quatsino Narrows).

APPROACH At LW from the NW once in Hecate Cove.

ANCHOR Hecate Cove is more of a bay. The "lower cove" offers good protection from the SE but is open to the NW. Swing along the eastern shoreline or take a stern line to the log conveniently chained to Kitten Islet. The holding is good in gravel and mud in 3–8 m (10–26 ft). Alternative anchorage is possible at the head of the cove.

Note: Quatsino Boat Yard in Hecate Cove has closed (2008) and is now a private residence.

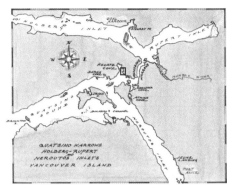

✽50°32.60'N 127°35.62'W

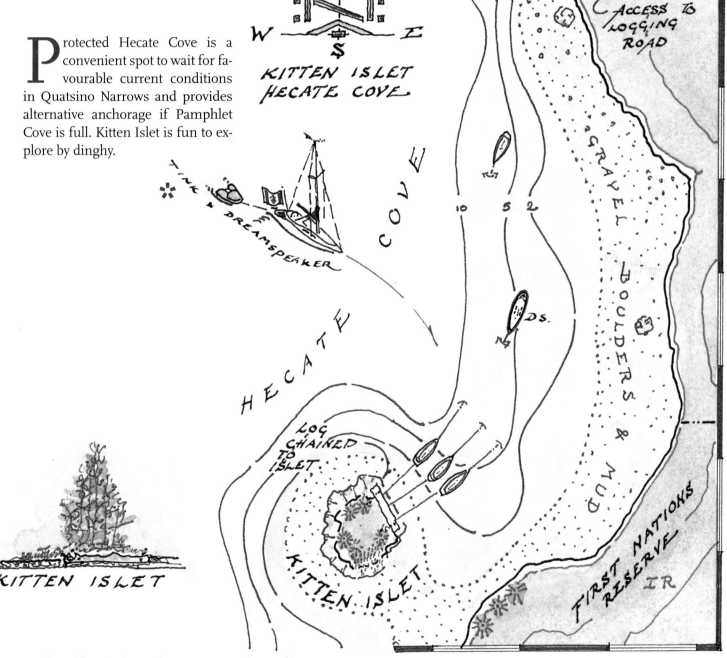

Protected Hecate Cove is a convenient spot to wait for favourable current conditions in Quatsino Narrows and provides alternative anchorage if Pamphlet Cove is full. Kitten Islet is fun to explore by dinghy.

Not to be used for navigation. Depth contours are approximate and in metres.

4.3 COAL HARBOUR, HOLBERG INLET

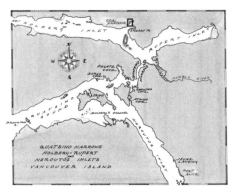

✽ 50°35.85'N 127°34.83'W

CHARTS 3679. 3681 (detail Coal Harbour).

APPROACH From the SW (Waypoint is S and W of the wharfhead). The approach is clear.

ANCHOR E of the public wharf only.

PUBLIC WHARF Extensive floats available for visiting boats. Power and water are available on the dock. Washroom and shower facilities are close by.

MARINA A small private marina lies W of the public wharf.

FUEL Fuel barge at W end of the public wharf has diesel and gas.

LAUNCH Private.

Approaching the wharfhead.

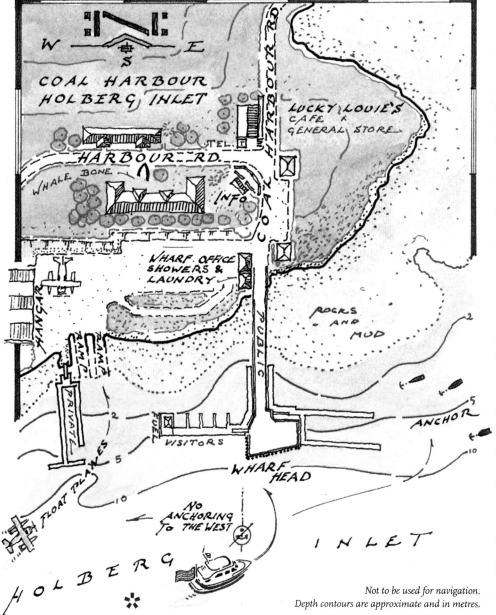

Not to be used for navigation.
Depth contours are approximate and in metres.

Coal Harbour takes its name from the coal deposits discovered in the area in 1883. During the Second World War, Coal Harbour was a base for the Royal Canadian Air Force, and the wartime buildings are still in use today. A whaling station operated here from 1947 to 1967; it was the last one on the North American coast when it closed. The station is now a shipyard and float plane hangar.

With the expansion of the public wharf and the addition of a much-needed fuel dock, Coal Harbour has become more attractive to visiting boaters.

The community has an unusual monument—the massive jawbone of a blue whale, almost 7 metres (23 ft) long and believed to be the largest in the world! If you haven't had an ice cream in weeks, head up from the wharf to Lucky Louie's Café and General Store, where you will find friendly service, groceries, fresh and frozen produce, soup and sandwiches, and specialty pizzas to go. A government liquor store outlet is planned for 2008–09.

It's just 17 km (11 miles) by road from Coal Harbour to Port Hardy should you need to do some serious provisioning—get friendly with the locals or call North Island Taxi (250-949-8800).

VARNEY BAY, RUPERT INLET 4.4

CHARTS 3679.

APPROACH Enter between islet (1) southeast of Kenny Point and the rock that extends NE from islet (3). Round islet (2) into the anchorage.

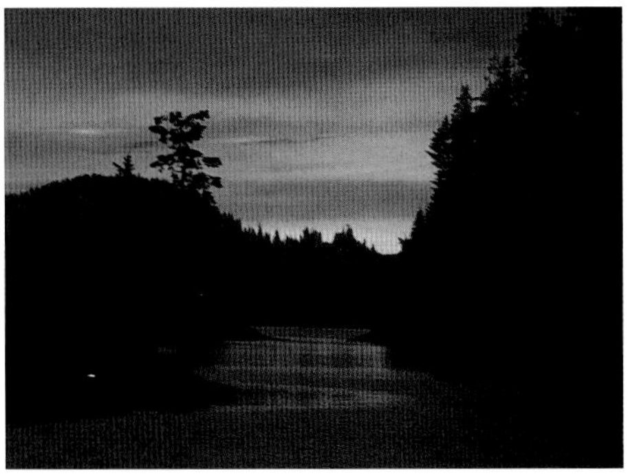

Sunset filters into Varney Bay.

ANCHOR Drop the hook in the NE cove, which offers good protection from the prevailing westerly winds out of Holberg Inlet. Alternatively, anchor along the southern shoreline as indicated. Note that this spot is more open and subject to the current, but affords excellent views to the Marble River Estuary. Good holding in mud and shell in 4–8 m (13–26 ft).

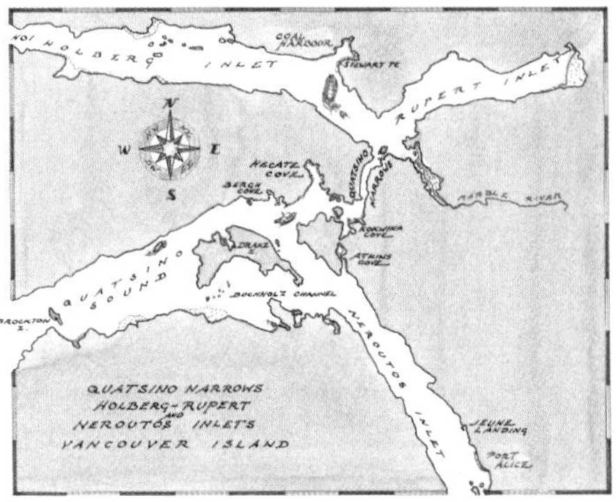

50°33.30'N 127°32.28'W

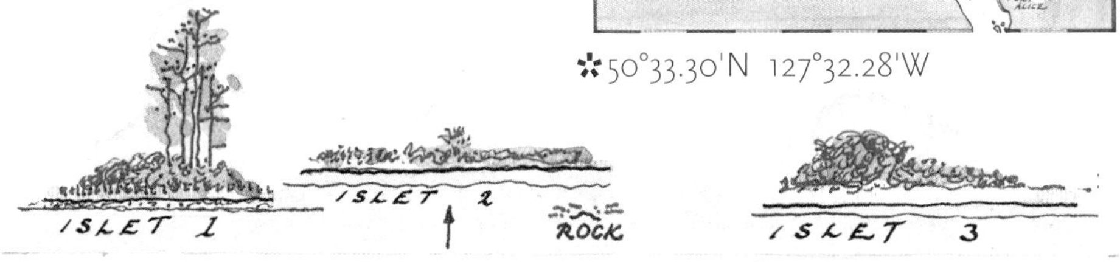

A pristine anchorage with a superb view, Varney Bay and the Marble River estuary are havens for migrating birds, ducks and boaters. Seals use the bay as a haul out and pupping area, and Marble River Provincial Park protects one of the most significant steelhead and chinook salmon runs in Quatsino Sound.

On our visit, the anchorage and surrounding forest were filled with a variety of bird sounds, from the piercing twitter of eagles to the laughter of loons, which were abundant. Sea otters fished and frolicked in the kelp while we amused ourselves for hours exploring the shoreline and islets.

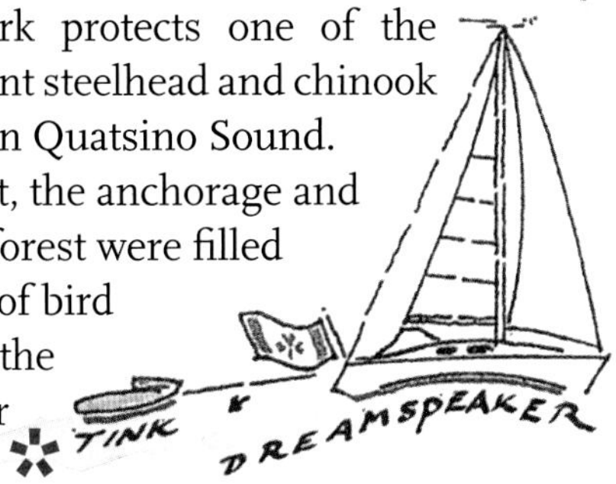

Note: Marble River runs from Alice Lake to Varney Bay. Kayaking friends and our anchorage neighbours with a small boat and outboard navigated the river before HW, following the flood tide up and returning with the ebb. Magnificent Marble Canyon, the most picturesque portion of the river flows between rocks eroded with caves and shaded by hanging branches and foliage.

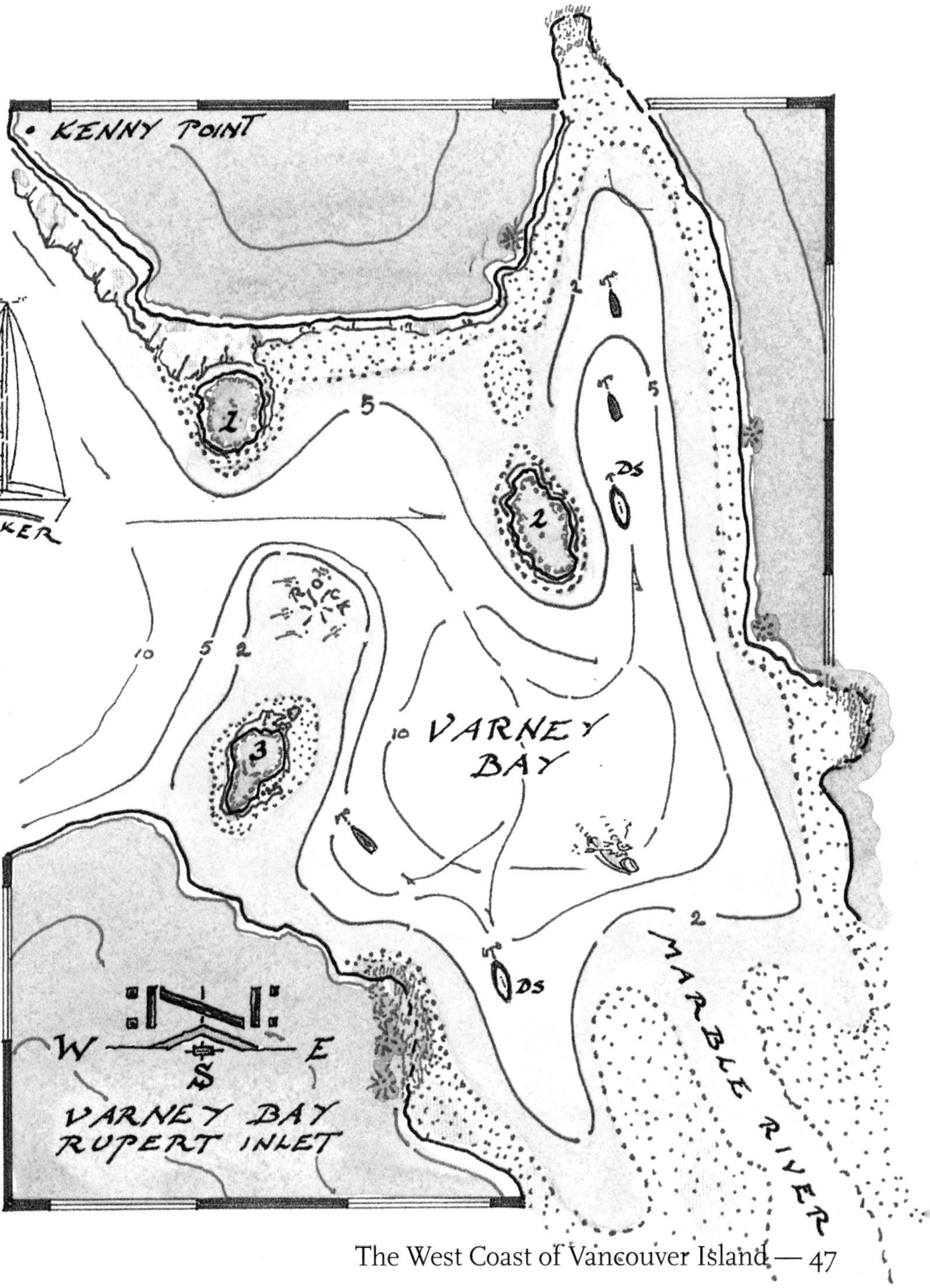

Not to be used for navigation.
Depth contours are approximate and in metres.

4.5 VILLAGE OF PORT ALICE, NEROUTSOS INLET

✲50°25.45'N 127°29.49'W

CHARTS 3679. 3681.

APPROACH From the NW, the Port Alice Yacht Club lies in a bight below Lion's Park. Leave the log breakwater to the N and tie up at the small marina or call ahead to arrange moorage and collect a gate key.

ANCHOR If space is unavailable or your boat is too long, temporary anchorage is possible off the park shoreline, where you can dinghy ashore and pull up on Rumble Beach. Depth and holding not recorded. Community Marina with ample visitor moorage is planned for 2009 (location illustrated).

MARINA Port Alice Yacht Club (call Errol Stewart 250-284-6100) welcomes visiting boaters and will make every effort to create temporary moorage (38–40 ft max). We were made very welcome in 2007.

FUEL Call Jack Masse (250-284-3379) and he will collect and deliver propane, gas and diesel to the ramp opposite the yacht club. He also runs the Port Alice Petroleum Products dock where propane and gas are available.

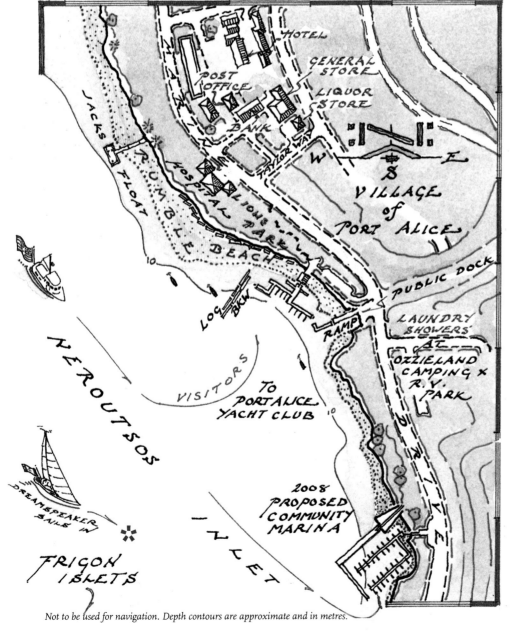

Not to be used for navigation. Depth contours are approximate and in metres.

The community of Port Alice is situated on the side of a mountain with a magnificent view out to Neroutsos Inlet and the west shore mountains. Port Alice was founded about 1917 with the building of the pulp mill, which is still the town's main employer and lifeblood. The town moved to its current location in 1965 to become British Columbia's first "instant" municipality.

The compact village of Port Alice is just a short walk through Lion's Park from the Port Alice Yacht Club. Here you will find the welcoming Visitor Information and Heritage Centre, a bank, a post office and library with cable internet connection, a well-stocked grocery and hardware store, a government liquor store and a health clinic.

Excellent natural gas-powered showers (with double stalls) and laundry facilities are available at the friendly Ozzieland Camping and RV, which also has a small café that serves delicious waffles, soup and sandwiches. If you have an overflowing bag of laundry call Ozzie (250-284-3422); you might be lucky enough to get a ride there and back if you are prepared to be flexible. Otherwise, it's a pleasant 15-minute walk along the village seawall.

Note: The village of Port Alice is marked on charts as "Rumble Beach." The location labelled "Port Alice" on the chart is the pulp mill.

Dreamspeaker *visits the Port Alice Yacht Club.*

4.6 JULIAN COVE, BUCHHOLZ CHANNEL

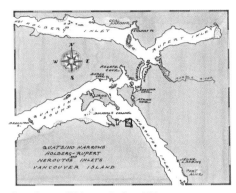

✳ 50°29.46'N 127°36.17'W

CHARTS 3679.

APPROACH From the NE. A one-tree islet and rocky outcrop lies W of the entrance. The approach is clear.

ANCHOR In the S of the cove where there is swinging room for a number of boats. Note that the bottom shallows rapidly. The anchorage affords good protection but is open to the N. Anchor in 4–8 m (13–26 ft) with good holding in mud.

Note: Although the cove is open to the NW, winds from that direction tend to dissipate within the cove.

Morning departure, Julian Cove.

From intimate Smith Cove we ventured on a ten-minute jaunt to anchor in the more roomy waters of protected Julian Cove; a one-tree islet and rocky outcrop indicates the entrance to the cove. We dropped anchor off the shallows that are backed by an extensive grassy marsh which provides a rich feeding ground for resident and migratory birds, ducks and geese. On our exploratory row we spotted a pair of nesting bald eagles hidden in a nearby tree, feeding and protecting their young.

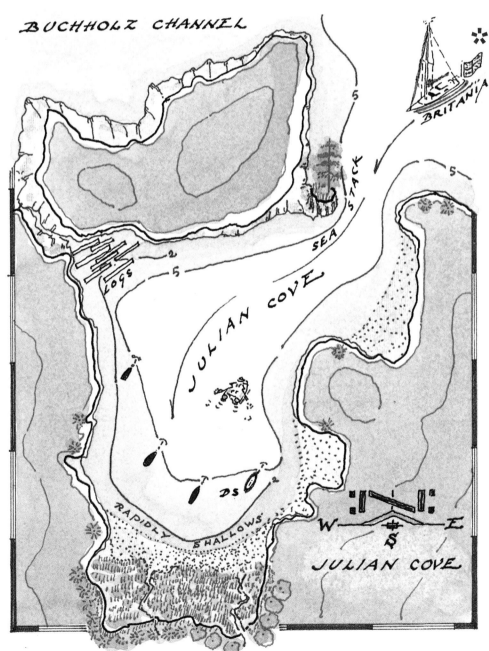

Not to be used for navigation. Depth contours are approximate and in metres.

CHARTS 3679.

APPROACH The entrance lies to the SE of Pender Point. Enter at LW when rocks are visible.

ANCHOR In the calm pool SE of the islet and rocky ledge. Good protection from all quarters with good holding in mud in depths of 3–7 m (10–23 ft).

✵ 50°29.49'N 127°35.55'W

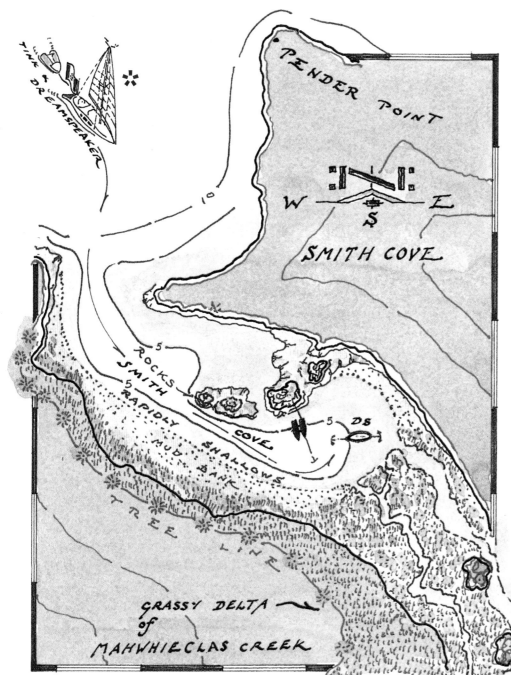

Not to be used for navigation. Depth contours are approximate and in metres.

A seal atop a hard-to-spot rock.

Entering Smith Cove at mid-tide, we were thankful to find a plump basking seal on the outermost rocks because there was no sign of kelp to indicate the dangerous extent of the rocky ledge. The sheltered cove is almost land-locked and offers a peaceful hideaway encircled by forest filled with bird chatter; tree branches tangled with moss skim the tranquil waters. Anchoring in the cozy SE pool, we disturbed a skittish family of mergansers slipping along the shallows—they disappeared into the grassy delta of Mahwhieclas Creek, only to reappear grace-fully when all was quiet.

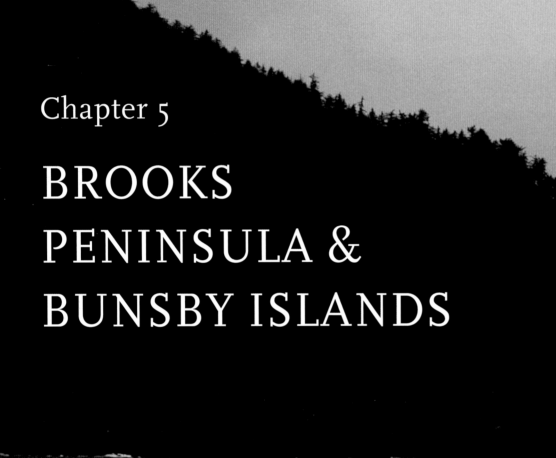

Chapter 5

BROOKS PENINSULA & BUNSBY ISLANDS

Brooks Peninsula lives up to its reputation—Cape Cook to port, Solander Island to starboard.

Chapter 5
BROOKS PENINSULA &
THE BUNSBY ISLANDS

TIDES
Volume 6, Canadian Tide and Current Tables
Reference Port: Tofino
Secondary Port: Bunsby Islands

CURRENTS
No current station for this area.

WEATHER
Weather Channel VHF WX1, Eliza Dome

Areas: West Coast Vancouver Island North—listen for Quatsino Lighthouse and South Brooks Marine Weather Buoy. For weather conditions to seaward of Brooks Peninsula, listen for wind strength and barometric pressure at Solander Island Light.

Note: Weather is dominated by Brooks Peninsula, a mountainous land mass that juts more than 10 km (6 miles) into the Pacific Ocean.

Green Head, a prominent sea stack in the Bunsby Islands.

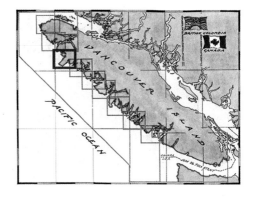

CAUTIONARY NOTES

Inshore navigation calls for careful avoidance of rocks and reefs. Watch for swell breaking over exposed rocks and kelp that marks submerged hazards. Exploring the northern shoreline of Brooks Peninsula is best done in southerly winds, when you may be sheltered in the lee of the peninsula. There are numerous unmarked but charted rocks here; however, due care will reward the adventurous.

Brooks Peninsula is the traditional dividing line between the territories of the Kwakwaka'wakw and Nuu-chah-nulth First Nations. The best conditions for rounding Brooks Peninsula are in light to moderate northwesterly winds. Conditions are seldom ideal offshore of Cape Cook and Solander Island, but waiting for a good weather window is essential for a safe, comfortable rounding.

If winds are SE and strong, there are three satisfactory anchorages to the east of Brooks Bay and NE of the peninsula. Tucked behind Anchorage Island is Klaskino Anchorage, a popular spot for boaters preparing to round Brooks Peninsula.

Named for the tribe that lived here, spectacular Klaskish Inlet is a deep, narrow channel some 20 m (66 ft) wide that leads to Klaskish Basin, with the near-pristine Klaskish River Estuary at its head. Klaskish Anchorage, E of McDougal Island in the mouth of this inlet, is used mainly by larger vessels but also offers good protection for smaller craft. This is the closest anchorage to Cape Scott.

Brooks Peninsula was untouched by the last ice age and its mountainous landscape is unique. The islets, reefs and rocks off its northern shore are rich with wildlife, and many of the rarest, most exotic birds of British Columbia's coast nest here. We were thrilled to view our first tufted puffins swimming alongside *Dreamspeaker*, and huge colonies of magnificent fur seals feeding off the wave-pounded reefs.

The offshore route around Brooks Peninsula lies well outside Cape Cook and Solander Island, giving Clerke Point plenty of sea room. The run E to the anchorages of Checleset Bay is usually a relief; however, don't let your guard down because there are still a few rocks and reefs to avoid here.

Columbia Cove, a small all-weather anchorage on the SE side of Brooks Peninsula, provides a safe refuge for pleasure craft and commercial vessels. Tucked in behind Jackobson Point and "Protection Island," the cove has two mooring buoys and space for six to eight boats.

Expansive Battle Bay has inviting sandy beaches that make for an exciting "day out," rain or shine. The sweeping crescent beach to the north is backed by sun-bleached driftwood.

Surrounded by numerous reefs, rocks and pocket beaches, the low-lying Bunsby Islands are a delight to explore by kayak or, if you've settled in one of the four anchorages, by motorized dinghy.

FEATURED DESTINATIONS

Not to be used for navigation. Depth contours are approximate and in metres.

5.1 KLASKINO ANCHORAGE, SCOULER ENTRANCE

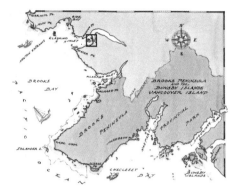

⁂ 50°18.37'N 127°49.87'W
(just to the west of buoy)

50°18.38'N 127°49.95'W

CHARTS 3651 (detailed) Scouler Entrance.

APPROACH From Scouler Entrance between Mocino Point and the starboard-hand (red) buoy. The channel to the small boat basin and Klaskino Anchorage should be navigated with care to avoid two large rocks that lie off the NE shore of Anchorage Island.

ANCHOR (1) In the small basin between Anchorage Island and the string of islets to the E. (2) Off the waterfall or creek delta in Klaskino Inlet in depths of 8–10 m (26–33 ft) with good holding in mud. Alternatively pick up one of the four mooring buoys to the S. (See note on buoys below.)

Note: Visiting boaters have reported that the condition of the mooring buoys is deteriorating (2008).

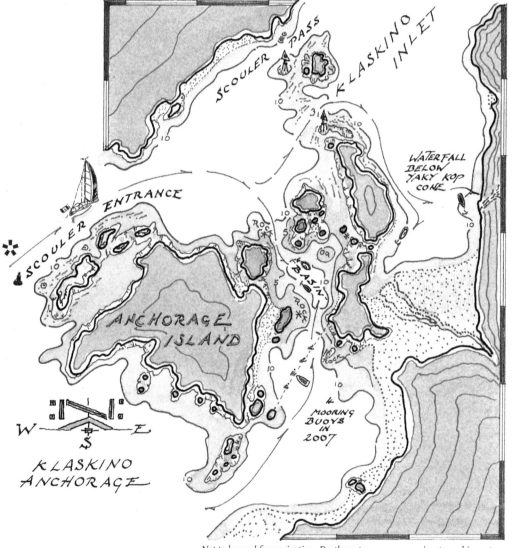

Not to be used for navigation. Depth contours are approximate and in metres.

Pilgrims Wake—*a variety of craft challenge the West Coast.*

Tucked behind Anchorage Island and backed by the steep cliffs of Yaky Kop Cone is Klaskino Anchorage, a popular spot for boaters preparing to round Brooks Peninsula. Klaskino Inlet curves northeast for about 5 km (3 miles) into the mountains of Vancouver Island and is an important stopover for migratory birds. The inlet also provides year-round protection for seabirds, ducks and shorebirds, and its streams support good stocks of coho and chum salmon.

In Scouler Entrance we witnessed a remarkable sight—a full-grown bald eagle "swimming" to the rocky shore with its white head and powerful wings barely above water. Clutched in his talons was a good-sized salmon that he dragged up onto the rocks to feast on.

CHARTS 3680.

APPROACH The waypoint lies S of the unnamed rock, W of the hook-shaped peninsula that defines the NW edge of the entrance. The entrance channel is deep and free of obstructions.

ANCHOR SW or NE of the line of four mooring buoys in 4–8 m (13–26 ft) with good holding in sticky mud. Alternatively pick up a mooring buoy. (See note on buoys page 56.)

Note: Waypoint is south and west of the rock as indicated.

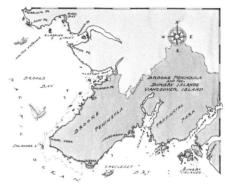

✳50°14.46'N 127°44.09'W

In bad weather, a handy buoy—Anne visits to catch up on cruising news.

Spectacular Klaskish Inlet is a deep, narrow channel some 20 m (66 ft) wide that leads to Klaskish Basin, with the near-pristine Klaskish River Estuary at its head. The river is navigable by kayak and protected by the Klaskish River Ecological Reserve, which encompasses the lower 1.5 km (1 mile) of the river, half of the basin and the neighbouring uplands. Watch for black oystercatchers, surf scoters and pigeon guillemots. The reserve shelters waterfowl in the winter months and the river supports a variety of salmon species.

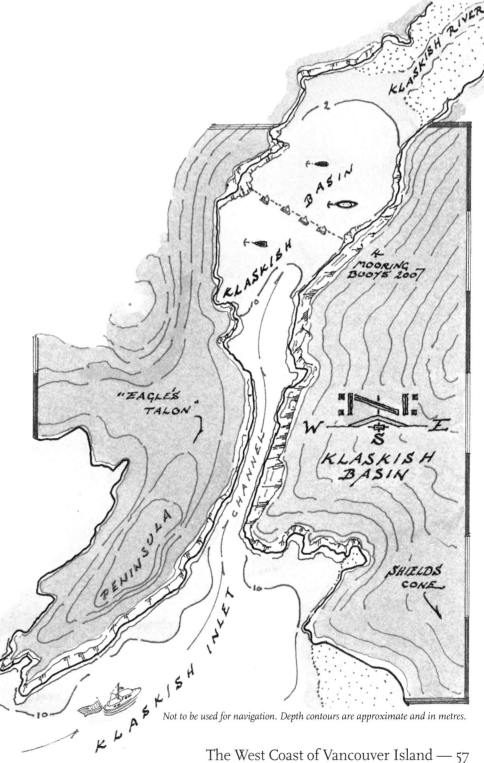

Not to be used for navigation. Depth contours are approximate and in metres.

5.3 KLASKISH ANCHORAGE

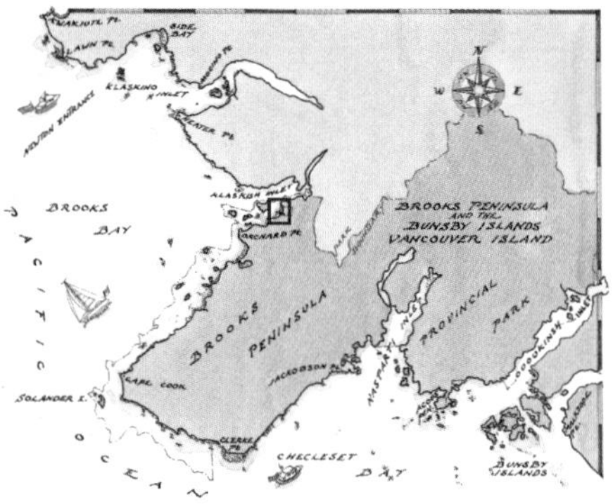

✲ 50°14.22'N 127°45.84'W

CHARTS 3690.

APPROACH From the N, leaving the port-hand (green) mark to the E.

ANCHOR Tuck in between the rock and the delta where the creek current keeps the boat off the shallows. Holding is good in very sticky mud in 6-10 m (20–33 ft).

Note: The anchorage shallows rapidly.

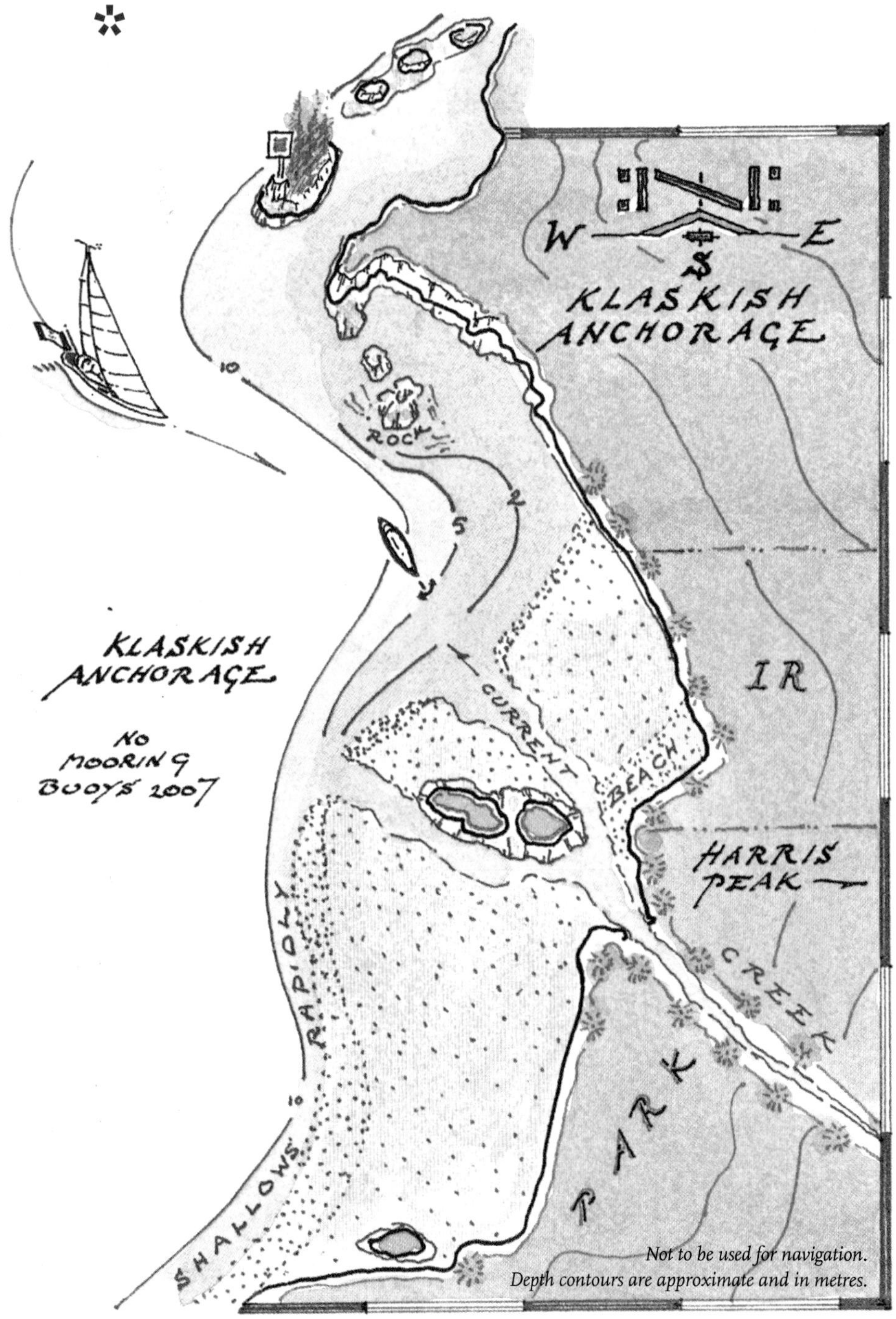

Not to be used for navigation. Depth contours are approximate and in metres.

The Klaskish Anchorage east of McDougal Island is used mainly by larger vessels but also offers good protection for smaller craft. Tucked in behind Brooks Peninsula, this is the closest anchorage to Cape Cook. We dropped our hook off the shallows for the night because we planned an early-morning start to round Cape Cook and Brooks Peninsula ahead of deteriorating weather. *Dreamspeaker* was well protected from the strong SE winds and swell.

Just up from the beach, the Brooks Peninsula Provincial Park shelter contains a map of the park and its boundaries.

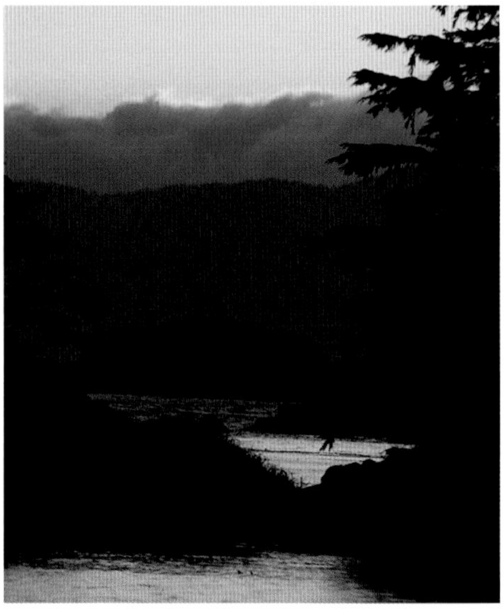

Morning after a stormy night in Columbia Cove.

CHARTS 3683.

APPROACH From the E staying well clear of Jackobson Point. The anchorage lies to the NW of "Protection Island."

ANCHOR This anchorage is protected in all weather. Three or four boats can anchor in relatively shallow water to the W of the two mooring buoys. Good holding in a sand and shell bottom in depths of 3–4 m (10–13 ft).

Note: There were two mooring buoys in commission in 2007—#1 in 2 m (6 ft) and #2 in 2.5 m (8 ft) at zero tide (See note on buoys page 56) It's possible to raft two or three boats to the mooring buoys.

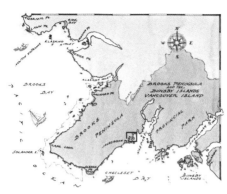

✻ 50°08.09'N 127°40.97'W

A small, all-weather cove on the E side of Brooks Peninsula is named in the *Sailing Directions* as Columbia Cove and by locals as "Peddlar's Cove." It offers safe refuge for pleasure and commercial vessels; it is a Provincial Boat Haven. Tucked behind Jackobson Point and "Protection Island," the cove offers two mooring buoys and space for up to seven or eight boats, depending on how many boaters choose to raft together.

Named "Columbia's Cove" by Captain Robert Gray and the crew of *Columbia Rediviva,* which anchored here several times to trade with the Checleset people in the late 1700s, it retains a wild feel that's enhanced by the wreck of a coast guard cutter at its entrance.

In the SW corner of the cove, a sign marks the trail to a wide sandy beach that's usually filled with mounds of driftwood and a variety of beachcombing treasures. Take a dinghy ashore and hike the trail to the ocean. The sight of the ocean beach being swept by gale-force waves will make you appreciate the shelter of the cove.

Note: Consider the state of the tide when looking for a good spot to secure your dinghy.

5.5 BATTLE BAY AND "WEST" BATTLE BAY

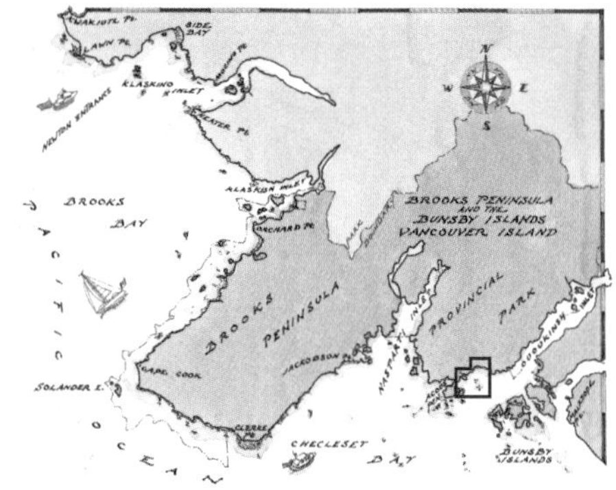

✣ (A) 50°06.66'N 127°34.05'W
to SE of Skirmish Islets

CHARTS 3683.

APPROACH Best navigated at LW keeping O'Leary and Cuttle islets to the north. Approach (A) Battle Bay NE of the Skirmish Islets and (B) "West" Battle Bay W of the Skirmish Islets.

ANCHOR

(A) Good protection from NW winds and swell in "West" Battle Bay.

(B) Good protection from N winds but less protection from swell.

Both have good holding in shingle and mud in 4–12 m (13–40 ft).

Battle Bay is said to have been named for the many skirmishes that took place here between the local Checleset tribe and the powerful Haida Nation, which built large ocean-going war canoes and were known to paddle south from the Queen Charlotte Islands (Haida Gwaii) to make war on southern tribes.

Acous Peninsula to the S is Indian Reserve. The Checlesets (the northernmost band of the Nuu-chah-nulth) moved here in the early 1800s and evidence of the village, five longhouses and crumbling house posts, can still be seen today. Because this is private land, permission must be obtained to visit the area. Inquire at the village of Houpsitis in Walters Cove.

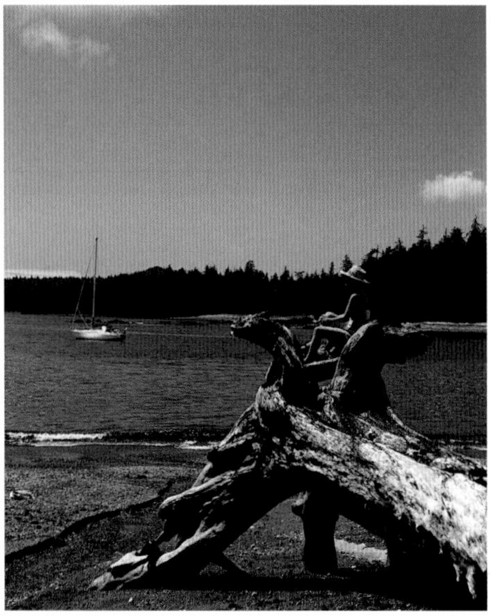

A big log makes for a good view.

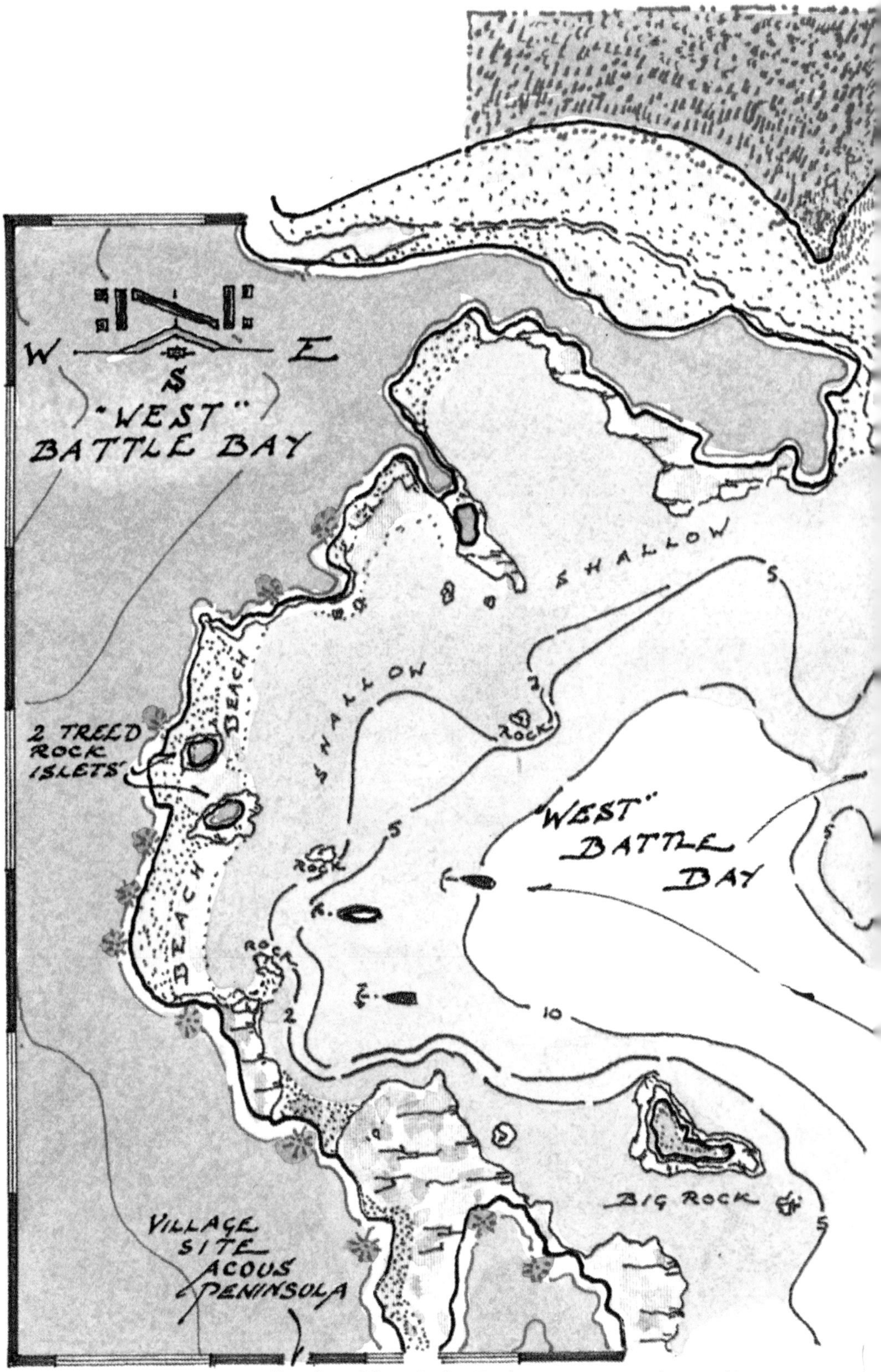

Not to be used for navigation. Depth contours are approximate and in metres.

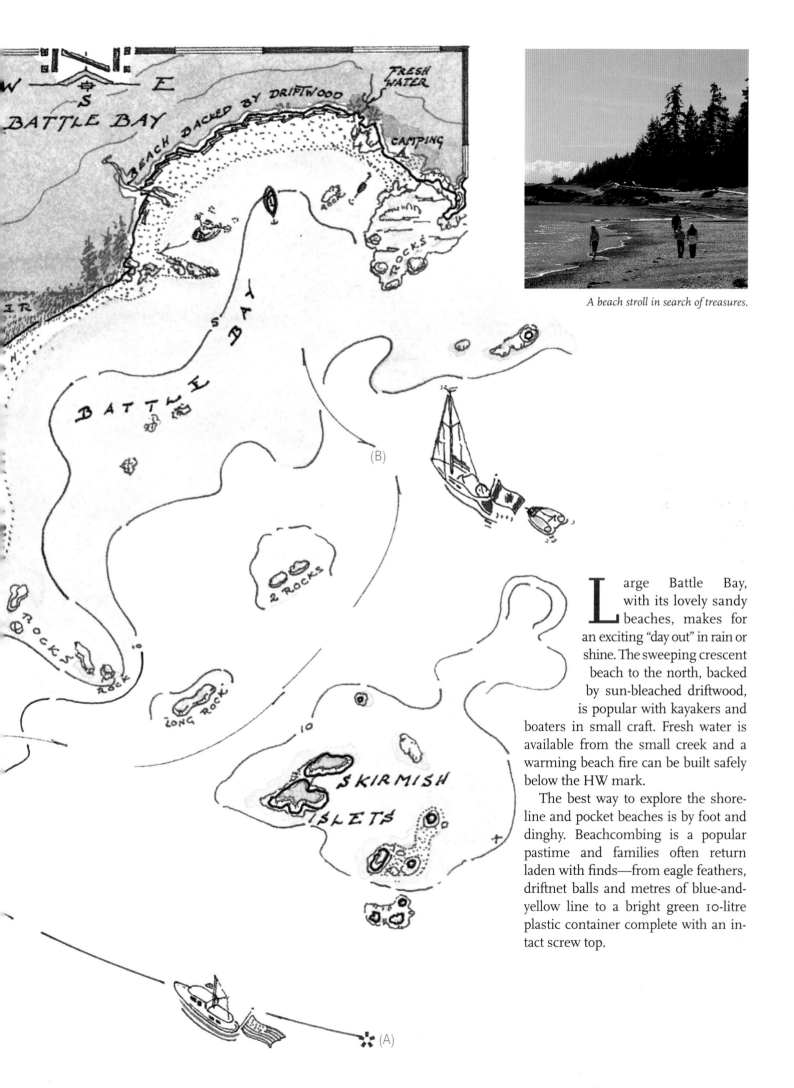

A beach stroll in search of treasures.

BATTLE BAY

FRESH WATER

CAMPING A

BEACH BACKED BY DRIFTWOOD

W E N S

ROCKS

I R

BATTLE BAY

BATTLE BAY

(B)

2 ROCKS

ROCKS ROCK

LONG ROCK

SKIRMISH ISLETS

(A)

Large Battle Bay, with its lovely sandy beaches, makes for an exciting "day out" in rain or shine. The sweeping crescent beach to the north, backed by sun-bleached driftwood, is popular with kayakers and boaters in small craft. Fresh water is available from the small creek and a warming beach fire can be built safely below the HW mark.

The best way to explore the shoreline and pocket beaches is by foot and dinghy. Beachcombing is a popular pastime and families often return laden with finds—from eagle feathers, driftnet balls and metres of blue-and-yellow line to a bright green 10-litre plastic container complete with an intact screw top.

5.6 THE BUNSBY ISLANDS

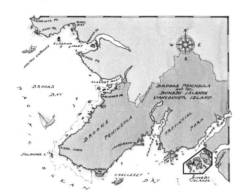

❖ (A) 50°06.68'N 127°31.89'W
❖ (B) 50°05.61'N 127°30.38'W

Unique rock formations mark the view south from the Bunsbys.

Cruising sailboat in "Scow Bay," Big Bunsby.

Sea otters were reintroduced to the West Coast in Checleset Bay Ecological Reserve between 1969 and 1972.

Surrounded by numerous reefs, rocks and pocket beaches, the low-lying Bunsby Islands are a delight to explore by kayak or, if you've settled in one of the four anchorages, by motorized dinghy. The Bunsbys were named by Captain George H. Richards of the Royal Navy survey ship *Hecate* for Jack Bunsby, a ship commander who was regarded as an oracle by retired Captain Cuttle in the Charles Dickens novel *Domby and Son*. Cuttle Islets were named for Captain Cuttle and Gay Passage for Walter Gay, while many other islets and points bear the names of characters in the Dickens work.)

The Bunsbys have a significant recent history of their own—they were the first site for the reintroduction of the sea otter, whose population was decimated by the fur trade in the early 19th century. Between 1969 and 1972, 89 sea otters were relocated from Alaska to the nearby Checleset Bay Ecological Reserve. Theirs is a success story: the last count on the West Coast found 2,700 of these "sea urchin guzzlers," whose eating habits help to sustain kelp forests—vital spawning grounds for an abundance of sea life.

The topcoat and dense underfur of the sea otter is composed of 100,000 hairs per square centimetre and is kept aerated by grooming and blowing on it to insulate its body from the chilly Pacific waters. Because of the insatiable European and Chinese market for the luxuriant thick fur pelts, the wild sea otter, *Enhydra lutris*, vanished from Canada in the 1920s–from 1741 to 1867, hunters took over 800,000 from North Pacific waters.

Between 1969 and 1972 eighty-nine Alaskan otters were transplanted to Checleset Bay on the west coast of Vancouver Island. Here they thrived on the abundance of sea urchins, which in their absence had caused serious damage to the vital kelp forests along the west coast; kelp beds help buffer the unprotected shorelines and provide significant spawning areas and hidey-holes for an assortment of sea life–from a variety of fish to octopuses and grey whale calves.

Happily these playful, urchin-munching creatures have thrived, and recent boat and air counts recorded up to 3,200 sea otters on the BC coast, 2,700 being sighted on the west coast of Vancouver Island.

CHARTS 3683.

APPROACH There are two passages between the Bunsby Islands:

(A) Gay Passage is the main artery and preferred route through the Bunsbys. Approach from the N at the entrance to Ououkinsh Inlet. Gay Passage leads to 5.9 "Scow Bay" and 5.8 "West Nook." Alternatively, approach Gay Passage from the S, south of Upsowis Point. Although Gay Passage is the main channel, it has a number of rocks and should be navigated with caution.

(B) "False Gay Passage" is often mistaken for Gay Passage; in fact, it is a rock-strewn secondary channel. It should be navigated with extreme caution at LW when the rocks are visible. From the N it will lead to 5.7 "Green Head Cove."

The view from "West Nook," "Middle Bunsby Island."

Not to be used for navigation. Depth contours are approximate and in metres.

BUNSBY ISLAND ANCHORAGES

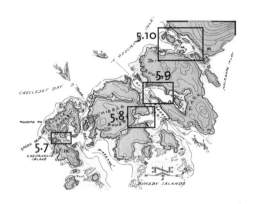

5.8 "WEST NOOK," "MIDDLE BUNSBY"

APPROACH From Gay Passage, enter centre, then favour the N or S side.

ANCHOR As indicated—good protection from northerly winds and swell, and moderate protection from the S. Anchor in depths of 6–12 m (20–40 ft) with moderate holding in a mix of gravel, rock and kelp.

Note: The nook provides anchorage for two to three boats on short scope.

A sizable native village occupied the SW shore of "Middle Bunsby Island" but after intensive logging, little remains today except a quiet, sheltered nook to explore or drop the hook for the night—and the wildlife.

Not to be used for navigation. Depth contours are approximate and in metres.

5.7 "GREEN HEAD COVE"

APPROACH If approaching from the N via "False Gay Passage," do so with extreme caution. The southern approach is straightforward except for the charted rock in its centre.

ANCHOR Good protection from northerly winds and swell in depths of 4–8 m (13–26 ft) with good holding in sand and mud. A shallow area extends out from the gap in the NW corner.

Note: The nook has room for one or two boats to swing on short scope.

Protected by the reefs of Checkaklis Island Indian Reserve to the south, "Green Head Cove" is a delight in favourable weather conditions. Green Head, a prominent sea stack to the west of the pocket shell beach, guards the anchorage. We stayed for two nights and could have stayed longer—the cove was filled with constant birdsong, and playful sea otters popped up within yards of *Dreamspeaker*.

Not to be used for navigation. Depth contours are approximate and in metres.

Wind whistles between "Little Bunsby" and Checkaklis islands.

Drying out after torrential rain, "West Nook."

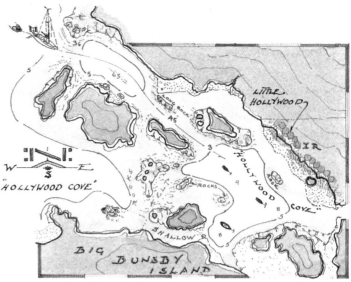

Not to be used for navigation. Depth contours are approximate and in metres.

5.10 "HOLLYWOOD COVE," LITTLE HOLLYWOOD

APPROACH From the NW at LW. The passage in is straight except for a kelp patch that requires careful navigation.

ANCHOR The cove has good protection from southerly winds and swell

and moderate protection from the N. Good holding in depths of 4–10 m (13– 33 ft) in sand/mud.

Note: Room for two or three boats on moderate scope— note the location of the rock that covers at HW.

The village of Little Hollywood, on the N shore of the mouth of Malksope Inlet, was home to the Checleset First Nation after they left Acous Peninsula and Battle Bay. The village site is now overgrown but the midden is bordered by salal and salmonberry bushes, soft green grass and fresh sea asparagus. When we visited, seal pups frolicked in the creek, a family of mergansers marched along the pebble beach, and a pair of bald eagles perched on their large family nest feeding their young.

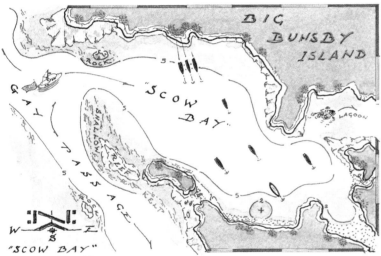

Not to be used for navigation. Depth contours are approximate and in metres.

5.9 "SCOW BAY," BIG BUNSBY PROVINCIAL MARINE PARK

APPROACH From Gay Passage. Enter from the N, close to the charted rock.

ANCHOR Swing W of the islet as indicated. Good all-round protection and the preferred anchorage in bad weather. Anchor in depths of

6–12 m (20–40 ft) with good holding in mud and gravel below the kelp.

Note: This is the largest of the four anchorages with room for six or seven boats on moderate scope.

Big Bunsby Island offers boaters a large protected cove known locally as "Scow Bay" and a lovely lagoon to explore at HW. The provincial park has no trails for hiking so our daily rowing exercise took us on exploratory trips between the kelp and into Gay Passage to photograph the elusive sea otters who love to play "hide and seek" with the lens.

Looking south from the Bunsbys, calm after the storm.

Chapter 6

KYUQUOT SOUND

The beach at Rugged Point Marine Park is a paradise for all, including joggers.

Chapter 6
KYUQUOT SOUND

TIDES

Volume 6, Canadian Tide and Current Tables

Reference Port: Tofino

Secondary Ports: Kyuquot, Copp Island, Fair Harbour

CURRENTS

No current station for this area.

WEATHER

Weather Channel VHF WX1 Eliza Dome.

VHF reception is good in Kyuquot but deeper into the sound it may be difficult to obtain a signal.

Areas: West Coast Vancouver Island North—listen for Kyuquot Weather Station and South Brooks weather buoy for offshore conditions.

Note: This is the raincoast—the west coast of Vancouver Island needs no excuse to rain and when it does, it buckets down!

Kayak launching—part of the MV Uchuck III service.

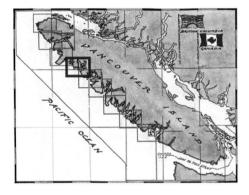

CAUTIONARY NOTES

The maze of off-lying shoals, rocks, islets and islands may be visually stunning, but skipper and crew should always be vigilant and watch ahead for any indication of covered reefs and rocks. In this chapter we were pointedly reminded that rocks don't make way for boats!

The run SE from the Bunsby Islands, inside the Barrier Islands, to the Mission Group and Walters Cove is nine nautical miles and calls for good visibility and careful navigation. If weather conditions and visibility are not ideal, it is prudent to take the offshore route, outside the Barrier Islands. Be sure to leave enough sea room to avoid the many islets, rocks and reefs that extend E from the Mission Group. This route takes 18 nautical miles before you can turn NE to Barter Cove via Nicolaye Channel.

Home to the Nuu-chah-nulth First Nations, Kyuquot Sound has a fertile ecosystem that includes beds of eelgrass in the lower intertidal zone that provide significant habitat for a variety of species, from shellfish to seabirds.

To gain safe access to Walters Cove and the small, friendly village of Kyuquot, Chart 3651 is essential—the sinuous passage is well marked but requires careful piloting. At Kyuquot, watch the artful unloading of provisions and kayakers in their craft from the MV *Uchuck III* on Thursdays; the best time to shop at the small market is Friday afternoon, when the newly arrived fresh produce is on display.

Barter Cove in the Mission Group of islands offers a great day stop or an alternative anchorage outside Walters Cove, where anchoring is not advised.

If you are in need of fuel or anchorage for the night, follow Kyuquot Channel into inner Kyuquot Sound, where you will find several anchorages worth exploring. Gas and diesel are available at the small marina at the head of Fair Harbour. While in Kashutl Inlet, visit the marshland below the creek in Hankin Cove, then enjoy a picnic on a nearby sandy beach with an open view down Kyuquot Sound.

Dixie Cove on Hohoae Island offers plenty of anchoring room. Divided into a sheltered "outer cove" and a bulletproof "inner cove," it is surrounded by parkland. The western shore of Amai Inlet, locally named "Blue Lips Cove" affords anchorage and shelter for three to four boats.

Discover some of the best sandy beaches on Vancouver Island at Rugged Point Marine Park. The park encompasses miles of accessible beach connected by a maintained trail.

FEATURED DESTINATIONS

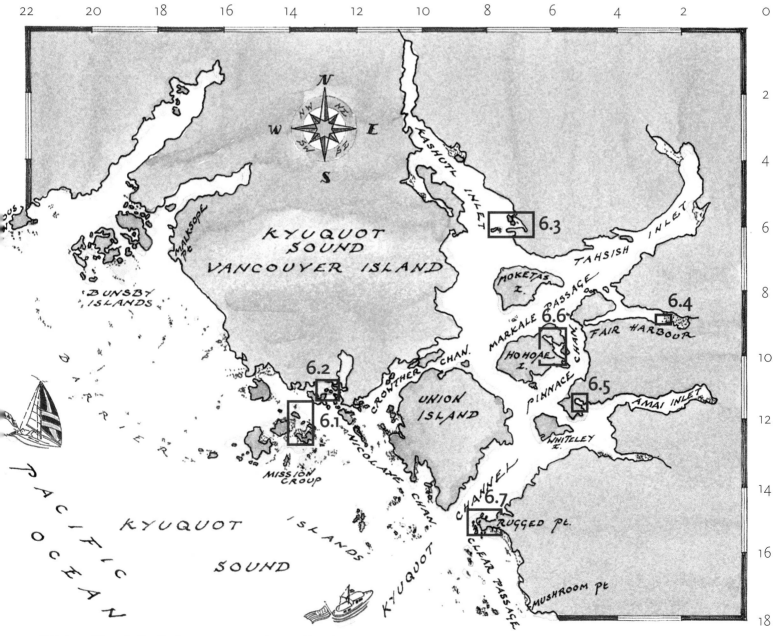

Not to be used for navigation. Depth contours are approximate and in metres.

6.1 BARTER COVE, MISSION GROUP OF ISLANDS

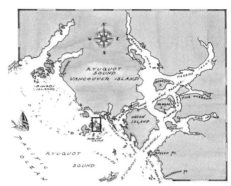

CHARTS 3682 (Kyuquot).

APPROACH From the N leaving Gayward Rock and light to the W. Enter favouring the islet shoreline.

ANCHOR Off Kamils Island with protection from moderate winds and swell. However, swell is still present and winds will whistle through the low-lying islands. Good holding in sand in depths of 4–6 m (13–20 ft).

✻ 50°01.17'N 127°23.08'W

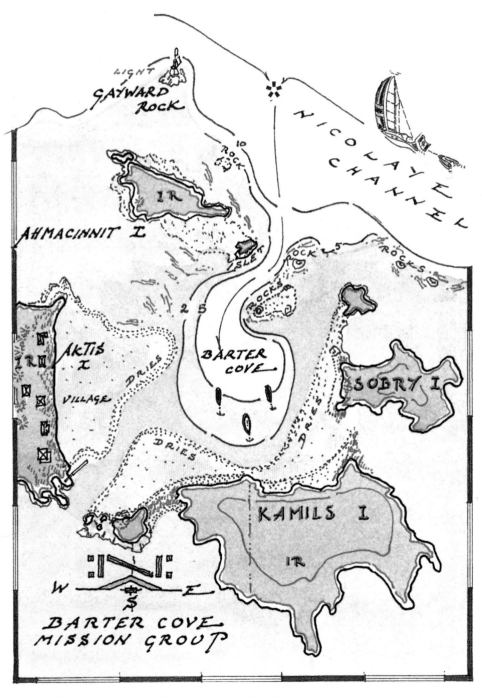

Surrounded by four islands that are all Indian Reserves, Barter Cove offers a great day stop or an alternative moorage to Walters Cove (Kyuquot), where anchoring is not advised. The grassy islet connected to Kamils Island by an isthmus is the only public section of the cove; its drying mud flats and sandy beach are worth exploring.

Aktis Island, known locally as Village Island, was the summer village of the Kyuquot people who moved there in the early 1800s because of the increasing fish oil and fur trade. Today, many of the houses are abandoned and only a small number of people live there.

Not to be used for navigation.
Depth contours are approximate and in metres.

A raft of female and young sea otters at Chief Rock.

6.2 COMMUNITY OF KYUQUOT, WALTERS COVE

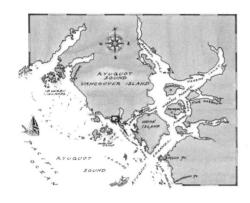

Kyuquot comes into view—leave the port-hand daymark to the west.

The public wharf is the centre of community activities.

Kyuquot Village and Houpsitas Indian Reserve (with its large school) occupy the south and north shores of Walters Cove and welcome visitors. Most of Kyuquot Sound's 200-plus residents live and work in these two villages.

The *Uchuck III* (known locally as the "Upchuck" during bad weather) is the lifeblood of Kyuquot, delivering fresh produce, groceries, fuel, appliances, locals, tourists and kayakers in their kayaks—it's a fun, fascinating time for all when she pulls into dock. Don't count on a quiet night but the well-stocked store the next afternoon makes all the commotion worthwhile. Kyuquot Market (250-332-5211) has a post office and accepts credit cards or direct debit cards.

In the small community stores on the West Coast we never asked prices—if we needed it or wanted it, we bought it (within reason). Transportation adds to the final price but we were always pleasantly surprised to find fresh fruit and vegetables in most stores.

Showers are available when the store owner's rental accommodation is not occupied—ask at the store. A floating, "motor-through" coffee shop called Java the Hutt is located at the entrance to Walters Cove.

Note: Miss Charlie, Walters Cove's adopted seal and mascot, was loved by all. In 2005, at the age of 41, she went out to sea and never returned. Miss Charlie was a playful character and brought much joy to the cove's residents and visitors. She is sorely missed.

MV Uchuck III is the lifeblood of Kyuquot.

CHARTS 3651 (detail Kyuquot).

APPROACH Enter the channel to Walters Cove NW of Rolston Island. Leave port-hand buoys (green) to port and starboard-hand buoys (red) to starboard.

ANCHOR Because of the network of cables that criss-cross the cove, anchoring is not recommended. The closest anchorage is in Barter Cove, Mission Group of Islands (see 6.1 page 70.)

MARINA All docks other than the public wharf are private.

PUBLIC WHARF Two long floating docks lie on either side of the causeway behind the wharfhead. The public wharf is used constantly by the community. They welcome visiting boaters but when it's busy, rafting is the norm. A donation for moorage to offset the cost of weekly garbage service is appreciated.

Note: Float planes use the cove regularly and moor at the base of the public dock. MV Uchuck III docks overnight at the wharfhead on Thursday evenings and departs Friday morning. See www.mvuchuck.com for the weekly itinerary. The best day to shop at the general store is Friday afternoon.

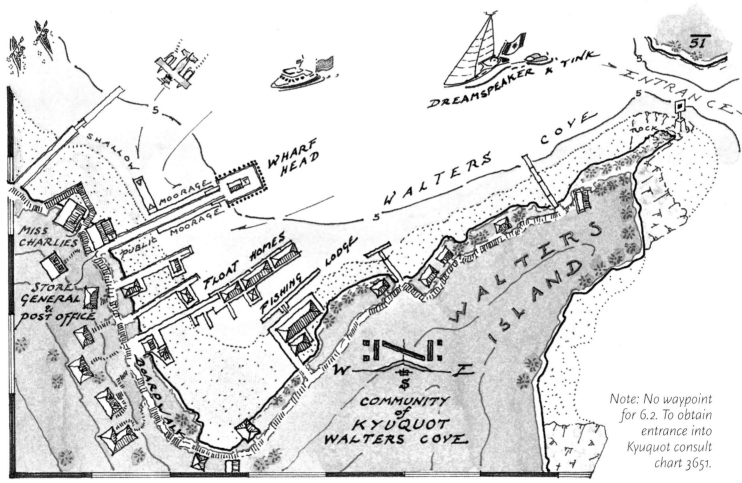

Note: No waypoint for 6.2. To obtain entrance into Kyuquot consult chart 3651.

Not to be used for navigation. Depth contours are approximate and in metres.

6.3 HANKIN COVE, KASHUTL INLET

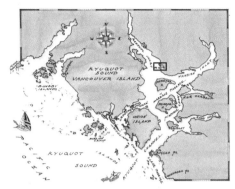

CHARTS 3682.

APPROACH From the S, midway between Expedition Islets and the promontory that juts out from the Vancouver Island shoreline; enter the cove along the promontory's N side.

ANCHOR Although the northern nook is favoured, good, all-weather protection can be found throughout the cove in 6–10 m (20–33 ft) with good holding in soft mud.

Note: The islet to the SW of the cove is low-lying and provides good protection from swell but only moderate protection from prevailing winds.

✿ 50°06.44'N 127°14.19'W

Cozy Hankin Cove is a delight on a sunny day. Visit the marshland below the creek where families of ducks, grebes and swans can be seen feeding, or settle on the large, grass-covered rock and build a fire ring for the evening's BBQ. Alternatively, take a trip north of the cove by motorized dinghy or kayak and enjoy a picnic on a lovely sandy beach with an open view down Kyuquot Sound.

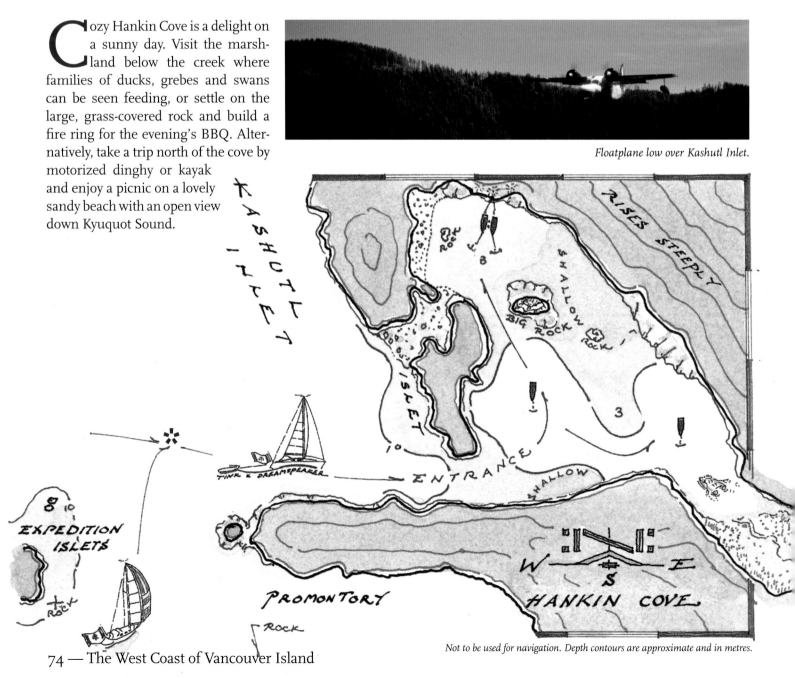

Floatplane low over Kashutl Inlet.

Not to be used for navigation. Depth contours are approximate and in metres.

A local fish boat departs Fair Harbour.

6.4 SWAN SONG AT FAIR HARBOUR

CHARTS 3682.

APPROACH Enter the harbour via a marked channel from Markale Passage. The public wharf (well used by local boats), fuel dock and moorage finger lie to the SE, at the head of the harbour.

ANCHOR No real anchorage available for small craft.

MARINA A small marina, consisting of a combined fuel dock and moorage finger, lies behind a log breakwater and is used mainly by sport fishing boats.

PUBLIC WHARF The finger stretches NW from the wharf head—moorage is sometimes available.

FUEL Gas, diesel, water are available year round except Christmas Day. Open 8 am–8 pm. Closed for an hour at dinner time (usually 5–6 pm). Pay at the store-office.

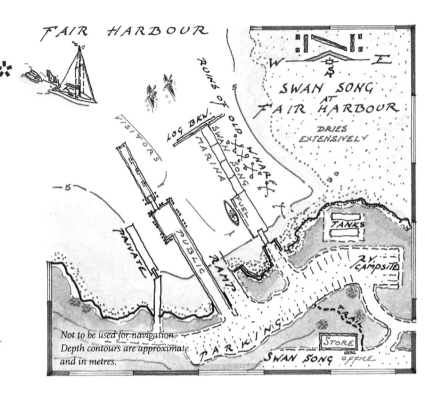

Not to be used for navigation. Depth contours are approximate and in metres.

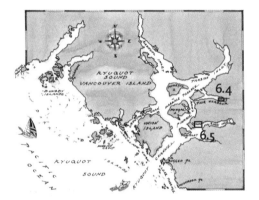

BOAT LAUNCH Private and used extensively by trailer boats and kayakers in the busy summer months—ask at the store, which stocks fishing gear, ice cream, milk and snacks.

Note: Unless fuel is a necessity, or you are picking up or changing crew and need road access, Fair Harbour offers the cruising boater few attractions.

6.4 ✿ 50°03.75'N 127°07.11'W
6.5 ✿ 50°01.35'N 127°10.41'W

"BLUE LIPS COVE," AMAI INLET 6.5

Not to be used for navigation.
Depth contours are approximate and in metres.

CHART 3682.

APPROACH From the SE. The cove is not named on the chart and lies NW of the entrance to Amai Inlet. The entrance is deep and free of obstructions.

ANCHOR In 7–9 m (23–30 ft) over a relatively even, soft mud bottom. Good shelter from all directions.

Known locally as "Blue Lips Cove," this snug anchorage affords shelter for three to four boats if one or two stern lines are taken ashore. Amai Inlet was marked as "Deep Inlet" on the original British Admiralty chart before the Canadian Hydrographic Service changed the name in 1947. Amai Point is a favourite haul-out for seals and sea lions.

DIXIE COVE PROVINCIAL PARK, 6.6
HOHOAE ISLAND

CHARTS 3682.

APPROACH From the SE the entrance channel lies between Copp Island and Hohoae Island. The outer cove is deep and the channel to the inner cove is 25 m (82 ft) wide with a minimum depth of 6.3 m (21 ft). The channel is clear.

ANCHOR The well-protected outer cove gives larger boats plenty of room to swing. Anchor in 8–14 m (26–46 ft) with good holding in mud. The all-weather inner cove requires shorter scope and offers good holding in mud in 6–10 m (20–33 ft).

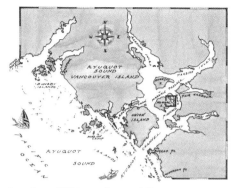

✿50°02.68'N 127°11.00'W

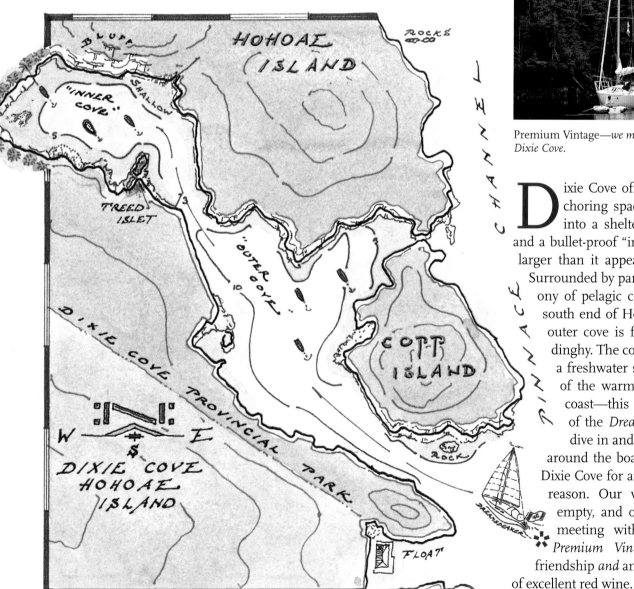

Premium Vintage—*we make a new friend in Dixie Cove.*

Dixie Cove offers plenty of anchoring space and is divided into a sheltered "outer cove" and a bullet-proof "inner cove" that is larger than it appears on the chart. Surrounded by parkland, with a colony of pelagic cormorants at the south end of Hohoae Island, the outer cove is fun to explore by dinghy. The cozy inner cove has a freshwater stream and some of the warmest water on the coast—this encouraged one of the *Dreamspeaker* crew to dive in and swim all the way around the boat. We remember Dixie Cove for another important reason. Our wine locker was empty, and our serendipitous meeting with the owner of *Premium Vintage* resulted in friendship *and* an adequate supply of excellent red wine.

Not to be used for navigation. Depth contours are approximate and in metres.

The anchorage north of Rugged Point offers boaters access to the park.

RUGGED POINT MARINE PARK 6.7

CHARTS 3682.

APPROACH From the NW after rounding the light on the tip of Rugged Point (give the point a wide berth).

ANCHOR Day anchorage is possible in the three coves defined by rock fingers that lie W to E between Rugged Point and Robin Point. Well protected from southerly and W to NW winds but open to the N. Strong summer outflow winds can develop at night and last through the morning hours. If staying overnight it is best to anchor well off the beach. Anchor in depths of 4–12 m (13–40 ft. Good holding in packed sand.

Note: Owing to the occurrence of strong outflow winds, we recommend overnight anchorage in 6.5 "Blue Lips Cove" or 6.6 Dixie Cove. Sightings of bear and cougar were reported in 2007.

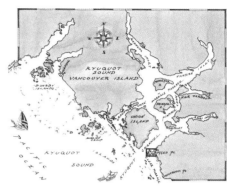

❂ 49°58.36'N 127°14.82'W

Lured by the prospect of exploring some of the best sandy beaches on Vancouver Island, we cautiously wound our way around the rocky shoreline of Rugged Point and dropped anchor in the clear waters of the easternmost cove of Rugged Point Marine Park. The white-sand pocket beaches glistened in the sunlight and campers played "driftwood hockey" on the firm-packed sand.

A favourite with kayakers, the marine park encompasses miles of accessible beach connected by a maintained trail that leads through old-growth Douglas fir. A wooden boardwalk covers the boggy sections. Your reward is a spectacular crescent beach of powder white sand backed by silver driftwood and littered with sand dollars. A "secret" warm salt-water pool is hidden in the rocky outcrop to the west of the first trailhead.

To the E a series of rocky outcrops interrupt the beach. Explore around the base of these outcrops, near the forest, and you'll find hidden trails with ropes, ladders and hand-holds to assist you on the steep climbs across these rocks. The trail around one of these outcrops leads through a forest of ancient cedar and spruce.

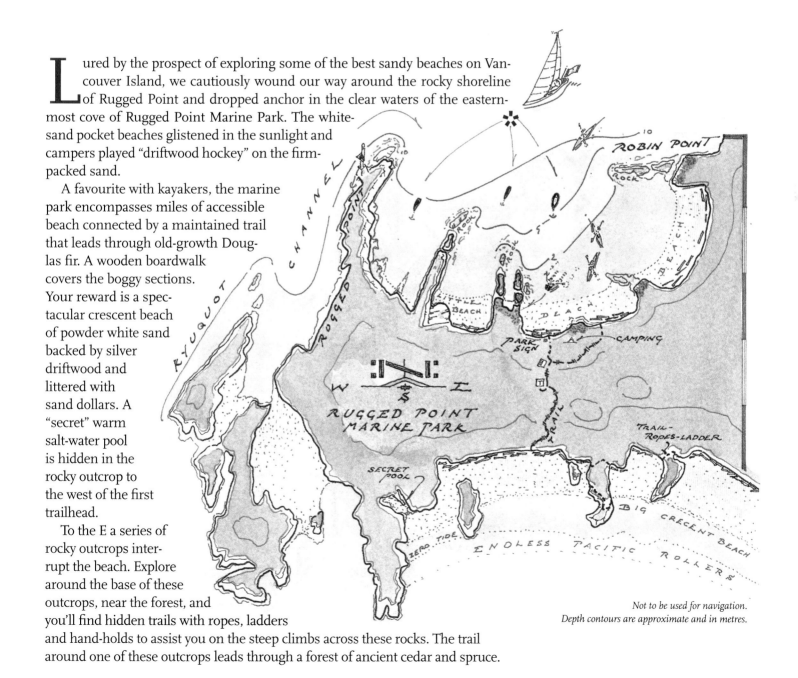

Not to be used for navigation.
Depth contours are approximate and in metres.

Chapter 7

ESPERANZA INLET

MV Uchuck III steams west in Tahsis Narrows.

Chapter 7
ESPERANZA INLET

The old mission church at Queens Cove Village.

TIDES

Volume 6, Canadian Tide and Current Tables
Reference Port: Tofino
Secondary Ports: Ceepeecee, Zeballos

CURRENTS

No current station for this area. Odd as it seems, Tahsis Narrows is free of strong tidal currents.

WEATHER

Weather Channel VHF WX1 Eliza Dome.

Areas: West Coast Vancouver Island South—listen for South Brooks and La Pérouse Bank for offshore weather and Nootka Lighthouse for the inlets.

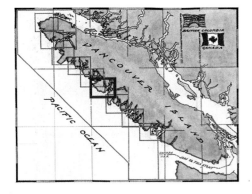

CAUTIONARY NOTES

The currents that swirl around Catala Island create confused seas—enter Rolling Roadstead only from the W in calm conditions. A maze of hazardous rocks and reefs fringe the entrance to Esperanza and Nuchatlitz inlets.

Note: For a shortcut to Tahsis Inlet (Chapter 8) follow Hecate Channel to Tahsis Narrows.

Heading SE from Kyuquot Channel, the offshore route takes you 20 nautical miles to Gillam Channel, which leads into Esperanza Inlet. Rolling Roadstead branches NW; Catala Island provides shelter from the Pacific swell.

The alternative inshore route from Rugged Point via Clear Passage rewards the boater with a spectacular West Coast seascape; we found ourselves surrounded by islets and reefs supporting uniquely shaped boulders and sea stacks. When exiting the passage, note the rock that dries 8 ft NE of McQuarrie Islets.

The triangular sand-and-pebble spit on the north side of Catala Island offers protected anchorage and accessible beaches, making it an enjoyable day stop for boaters; the marine park is very popular with campers in the summer. Anchor in the shelter of the spit and row ashore to investigate the sea caves.

Two well-protected anchorages are close by: peaceful Queen Cove at the entrance to Port Eliza, and the spacious anchorage in Nuchatlitz Marine Park. Walk along the park's sandy beach and isthmus at LW to the adjoining "kayaker's island" or take a HW dinghy trip to the outer islands to watch the sea otters at play.

Nuchatlitz Inlet offers an array of diverse anchorages. Port Langford is a deep bay with a choice of overnight spots to sample, pocket beaches to discover and sea caves to investigate by dinghy or kayak. Watch for the large eagle's nest and black bears feeding on the beach at dusk.

Farther E in Nuchatlitz Inlet is peaceful Mary Basin; we anchored off Laurie Creek estuary, opposite mottled cliffs and an exposed bluff. A dinghy ride up the creek rewarded us with a calming waterfall.

Louie Bay on the western tip of Nootka Island is often used by boaters prior to heading south on the outside. This is an inviting anchorage with extensive mud flats that finally become a tidal stream, which then connects to a storm channel before it reaches the Pacific Ocean.

Cruising farther N and E will bring you to Zeballos Inlet. Afternoon inflow breezes build to strong in Esperanza Inlet and will propel you smartly up Zeballos Inlet to the village of Zeballos. Here you will find fuel, a small general store and a BC Liquor Store; moorage at the public wharf could involve rafting up. With its many colourful, false-fronted buildings, this laid-back town has the ambiance of a Wild West movie. Take a walk to one of the pubs and enjoy a cold beer with the friendly locals.

FEATURED DESTINATIONS

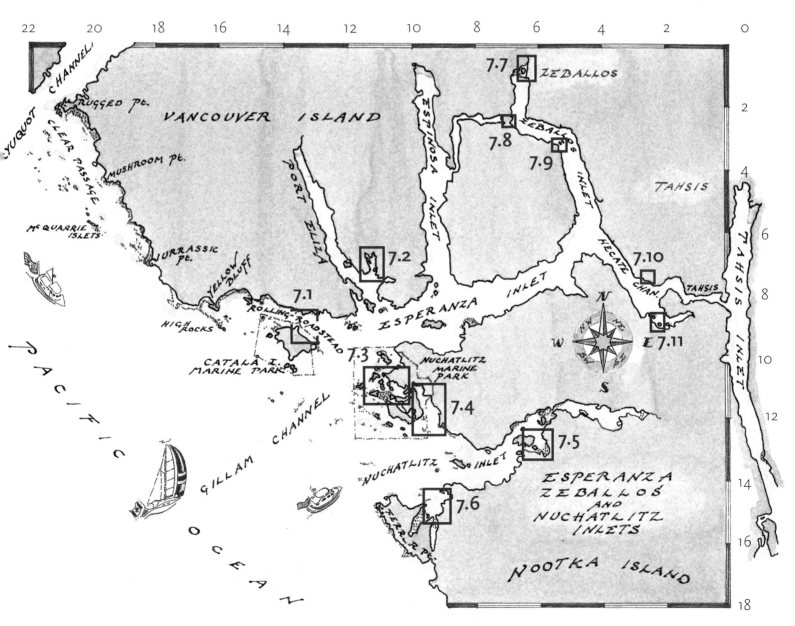

Not to be used for navigation. Depth contours are approximate and in metres.

7.1 "THE SPIT," CATALA ISLAND MARINE PARK

CHARTS 3676.

APPROACH From the NE out of Rolling Roadstead, where Catala Island's pebble-and-sand spit is highly conspicuous.

ANCHOR Tuck into the E side of the spit and anchor on a shelf in 3–5 m (10–17 ft). Good holding in gravel and sand. Not recommended as an overnight stop because the swell makes the anchorage uncomfortable.

✳ 49°50.76'N 127°02.55'W

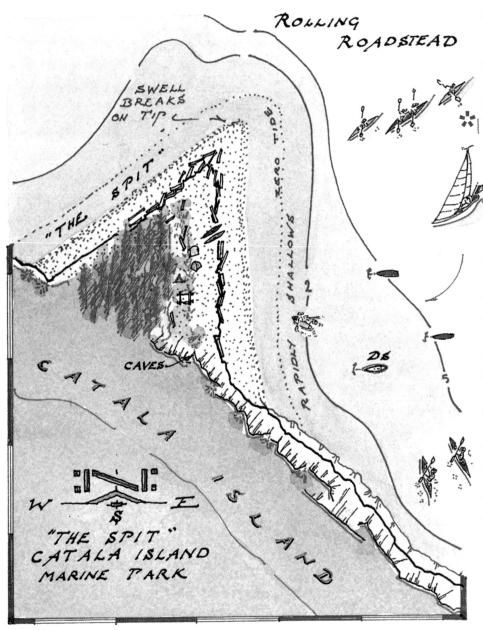

The triangular pebble-and-sand spit that has formed on the north side of Catala (KAT-a-la) Island provides a sheltered if rolly anchorage. For those who don't like the rolling, the spit is a great day stop. Nuchatlitz or Queen Cove, only a few miles away, provide quieter anchorages for the night. Catala Island Marine Park protects 850 hectares (2,100 acres) of the island plus other features close by: Halftide Reef, Twin Islands and White Rock, which supports a seabird breeding colony, one of the few in Nootka Sound.

Named for Rev. Magin Catala, a Franciscan monk and missionary, Catala Island is rocky and exposed on the outside but offers sheltered waters with accessible beaches on the inside, making it popular with kayakers and campers in the summer months. We anchored in the shelter of the spit and rowed ashore to explore the fascinating caves and sea stacks to the east of the spit. Near high water, the pebble beach is very steep, and wellies are required to get from your landing spot to the driftwood logs that enclose the campers' creatively constructed shelters and campsites.

Not to be used for navigation.
Depth contours are approximate and in metres.

CHARTS 3676.

APPROACH From Esperanza Inlet and Birthday Channel. The entrance to the cove lies NW of the small village of Queens Cove—the stone retaining wall along the foreshore is conspicuous. The approach is clear.

ANCHOR Excellent shelter from all quarters, but a slight swell does enter the bay. Anchor in 5–12 m (17–40 ft) with good holding in mud.

Note: Park River is navigable by dinghy and kayak at high water.

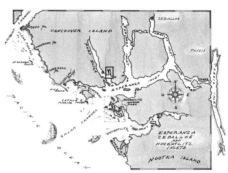

✷ 49°52.43'N 126°59.13'W

Peaceful and protected, Queen Cove is a favourite stop for cruising boaters circumnavigating Vancouver Island. Near the cove's entrance lies the small summer community known locally as Queens Cove; there are some abandoned homes on the waterfront and a weather-worn wooden church in the trees. The village was formerly occupied by members of the Ehattesaht Band; it was recorded in 1979 that Chief David John's grandfather, Chief Clakhoi, lived to be 115 years old in Queens Cove.

Houses hug the shoreline of the cove and a wrecked fishboat rests on the old cannery ways; old wooden pilings are sun-bleached and well camouflaged among the surrounding rocks. This is a lovely spot to spend a tranquil few days, especially if a northwesterly is up. Philip John, a former band chief councillor, notes: "This place is very well protected. We don't get wind unless it's doing thirty-five to forty miles per hour. Otherwise it bypasses us, over there."

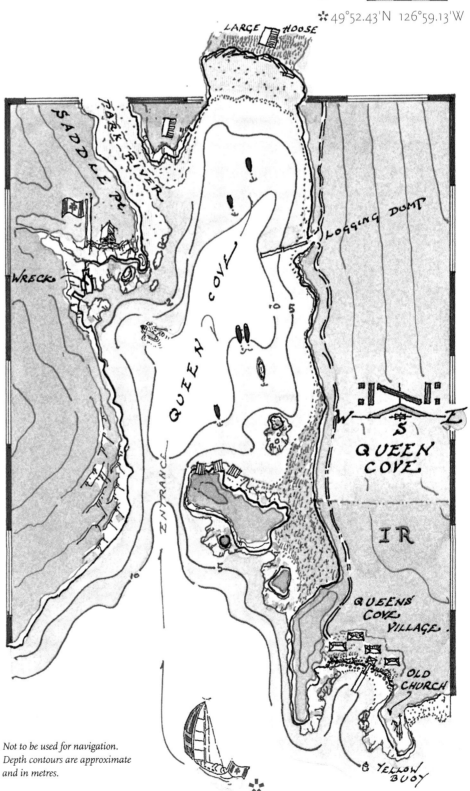

Not to be used for navigation.
Depth contours are approximate
and in metres.

The site of a summer village of the Nuchatlaht First Nations in the early 1900s, most of this area is now a provincial marine park, including the surrounding islands, islets and reefs, making it a favourite destination for kayakers. Bordering the park and anchorage are two Indian Reserves, and the private homes and oyster rafts of the small community of Nuchatlitz.

Tucked behind the abandoned "village islet," the roomy, protected anchorage offers beauty and serenity that encourage a longer stay.

Walk along the sandy beach and isthmus at HW to the adjoining "kayaker's island"—the loveliest of the surrounding islands—where trails cross over the headland between two beaches and allow a complete circumnavigation.

At HW take a dinghy trip to the outer islands to enjoy the sea otters at play and walk on mussel beaches. In the evening, watch the sun set over the islands to the NW and listen to the sound of surf on the outer islands as you enjoy this absolutely protected anchorage.

Dreamspeaker at anchor off the site of the original Nuchatlitz village.

NUCHATLITZ, NUCHATLITZ MARINE PARK, NOOTKA ISLAND

CHARTS 3676.

APPROACH Approach the entrance to the Nuchatlitz anchorage with caution from the W. The narrow entrance is marked by a white light on a pillar. Kelp lies across the entrance and in the channel. An alternative deeper channel winds S from Rosa Harbour between the island shore and rocks.

ANCHOR The "inner channel" lies NE of the two starboard-hand (red) buoys. Tuck in behind the abandoned village islet in 6–8 m (20–26 ft) with good holding in mud. The off-lying rocks, reefs and islets calm any westerly winds and swell.

Note: The channel is navigable at all states of the tide but we recommend a LW entrance if possible.

✱ 49°52.43'N 126°59.12'W

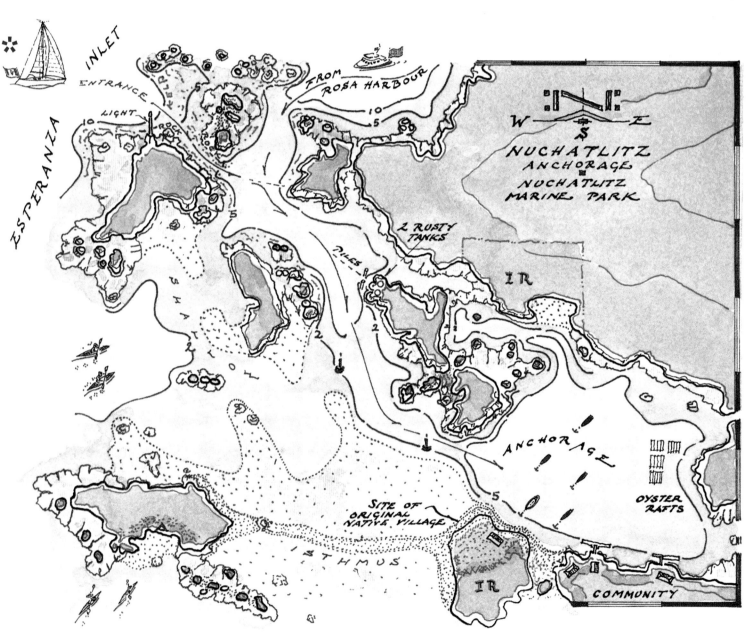

Not to be used for navigation. Depth contours are approximate and in metres.

7.4 PORT LANGFORD, NUCHATLITZ INLET, NOOTKA ISLAND

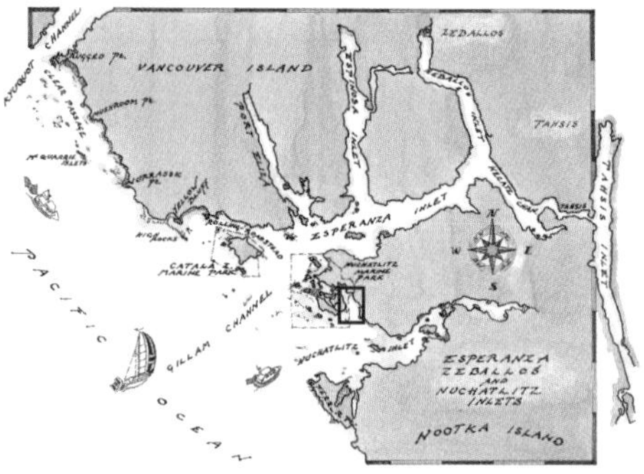

CHARTS 3676.

APPROACH Between Colwood Rocks and Belmont Point—the approach is clear to the head of the anchorage.

ANCHOR In a tranquil pool at the head or in the larger anchorage to the S. Protected from all quarters except the SE, as indicated by driftwood piled high on the beach.

49°47.36'N 126°55.99'W

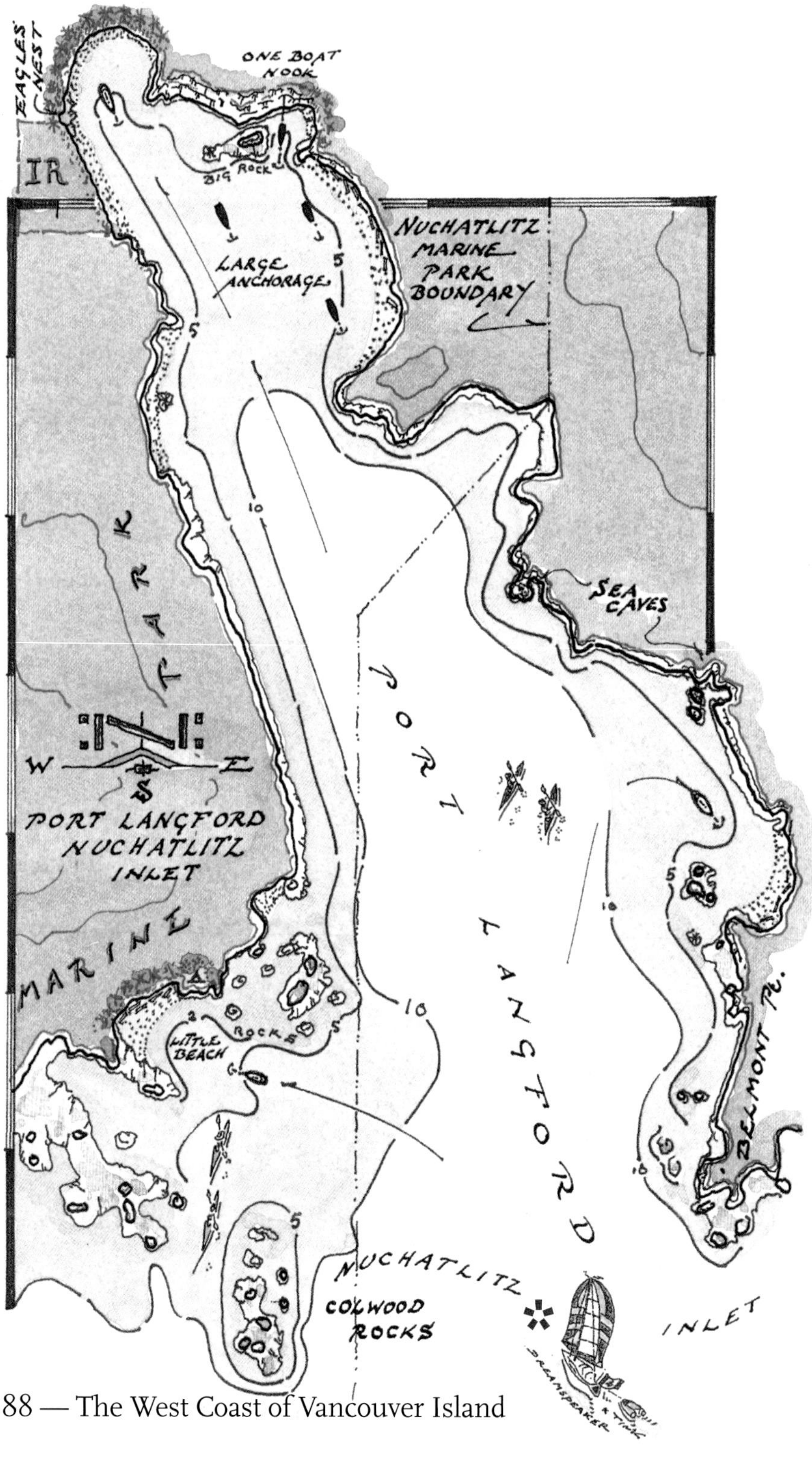

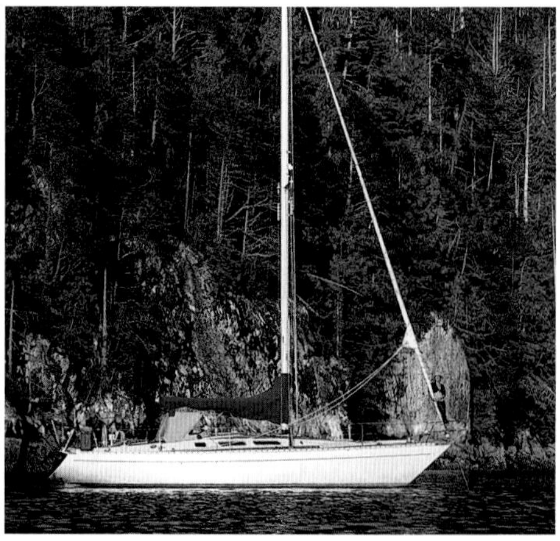

Dreamspeaker and Anne aglow in Mary Basin.

An explorer's haven, Port Langford is a deep bay with a choice of anchorages to sample, pocket beaches to discover, and sea caves to investigate by dinghy or kayak. Look for a beautiful cave with a waterfall that flows over its entrance, and an unusual white sea stack north of Belmont Point.

While anchored at the head of the bay we spied a particularly large eagle's nest, perhaps generations old, occupied by a hard-working pair of bald eagles and their young. A black bear visited the crescent beach at dusk, overturning rocks in search of supper, while sea otters romped in the kelp, munching on seafood morsels.

Not to be used for navigation.
Depth contours are approximate and in metres.

MARY BASIN, NUCHATLITZ INLET, NOOTKA ISLAND 7.5

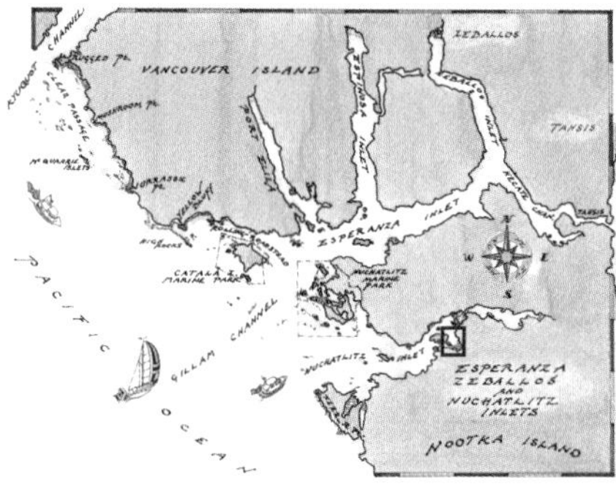

✲ 49°47.29'N 126°50.88'W

CHARTS 3676.

APPROACH Mary Basin is entered mid-channel between Lord Island and a sand beach off Nootka Island. The basin is commodious.

ANCHOR Known by local fishermen as a storm hole, the basin has easy access from seaward. Lord Island and the adjoining islet both offer good protection—make your choice and anchor in 6–12 m (20–40 ft) with good holding in sticky mud.

Note: A local boater we spoke to spent his childhood in the area and said he and his family would visit a small waterfall and swimming hole up Laurie Creek.

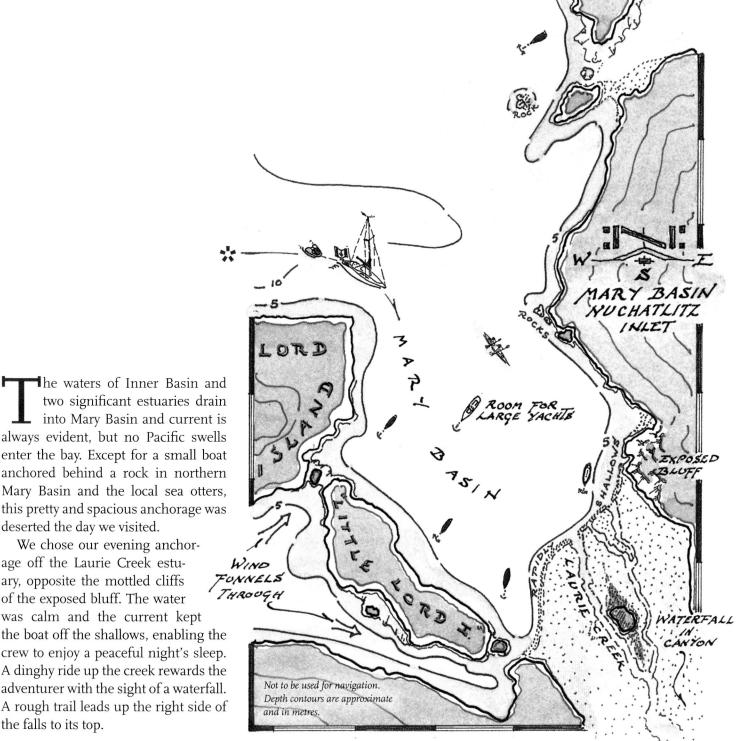

The waters of Inner Basin and two significant estuaries drain into Mary Basin and current is always evident, but no Pacific swells enter the bay. Except for a small boat anchored behind a rock in northern Mary Basin and the local sea otters, this pretty and spacious anchorage was deserted the day we visited.

We chose our evening anchorage off the Laurie Creek estuary, opposite the mottled cliffs of the exposed bluff. The water was calm and the current kept the boat off the shallows, enabling the crew to enjoy a peaceful night's sleep. A dinghy ride up the creek rewards the adventurer with the sight of a waterfall. A rough trail leads up the right side of the falls to its top.

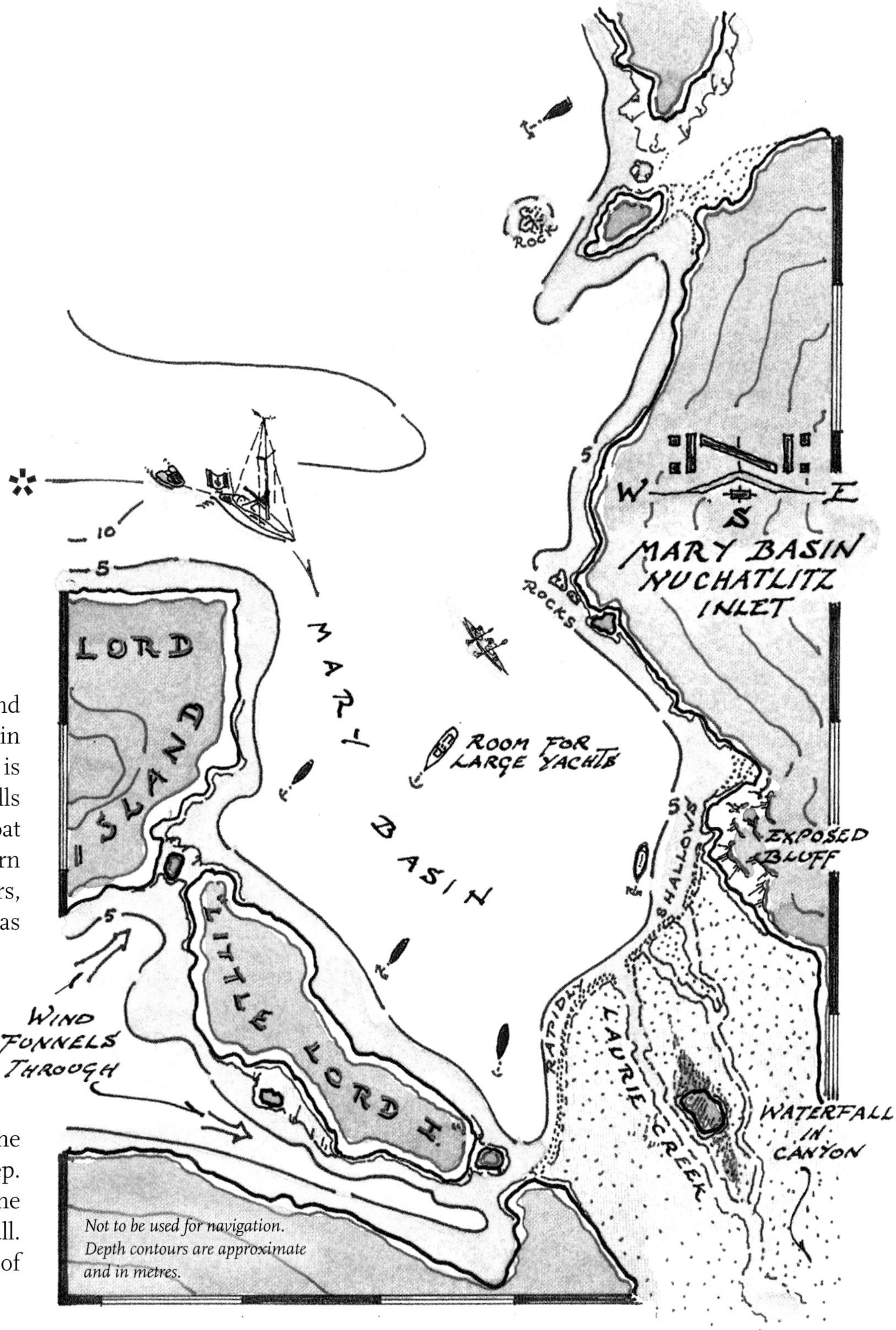

Not to be used for navigation. Depth contours are approximate and in metres.

7.6 LOUIE BAY, NUCHATLITZ INLET, NOOTKA ISLAND

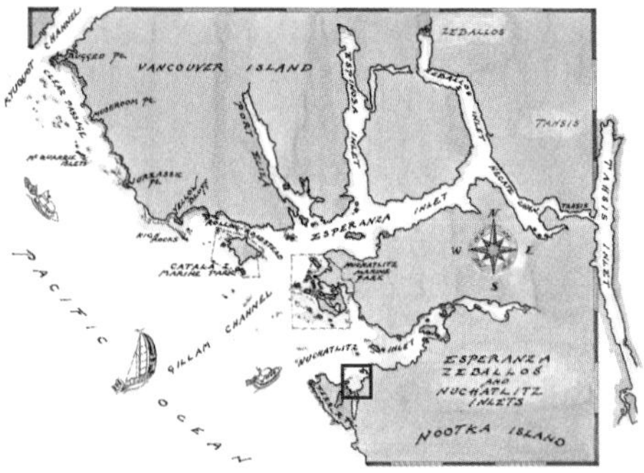

CHARTS 3676.

APPROACH From the N between Florence and Tongue points.

ANCHORAGE The LW picnic anchorage off the beach is open to westerly winds and swell. Good holding in sand in 4–6 m (13–20 ft). For better protection from the swell, strong SE winds and moderate westerly winds, anchor between the wreck and the tidal falls in depths of 4–8 m (13–26 ft). Good holding in mud and sand, while the current from the tidal falls steadies the boat.

✲ 49°45.46'N 126°56.00'W

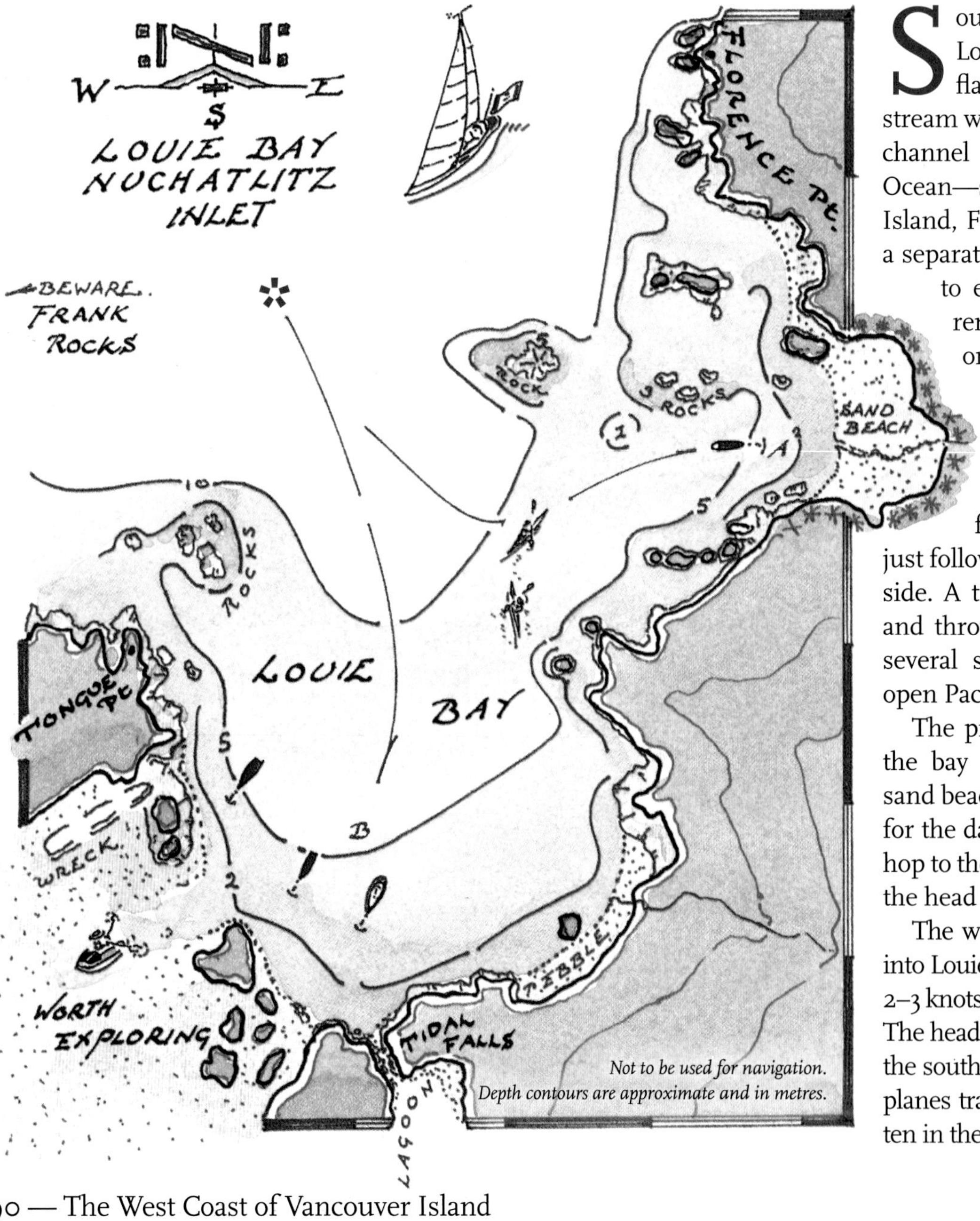

Not to be used for navigation.
Depth contours are approximate and in metres.

South and W of Tongue Point, Louie Bay has significant mud flats that finally become a tidal stream which then connects to a storm channel before it reaches the Pacific Ocean—so the western tip of Nootka Island, Ferrer Point, is technically not a separated island. At mid-tide it's fun to explore the shallows and the remains of a shipwreck lying on the beach, where it grows more weathered each year. *The Wild Coast* by John Kimantas suggests that "if you want to see the outer coast from the shelter of Louie Bay, just follow the storm channel to the far side. A trail runs along the shoreline and through a pretty rocky area with several sea stacks and views to the open Pacific."

The picnic anchorage to the NE of the bay lies off a charming packed-sand beach and provides a blissful spot for the day. From here it's only a short hop to the more sheltered anchorage at the head of Louie Bay.

The waters of an inland lagoon flow into Louie Bay and the current can reach 2–3 knots at the entrance to the tidal falls. The head of the Nootka Trail is located at the southern end of the lagoon and float planes transporting hikers land here often in the summer months.

A humpback whale shows its flukes, a common sight on the West Coast.

Approaching the marine facilities of Zeballos—the public wharf is right of centre.

CHARTS 3676.

APPROACH The marine facilities and public wharf lie in the eastern corner, at the head of Zeballos Inlet. The area around the public wharf has been dredged to 2.4 m (8 ft) but the area to seaward may be shallow. Chart 3676 shows a spot depth of 1.2 m (4 ft).

ANCHOR Zeballos Inlet is steep-sided and deep, with few opportunities for anchoring (see 7.8, 7.9 and 7.11 for possible temporary anchorages).

PUBLIC WHARF Zeballos Small Craft Harbour has two long fingers to accommodate commercial and sport fishing boats. The outside of the E finger is shallow. Visiting boaters are welcome but rafting is the norm. Call on VHF Channel 06 or 250-761-4333.

FUEL Weston Enterprises Ltd. operates a fuel dock inboard of the float plane dock. Excellent water is available. Call on VHF Channel 68 or 250-761-4201.

LAUNCH Public at the Small Craft Harbour

Note: The Village of Zeballos dock to the N of the seaplane and fuel dock is a short-stay moorage for loading and unloading.

✺ 49°58.63'N 126°50.71'W

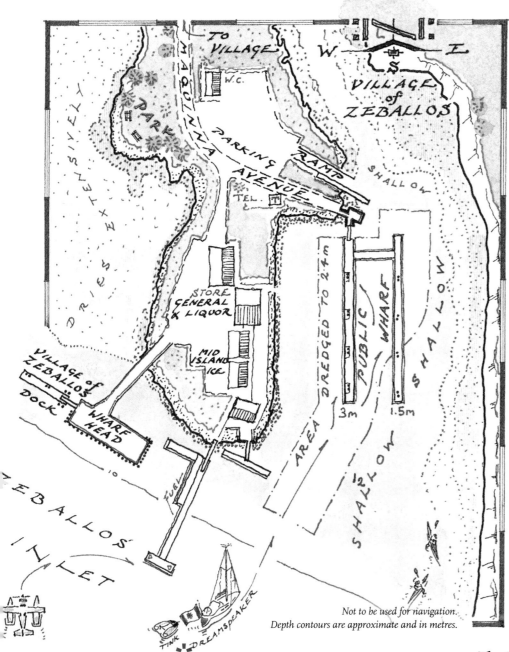

Not to be used for navigation.
Depth contours are approximate and in metres.

The town of Zeballos developed when gold was found there in the 1930s; its population quickly grew to more than 5,000 people but all mining activities were brought to a halt by the war in 1939. An iron mine operated here for a short time in the early '60s but it too closed and, like other small towns on the West Coast, Zeballos became a fishing and logging town. It is now a noted sport fishing centre.

Zeballos offers moorage, a small library and museum, a general store with ice, basic groceries and a BC Liquor outlet. Fresh provisions and other merchandise are trucked in by road each week, and the coastal freighter MV *Uchuck III* visits on Mondays.

After a good sail or a scenic cruise up Zeballos Inlet, the public wharf is the only place to tie up for the night—so relax, walk to one of several pubs and cafés, and enjoy a cold beer with the locals and visiting sport fishermen. The town's many colourful, false-fronted buildings lend it the ambiance of the "wild west," and the pub in Zeballos Hotel carries on the theme.

Although the Zeballos Museum has limited hours, a sign on the door invites visitors to call or stop at the village office for tours outside posted hours, and a visit is worthwhile.

7.8 RESOLUTION PARK RECREATION SITE—ZEBALLOS INLET

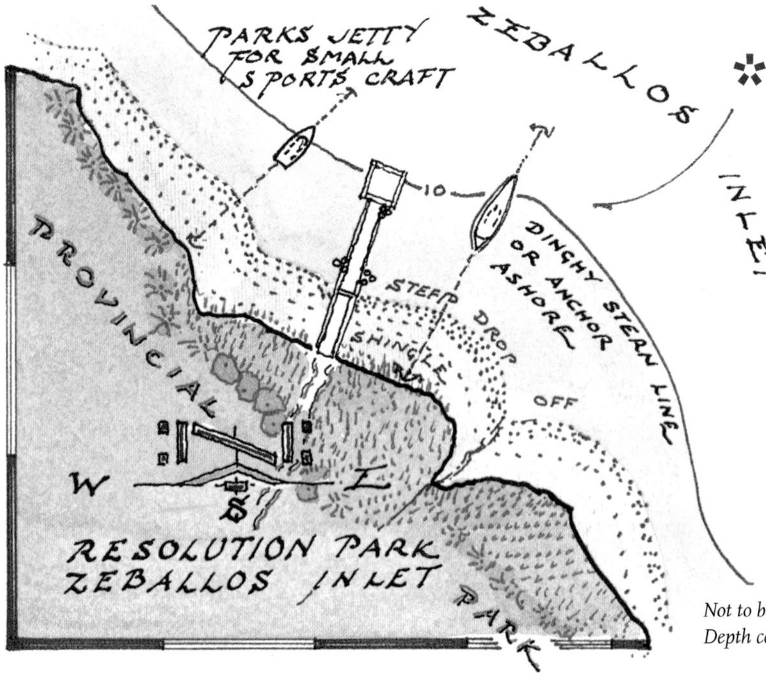

Not to be used for navigation.
Depth contours are approximate and in metres.

CHARTS 3676.

APPROACH At LW—tuck in behind the inshore islet with a small gravel beach and grassy knoll.

ANCHOR With a taut stern line ashore—this will provide some protection from up-inlet winds. Holding is moderate in gravel and mud in 5–12 m (16–40 ft).

A lovely LW picnic stop.

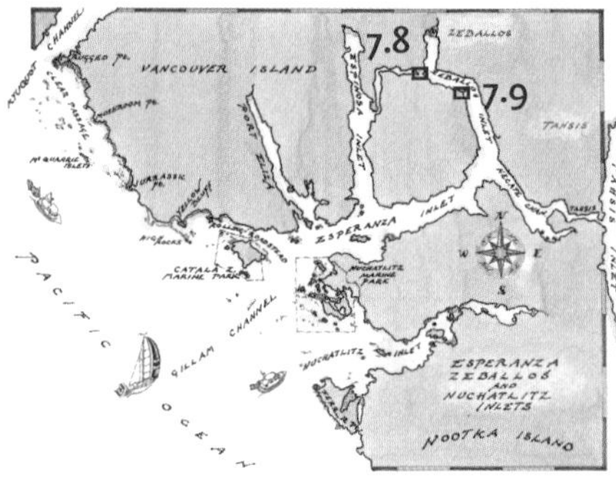

7.8 ✣ 49°57.35'N 126°51.44'W
7.9 ✣ 49°56.84'N 126°49.30'W

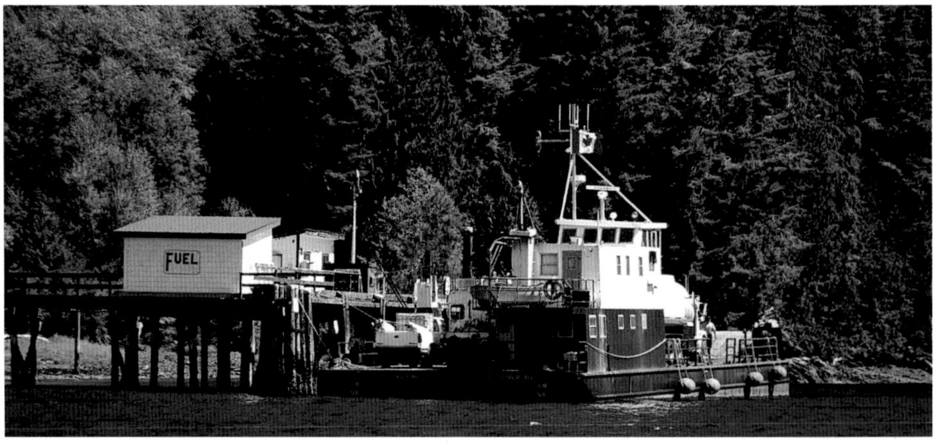

Approaching the fuel dock at Esperanza Mission (7.10), refuelling barge at the wharfhead.

7.9 TWIN ISLETS, ZEBALLOS INLET

CHARTS 3676.

APPROACH A small-craft float juts out from a steep gravel beach. The water is deep until the end of the dock is abeam.

ANCHOR Either side of the float with a taut stern anchor or line ashore. Anchor in 8–12 m (26–40 ft) with moderate holding in gravel and mud.

A pooch or picnic stop or just a place to get ashore.

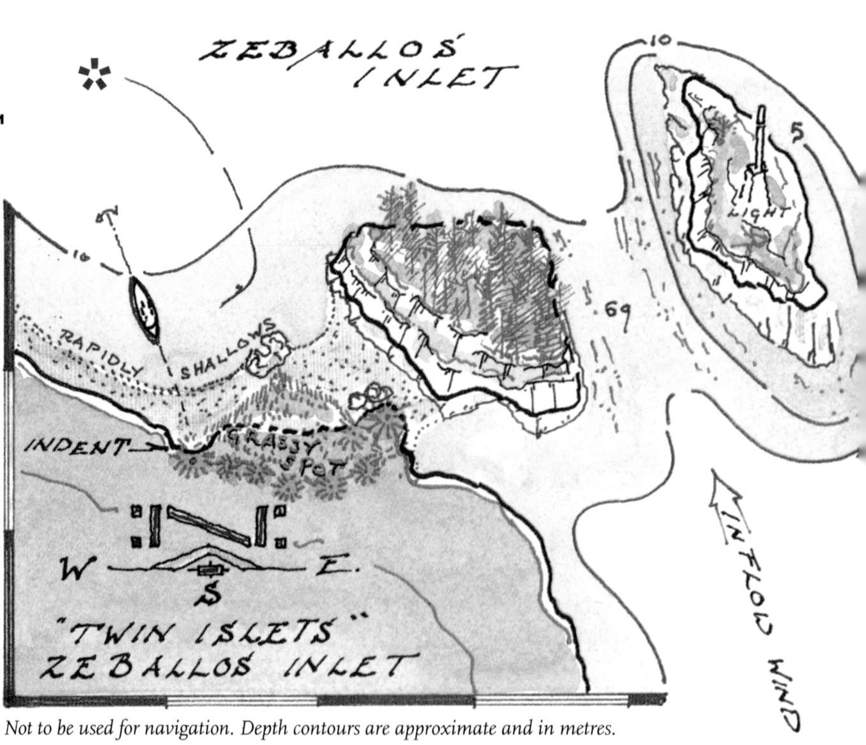

Not to be used for navigation. Depth contours are approximate and in metres.

7.10 ESPERANZA MISSION, HECATE CHANNEL

CHARTS 3676.

APPROACH The mission fuel dock lies to the E of a substantial wharfhead on the N shore of Hecate Channel.

FUEL An orderly fuel dock that can accommodate large commercial barges at the wharfhead and recreational boats on either side of the finger. Larger boats go on the outside.

Conveniently situated between Zeballos and Tahsis, the mission fuel dock provides revenue to support the ongoing outreach program the mission offers to children and families. The small store stocks canned drinks, ice cream, treats and the *Mission Cook Book*. If the mission staff have time they will take visitors on a tour of the facilities.

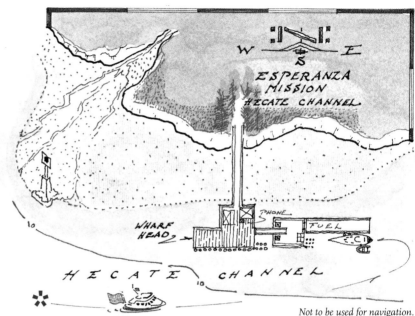

Not to be used for navigation.
Depth contours are approximate and in metres.

7.10 ✻ 49°52.22'N 126°44.70'W
7.11 ✻ 49°50.99'N 126°44.10'W

7.11 "NINE-METRE SHELF"

CHARTS 3676.

APPROACH At LW, a shelf of 9 m (30 ft) depth lies on the SW shore in the entrance to McBride Bay. Tuck in behind the "Big Rock."

ANCHOR With the bow facing the Esperanza Mission camp and a taut stern anchor to hold the bow into the chop from Hecate Channel and prevent current from swinging the boat around.

This two-boat anchorage offers protection in moderate conditions, and we spent a comfortable night at anchor in glassy calm water. When we took *Tink* out the next morning, we found seals sunning themselves on the rocks, a pair of bald eagles and multicoloured sea stars clustered in a rock pool.

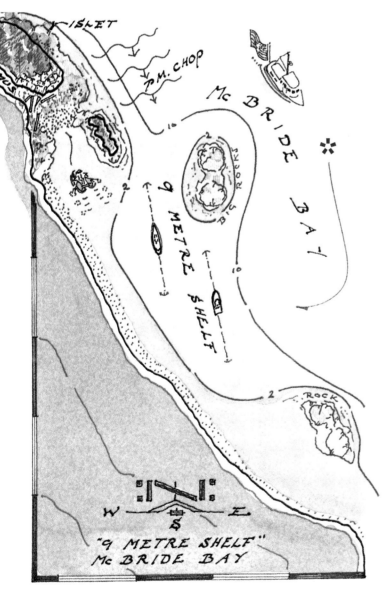

Not to be used for navigation. Depth contours are approximate and in metres.

Chapter 8

NOOTKA SOUND AND TAHSIS INLET

After a diversion north in Tahsis Inlet, Westview Marina and the community of Tahsis offer a welcome stop.

Cafés on the West Coast are few and far between.

Chapter 8
NOOTKA SOUND & TAHSIS INLET

TIDES

Volume 6, Canadian Tide and Current Tables

Reference Port: Tofino

Secondary Port: Saavedra Island

CURRENTS

No current station for this area. Note that currents reach 3 knots at Tsowwin Narrows in Tahsis Inlet.

WEATHER

Weather Channel VHF WX2 Nootka.

Areas: West Coast Vancouver Island South—listen for marine reporting stations at Nootka Lighthouse and Estevan Point. Listen for La Pérouse Bank and South Brooks weather buoys for offshore conditions.

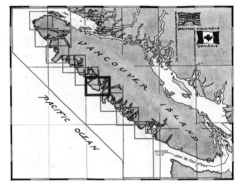

CAUTIONARY NOTES

When leaving Nuchatlitz Inlet, give Ferrer Point plenty of sea room; the ebb current meeting the Pacific swell creates very confused seas off this tip of Nootka Island.

WEATHER NOTE

In the summer months, outflow winds will commence in the evening and continue to the morning hours. They can be light, moderate or strong, and it's prudent to use them to your advantage: ride the inflow wind on a passage north, and the outflow wind when heading south. Inflow winds begin around noon and build in strength during the afternoon.

Note: Muchalat Inlet extends E 12 nautical miles to the Gold River Mill where you will find a very busy launch ramp. However, the inlet's waters are deep and offer no protected anchorages for the cruising boater.

From Nuchatlitz Inlet to the entrance to Nootka Sound is 25 nautical miles. Stay to seaward of Bajo Reef. Vancouver Island and British Columbia's pioneering history had its early beginnings in Nootka Sound, home of the Mowachaht First Nations who were the first to trade valuable sea otter pelts with Europeans. For cruisers, the highlights of Nootka Sound are the village of Yuquot in Friendly Cove and Bligh Island Marine Park.

Archaeological records suggest the main village of Yuquot was settled at least 4,200 years ago; it is one of the earliest and longest continuously populated sites on the west coast of Vancouver Island. Today the Williams family are caretakers of their ancestral village. Look for the impressive fallen totem pole in the long grass N of the Williams' house, and visit the pretty church-museum and the impressive Nootka lighthouse.

Just north of Friendly Cove, off Cook Channel, lies protected Santa Gertrudis Cove. The cove is used primarily by sport fishing boats which depart early and return late, leaving you free to choose the best spot to drop the anchor. Explore the park trail, which leads to the warm waters of Jewitt Lake.

The largest island in Nootka Sound, Bligh Island is largely preserved as a provincial marine park. The park encompasses the neighbouring Spanish Pilot Group—this area is favoured by fishing parties, kayakers, divers and sea otters. In 1778 Captain Cook, in search of the Northwest Passage, was the first European to set foot in Nootka Sound when he anchored his ships *Resolution* and *Endeavour* off Bligh Island, in what we now know as Resolution Cove.

If you venture W through Eliza Passage, stop off at Critter Cove Marina where you will find fuel (gas only) and handmade waffle cones filled with banana fudge ice cream at the Critter Café.

To the N and E, two enchanting anchorages await the cruising boater near the head of Kendrick Inlet. "Bodega Cove" rates high on our list of blissful spots to anchor overnight, while the two-boat bight between Bodega and Strange islands in Princesa Channel makes for a pleasant stop for lunch or to await favourable tides and winds for the run up Tahsis Inlet.

Our final destination in this chapter is welcoming, family-friendly Westview Marina and the community of Tahsis. A courtesy van is available for the quick trip into the small town to provision at the general store.

FEATURED DESTINATIONS

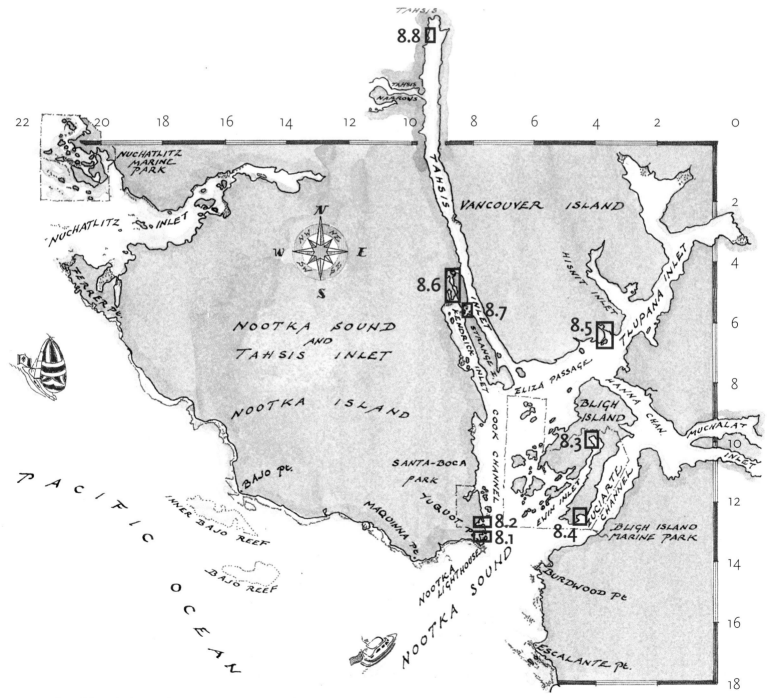

Not to be used for navigation. Depth contours are approximate and in metres.

8.1 VILLAGE OF YUQUOT AND FRIENDLY COVE, NOOTKA ISLAND

✤ 49°35.72.N 126°36.77'W

Nootka Lighthouse signals your arrival in Nootka Sound.

Dreamspeaker against the backdrop of the Yuquot church.

The Williams' family float extends out into Friendly Cove.

Archaeological records suggest the main village of Yuquot ("place of many winds") was settled at least 4,200 years ago and is one of the earliest and longest continuously populated sites on the West Coast of Vancouver Island. When Captain Cook visited the West Coast, approximately 1,500 Mowachaht lived in the 13 majestic big houses that overlooked Friendly Cove. They were a commanding nation led by powerful Chief Maquinna and developed a monopoly on the lucrative fur trade with visiting European ships. (For in-depth history read *Nootka Sound Explored*, Laurie Jones, see page 190)

Today the people of Yuquot live near Gold River in Muchalat Inlet, although the cove is part of the Mowachaht reserve and year-round home to Ray Williams and his wife Terry. Visitors are welcome and a small fee is charged for coming ashore—if you don't find Ray, he or one of the summer workers will find you!

Ray's son Sanford Williams is an accomplished master carver whose exquisite masks are exported around the world. In the summer months he can be found in his seaside carving shed near Ray Williams' float. Look for the impressive fallen totem pole in the long grass to the N of the Williams' house—it watched over the village from 1929 until 1993, when it toppled in a storm.

Allow time to visit the pretty village church-museum that was rebuilt in 1956 after the 1889 structure burned down. It houses colourful replica totems from the village of Yuquot and two detailed stained glass windows, gifts from the Spanish government. One depicts a Franciscan monk giving a sermon to the natives, while the other shows the cove being transferred from Spain to England by Captain Quadra and Captain Vancouver. North of the church is a lovely open "tenting" meadow used in the summer by returning members of the Mowachat Band, youth organizations, and hikers entering or exiting the Nootka Trail. Walk to the fascinating village cemetery and enjoy a swim in the warm waters of Jewitt Lake.

And be sure to climb up to the 1911 Nootka Lighthouse that stands tall on the rocks of Yuquot Point.

Note: In the summer months the MV Uchuck III visits Friendly Cove on Wednesdays and Saturdays—visit www.mvuchuck.com for its schedule.

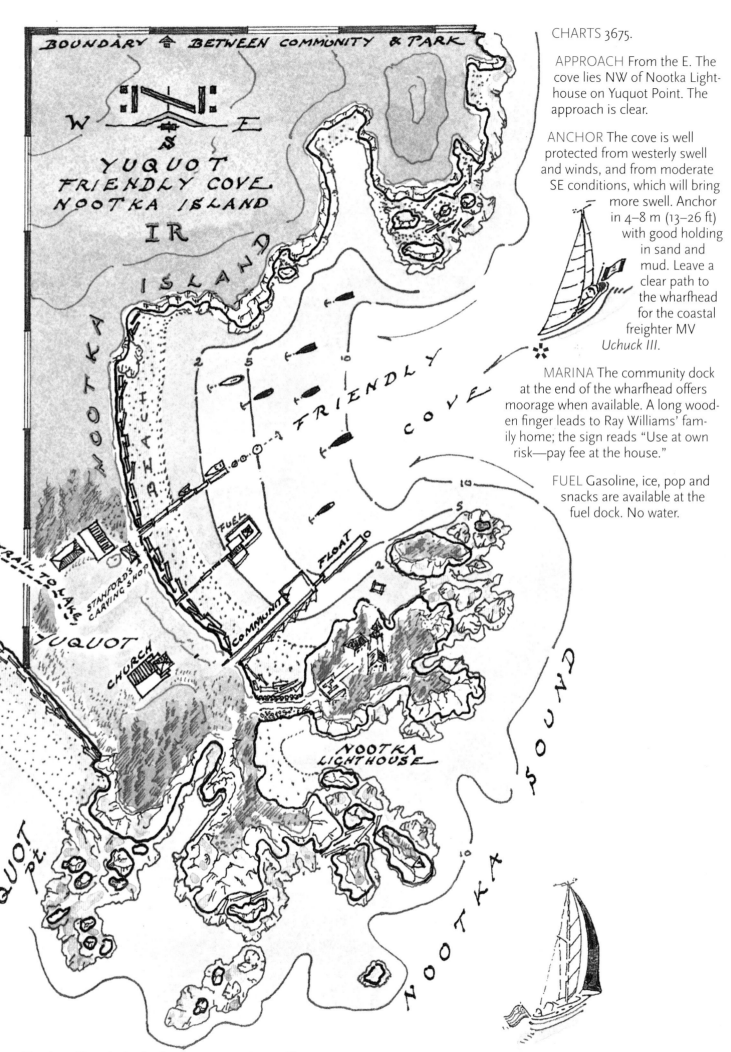

BOUNDARY ⛩ BETWEEN COMMUNITY & PARK

YUQUOT
FRIENDLY COVE
NOOTKA ISLAND
IR

NOOTKA ISLAND

TAHWA

STANFORD'S CARVING SHOP

TRAIL TO LAKE

YUQUOT

CHURCH

FUEL

FLOAT

COMMUNITY

FRIENDLY COVE

NOOTKA
LIGHTHOUSE

NOOTKA SOUND

YUQUOT PT.

NOOTKA

CHARTS 3675.

APPROACH From the E. The cove lies NW of Nootka Light-house on Yuquot Point. The approach is clear.

ANCHOR The cove is well protected from westerly swell and winds, and from moderate SE conditions, which will bring more swell. Anchor in 4–8 m (13–26 ft) with good holding in sand and mud. Leave a clear path to the wharfhead for the coastal freighter MV *Uchuck III*.

MARINA The community dock at the end of the wharfhead offers moorage when available. A long wooden finger leads to Ray Williams' family home; the sign reads "Use at own risk—pay fee at the house."

FUEL Gasoline, ice, pop and snacks are available at the fuel dock. No water.

Not to be used for navigation. Depth contours are approximate and in metres.

8.2 SANTA GERTRUDIS COVE, NOOTKA ISLAND

✿ 49°36.15'N 126°36.87'W

CHARTS 3675.

APPROACH With caution at LW when "Danger Rock," which lies centre channel, is visible. Leave the rock to the N.

ANCHOR (A) The S basin affords good protection from all quarters. A stern line to shore is recommended if swinging room is limited. Anchor in 4–8 m (13–26 ft) with good holding in mud.

(B) The N basin is protected but shallow and best left to shoal-draft sport fishing boats.

LW looking east—this rock is for real!

With a spectacular view to Nootka Sound, Santa Gertrudis Cove is used primarily by sport fishing boats, so it's early to bed, early to rise in this charming spot. The cove is delightful to explore by dinghy and kayak, and at LW many of the islets are connected to Nootka Island. A trail to the warm swimming waters of Jewitt Lake can be found behind the southwesternmost pebble beach.

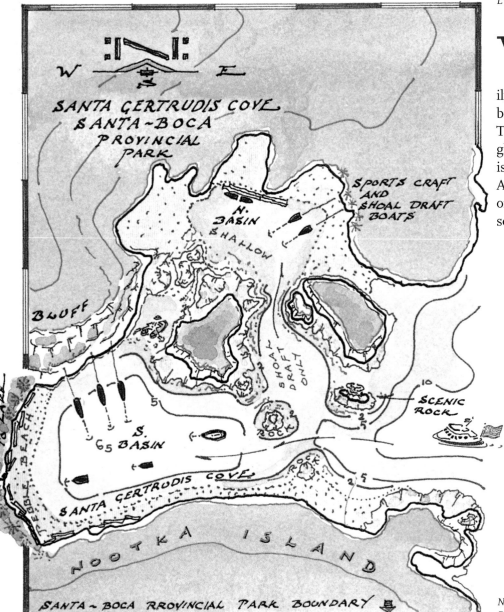

Not to be used for navigation.
Depth contours are approximate and in metres.

BLIGH ISLAND MARINE PARK 8.3

CHARTS 3676.

APPROACH Ewin Inlet runs NE without obstruction. Enter the anchorage by leaving the islet and rock to the S.

ANCHOR Good all-weather protection

Tucked into the southeast corner.

except from the SE and SW. Moderate holding in soft mud in depths of 6–8 m (20–26 ft).

Note: Strong afternoon up-inlet winds do reach into the head of Ewin Inlet.

✳ 49°38.74'N 126°30.96'W

The largest island in Nootka Sound and a key area for harvesting shrimp, Bligh Island is largely preserved as a provincial marine park. The park includes the neighbouring Spanish Pilot Group—this area is favoured by fishing parties, kayakers, divers and sea otters. The most protected spot to drop the hook is at the head of Ewin Inlet, which extends 5 km (3 miles) along Clerke Peninsula, offering an alternative anchorage to Friendly Cove and Santa Gertrudis Cove. In settled weather, boaters can also find a number of less protected anchorages among the Spanish Pilot Group.

Anchor off the camping beach (fresh water is available from the creek) and explore the rocks and treed islet by dinghy or kayak, or simply laze in the cockpit with a good book—perhaps a read about Captain Cook's voyages of discovery—before moving onto famed Resolution Cove (see page 104). Bligh Island was named for Lieutenant, later Vice Admiral, William Bligh, master of HMS *Resolution* on Cook's voyage to find the Northwest Passage, and the captain of HMS *Bounty* who was set adrift by his mutinous crew.

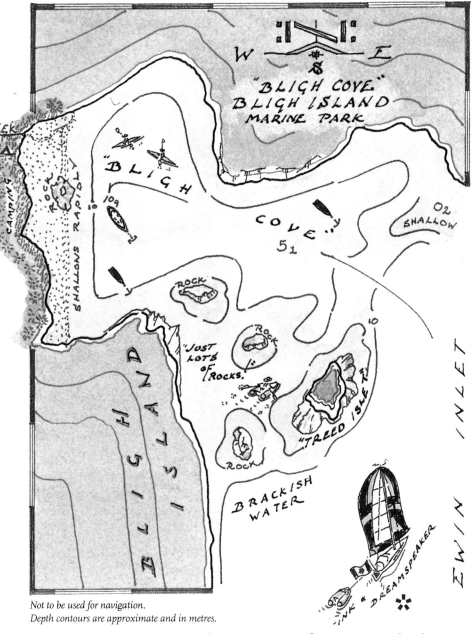

Not to be used for navigation.
Depth contours are approximate and in metres.

8.4 RESOLUTION COVE, BLIGH ISLAND MARINE PARK

✳ 49°36.32'N 126°31.79'W

CHARTS 3675.

APPROACH From the SW out of Zuciarte Channel. Head for the NW corner, which is marked by the profusion of driftwood that fronts the shingle-and-boulder beach. The water is deep close to shore.

ANCHOR In the NW corner. We recommend a taut stern anchor or stern line ashore to counter the surge entering the cove—wind and current will also swirl the boat around. Drop the bow anchor in 10–12 m (33–40 ft) over stone and rock and the stern anchor in 5–6 m (16–20 ft) in mud and shell.

Note: When taking the dinghy to shore to visit the commemorative plaques here be aware that the continuous surge into the cove makes landing tricky.

I n 1778 Captain Cook, in search of the Northwest Passage, was the first European to set foot in Nootka Sound when he anchored his ships *Resolution* and *Endeavour* off Bligh Island, in what we now know as Resolution Cove. He, too, took lines ashore to counter the surge in the cove.

Cook and his men spent a month repairing damage to their ships caused by a severe Pacific storm. One of the *Resolution's* masts and other damaged spars had to be replaced and there was no lack of excellent timber on the island. The crews traded with the local First Nations, exchanging buttons, knives, iron and tin, nails and other metals for carvings, spears, and clothing made of tree bark and a variety of animal skins, including luxurious sea otter pelts.

Two bronze plaques commemorate Cook's visit to what he called "Ships Cove"—they are set into a steep rock cliff at the top of a mossy knoll. We enjoyed our overnight stay here, including an unexpected visit by two seasoned kayakers, Mary Gazetas and Phoebe Dunbar—twins, writers and artists. *Around One More Point* by Mary Gazetas is a delightful read (see page 190.)

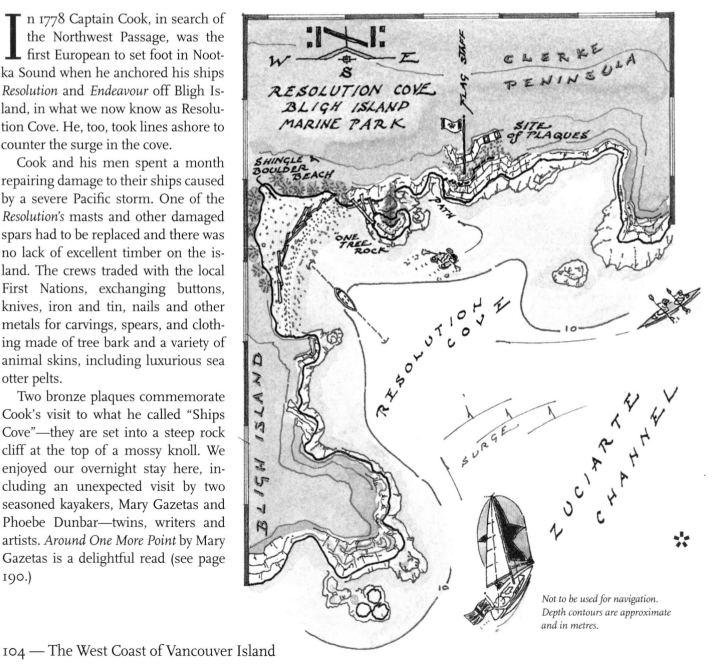

Not to be used for navigation. Depth contours are approximate and in metres.

A plaque in Resolution Cove commemorates the visit of Captain Cook and the crews of Resolution *and* Endeavour *in 1778.*

This motley crew was mighty impressed.

Mary Gazetas and Phoebe Dunbar—twins, artists and West Coast explorers.

Anne contemplates the events that took place in the cove.

Sport fishing boats are an integral part of West Coast scenery.

CHARTS 3675.

APPROACH

(A) From the SW to the "Hole in the Wall" anchorage—leave the marina to the E and stay in centre channel (see note below).

(B) From the SW to the marina guest dock. Leave the log breakwater to the W.

ANCHOR The well-protected "Hole in the Wall" anchorage has two float homes and is suitable for only two boats, with limited swinging room. Good holding in mud in 3–5 m (10–16 ft).

MARINA Critter Cove Marina is primarily a sport fishing camp but offers moorage for transient boats at the visitor dock. Pets are not allowed on the docks due to the marina's lack of a foreshore. Smoking is prohibited except on private boats. Call in advance in the busy summer months: 250-283-7364 or email info@crittercove.com.

FUEL Gasoline only at the fuel float. No diesel or water.

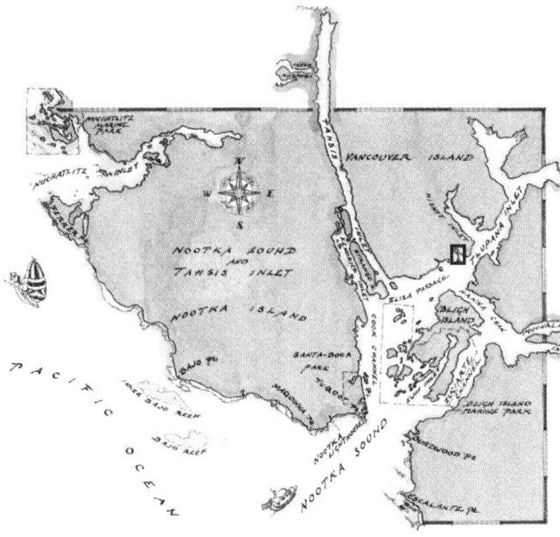

49°42.49'N 123°30.00'W

Critter Cove Marina guests return to this fishing camp year after year. The Critter Café offers excellent home-style cooking with favourites like roast beef, Yorkshire pudding and mashed potatoes, bread and butter pudding, blackberry apple pie and handmade waffle cones filled with banana fudge ice cream—just one more good reason to stay the night! The anchorage known locally as "Hole in the Wall" is considered by fishermen to be a great storm hole.

Note: On the N shore of the channel to "Hole in the Wall" anchorage there is a charted rock with a minimum depth of 1.5 m (5 ft) at zero tide. With 2 m (6.6 ft) of draft we entered the anchorage at LW on a moderate tide.

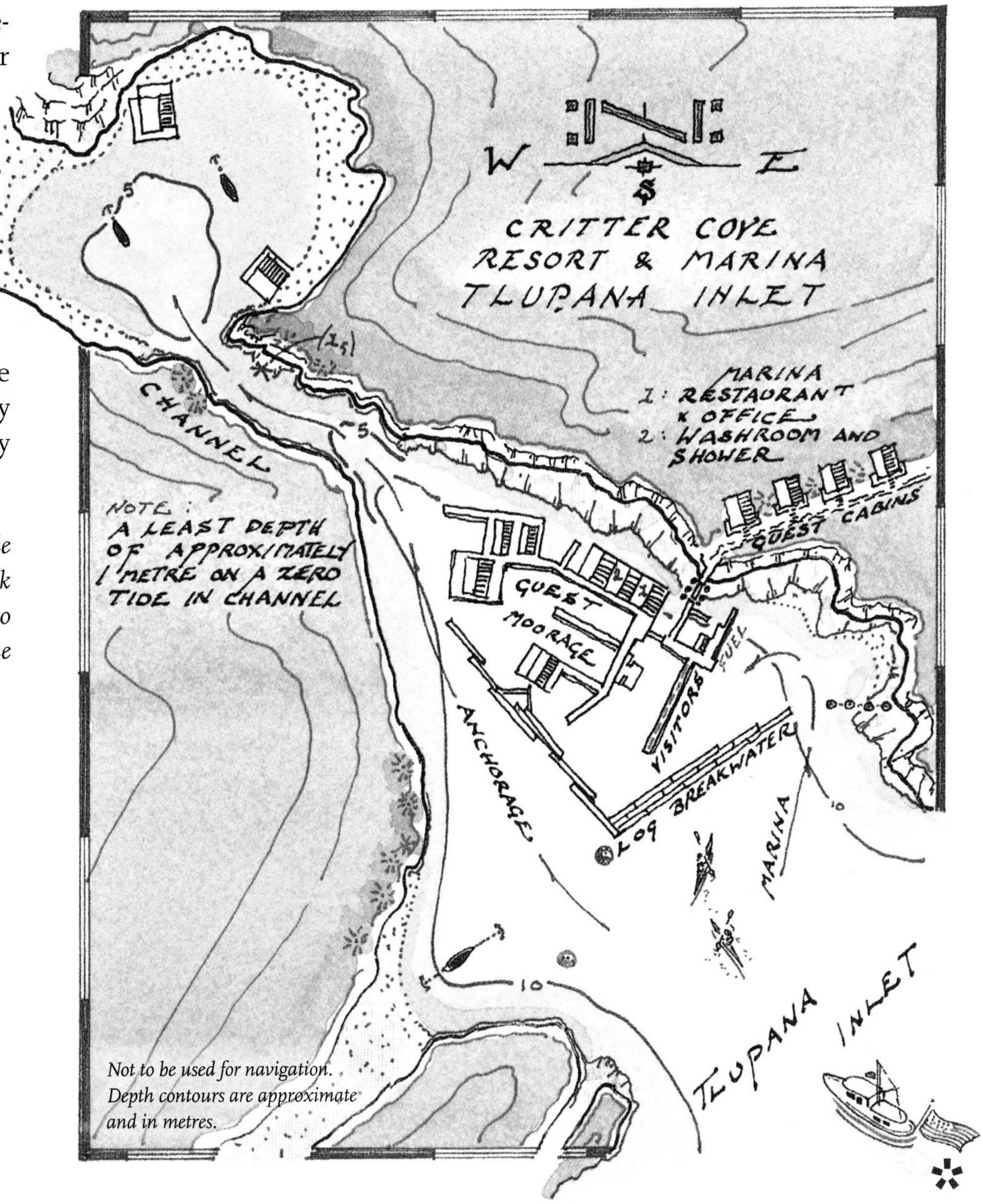

Not to be used for navigation. Depth contours are approximate and in metres.

8.6 "BODEGA COVE," HEAD OF KENDRICK INLET

✳ 49°43.61'N 126°38.23'W

All we could hear were birds chattering in the forest.

CHARTS 3675.

APPROACH The entrance channel lies off Bodega Island at the head of Kendrick Inlet—the approach is clear.

ANCHOR In the lower pool in 5–8 m (16–26 ft) with good holding in mud and rock. Or proceed to the upper pool at the head of the inlet where there is room for two boats to swing, bearing in mind that the channel to the basin has 2 m (6.6 ft) minimum depth. Anchor in 3–6 m (10–20 ft) with good holding in black, sticky mud.

Note: Dreamspeaker transited the channel at various states of tide and found suitable depths. We anchored for two nights in the cove.

Two enchanting anchorages await the cruising boater who takes time to explore the long, narrow channel to the head of Kendrick Inlet: "Bodega Cove" rates high on our list of blissful spots. Once clear-cut, it is now surrounded by green, and birds chatter constantly in the forest.

The upper anchorage contains a creek estuary that is abundant with wildlife, including kingfishers, pied-billed grebes, ravens, and the solitary vireo, which repeatedly warbles a question, then an answer, in the treetops. At HW, it's possible to row past the big rock at the mouth of the creek to the grassy meadows beyond and out to Tahsis Inlet.

Kendrick Inlet is an important herring spawning area and one of the major clam habitats in Nootka Sound; stocks of Dungeness crab also call this home. A huge logging operation on the western shore is well hidden from the anchorage.

Not to be used for navigation. Depth contours are approximate and in metres.

CHARTS 3675 (inset).

APPROACH Princesa Channel lies N of Strange Island and connects lower reaches of Tahsis Inlet with Kendrick Inlet. The channel is well marked but note the rock N of the port-hand (green) light.

ANCHOR The anchorage in the bight N of Princesa Channel is best approached from Kendrick Inlet at LW. Fair protection in moderate conditions with good holding in gravel and shell in 6–9 m (20–30 ft).

✿ 49°43.41'N 126°38.00'W

An unexpected treat in Princesa Channel.

A pleasant lunch stop, and well sheltered from overnight outflow winds, the two-boat bight between Bodega and Strange islands in Princesa Channel offers views out to Kendrick Inlet and the sport fishing boats that ply Tahsis Inlet. While we sipped our tea, a pair of bald eagles renovated their nest, snorting seals sunned on the flat rocks, and an elegant flock of sandpipers scurried along the pebble beach.

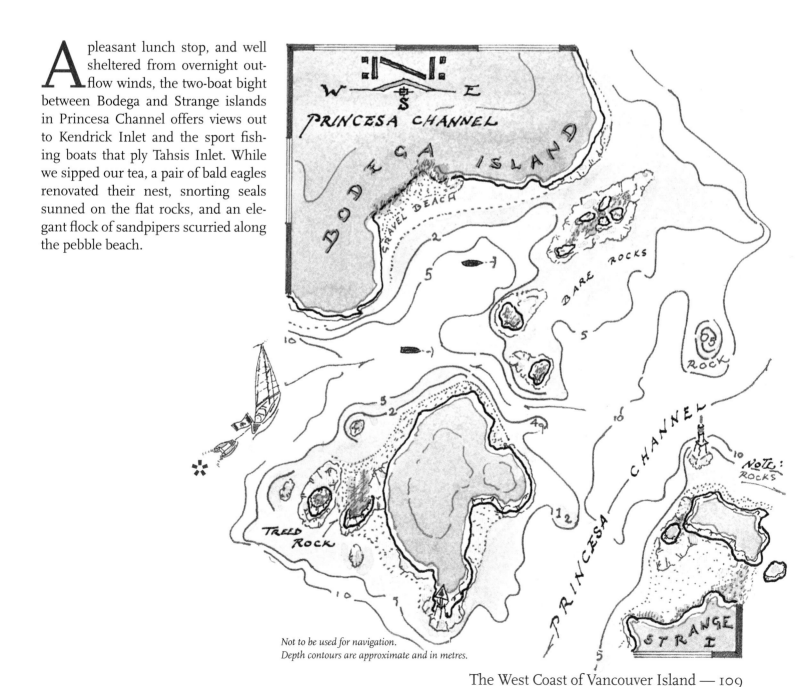

Not to be used for navigation.
Depth contours are approximate and in metres.

8.8 WESTVIEW MARINA AND THE COMMUNITY OF TAHSIS

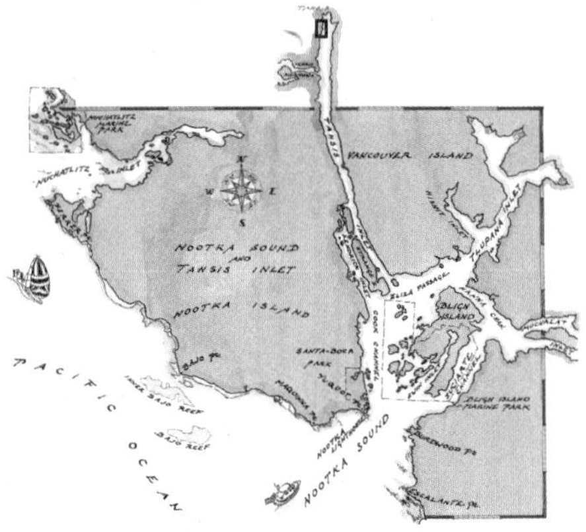

✲ 49°54.94'N 126°39.63'W

CHARTS 3676 (inset).

APPROACH The marine facilities of Tahsis lie along the W shore at the head of Tahsis Inlet.

ANCHOR The inlet is deep and shelter is limited, making it unsuitable for anchoring.

PUBLIC WHARF A single finger lies N of the wharfhead and moorage is limited to 24 hours.

MARINA Westview Marina is primarily a sport fishing centre with a restaurant, shower and laundry facilities. They welcome visiting boaters but call beforehand on VHF Channel 06 or 250-934-7672. Marine mechanic and wireless internet available.

FUEL Diesel and gasoline are available at the fuel dock. Propane tanks can be filled and the water is excellent.

BOAT LAUNCH Public, between the floatplane dock and public wharf.

"Welcome to civilization," John Daynes called out as we approached family-friendly Westview Marina and Lodge. Although the marina caters primarily to sport fishing boats, owners Cathy and John do their best to make space for transient cruisers. Tahsis is a former company town that is struggling to survive without an industrial base, but the community is optimistic and the marina is a welcoming spot to spend a few days.

Once you've started the laundry and indulged in a hot shower (both facilities are squeaky clean), laze on the patio with a mango ice cream cone, crushed ice margarita or a cold Mexican beer. The Marina Cantina restaurant serves delicious, authentic Mexican dishes.

The marina store stocks a good selection of marine supplies, gifts and clothing—and will also take your mail. A courtesy van is available for a quick trip into the small town to provision at the general store, which can be low on fresh produce a day or two before freight delivery on Fridays, when it's best to shop after 2 pm. The store also has a BC Liquor outlet. The highlight of our shopping spree was to discover that every Friday morning an industrious family from Gold River sets up a fruit and veggie stand with an excellent selection of produce—cash only.

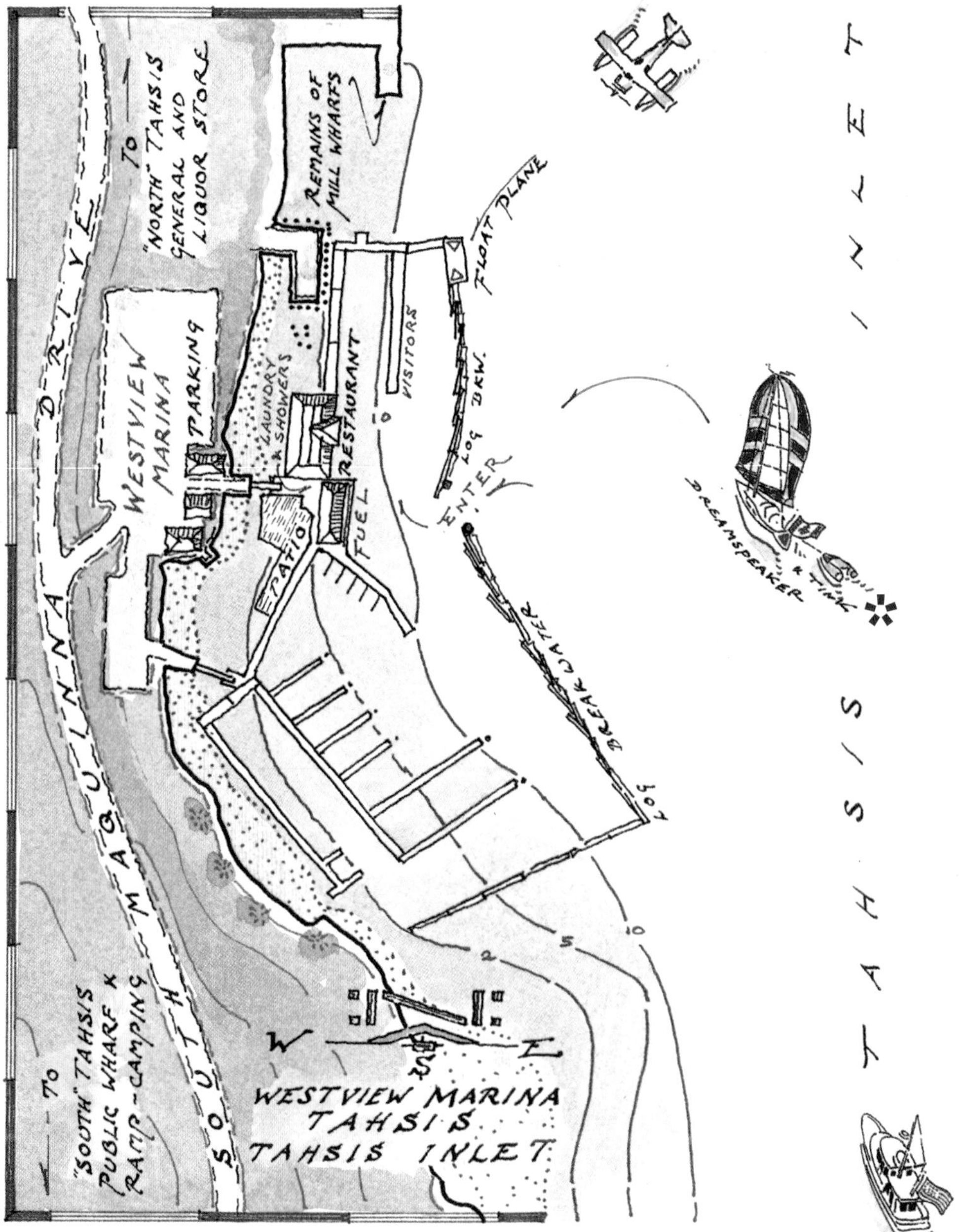

Not to be used for navigation. Depth contours are approximate and in metres.

*Sailing north in Tahsis Inlet—
the mountain scenery is
worth the trip.*

Chapter 9
WEST CLAYOQUOT SOUND

A misty day at Hot Springs Cove in Maquinna Provincial Park. Adrian Dorst photo.

Dreamspeaker *anchored in the lush surroundings of Young Bay.*

Chapter 9
ESTEVAN POINT TO WEST CLAYOQUOT SOUND

TIDES

Volume 6, Canadian Tide and Current Tables

Reference Port: Tofino

Secondary Ports: Sulphur Passage, Riley Cove, Herbert Inlet

CURRENTS

There is no current station for this area but currents in Hayden Passage—times of turn (slack), direction and velocity—are based on reference port Tofino.

Note: Currents run at up to 2–3 knots in

Hayden Passage and Sulphur Passage. Currents flood E in Hayden Passage and S in Sulphur Passage. It is always prudent to time your transit to take advantage of the currents.

WEATHER

Weather Channel VHF WX2 Nootka.

Areas: West Coast Vancouver Island South—listen for marine reporting stations from Nootka, Estevan Point and Lennard Island lighthouses. Listen for La Pérouse Bank and South Banks weather buoy for offshore conditions.

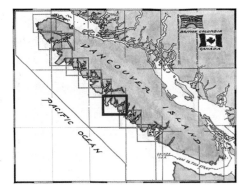

CAUTIONARY NOTES

Sulphur Passage has two navigable passes—the shortest is more difficult. It is always wise to time transit at LW slack as a rising tide is far more forgiving.

Although Hesquiat Harbour is pronounced "safe" as an anchorage by *Sailing Directions*, getting in or out across the bar in southeast weather with a moderate to heavy southwest swell running could be potentially hazardous to small craft as seas break across the bar. However in strong- to gale-force northwest winds, Hesquiat Harbour becomes a commodious safe haven.

Note: It's prudent to depart prior to the weather switching to the SE.

Before rounding Estevan Point, which is 15 nautical miles S of Nootka Sound, boaters first have to clear Escalante and Perez Rocks, staying at least two nautical miles off the Hesquiat Peninsula shoreline. Hesquiat Peninsula Park lies to the W and Maquinna Park to the E of Hesquiat Harbour, which is sheltered from the W and NW by Hesquiat Peninsula; the harbour offers miles of deserted beaches to explore by dinghy or kayak.

A pretty cove and a sandy beach backed by sun-bleached driftwood lie at the head of Rae Basin. Take the opportunity to visit renowned "Cougar" Annie's beautiful, five-acre garden in the rainforest from Boat Basin.

Not only is Hot Springs Cove a good storm hole, it is also home to Maquinna Provincial Park and the magnificent Ramsay Hot Spring. This 50-degree C geothermal spring tumbles into three tiered rock pools and has become a popular destination for non-boating tourists in the summer months. The tradition of bathing *au naturel* is now discouraged.

Across Sydney Inlet, on the western shoreline of Flores Island, Hootla-Kootla Bay provides a delightful hideaway. Sydney Inlet, Shelter Inlet and Millar Channel isolate Flores Island, the second largest on the West Coast after Nootka Island, creating sheltered inner passages and anchorages. Young Bay offers a cozy anchorage at its head, edged by old-growth forest and steep grassy bluffs.

Holmes Inlet leads north from Sydney Inlet at Adventure Point and ends at Ice River estuary. Protected, lagoon-like Bottleneck Cove lies at the south end of the inlet and is surrounded by steep, grassy cliffs.

A natural playground, Megin River Delta and nearby Bacchante Bay are two spots we would love to explore at leisure on a return visit. The Megin River is said to be navigable to picturesque Megin Lake where freshwater mussels have been reported.

Most boaters transit Sulphur Passage via the western route, but there are two alternative routes from the N and S on a rising tide.

The head of Matilda Inlet is known by the locals as one of the most sheltered anchorages in Clayoquot Sound. It's close to the Ahousat General Store, café and fuel dock. Nearby Ahousat Warm Springs is fed by the same kind of geothermal flow as Ramsay Hot Springs. From here a swampy creekbed trail leads to the spectacular sweep of Whitesand Beach.

FEATURED DESTINATIONS

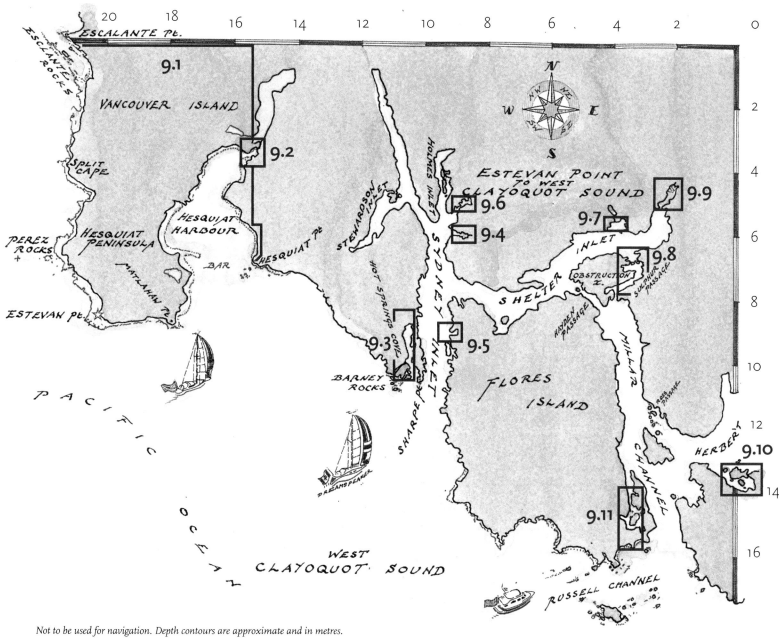

Not to be used for navigation. Depth contours are approximate and in metres.

9.1 ESTEVAN POINT AND HESQUIAT HARBOUR

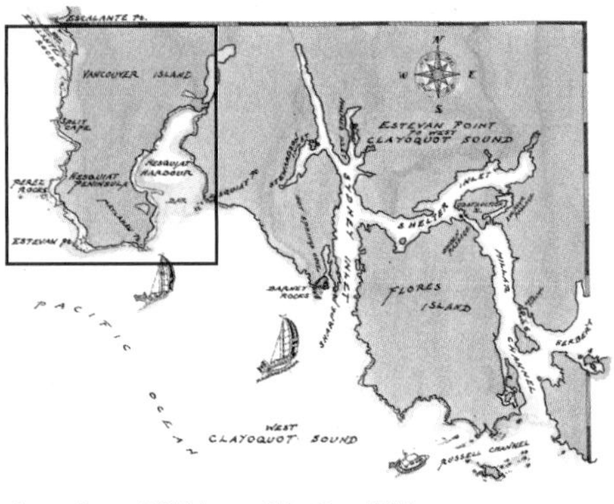

✣ 49°22.68'N 126°26.53'W

CHART 3674, 3603.

APPROACH Hesquiat Harbour in settled weather when winds are from W to NW. Best at LW with the tide flooding. Crossing The Bar (see note below). Give Antons Spit a wide berth.

ANCHOR In a W to NW wind tuck into the SW portion of Hesquiat Harbour off Antons Spit or farther N in the Boat Basin. The most protected spot is Rae Basin (see 9.2). Good holding in 5–10 m (16–33 ft) in sand.

Note: The Bar protects the anchorage from large ocean swells. However, "in strong to gale-force S to SE winds, seas break across the bar, but the anchorage is safe." (Sailing Directions British Columbia Coast (South Portion) Volume 1. Fifteenth Edition: 1990.)

Estevan Point is a forbidding stretch of low coastline with dangerous off-lying rocks and very few areas accessible from the water. It's wise to stay well offshore when rounding Estevan Point in all but the very calmest weather. The Spanish ship *Santiago*, captained by Juan Perez, anchored NW of Estevan Point in the vicinity of Perez Rocks on August 8, 1774—the first European vessel the Vancouver Island natives had set eyes on. Shortly after they anchored, a strong NW wind came up and the *Santiago* had to slip its anchor line, leaving the honour of being the first Europeans to set foot on Vancouver Island to Captain Cook four years later.

The First Nations who lived at Hesquiat Harbour represented several independent tribal groups. Only one or two families now live year-round at the village. Most have moved to Hot Springs Cove, which offers a more protected anchorage.

Hesquiat Peninsula Park lies to the W and Maquinna Park to the E of sheltered Hesquiat Harbour, which offers miles of deserted beaches to explore by dinghy or kayak.

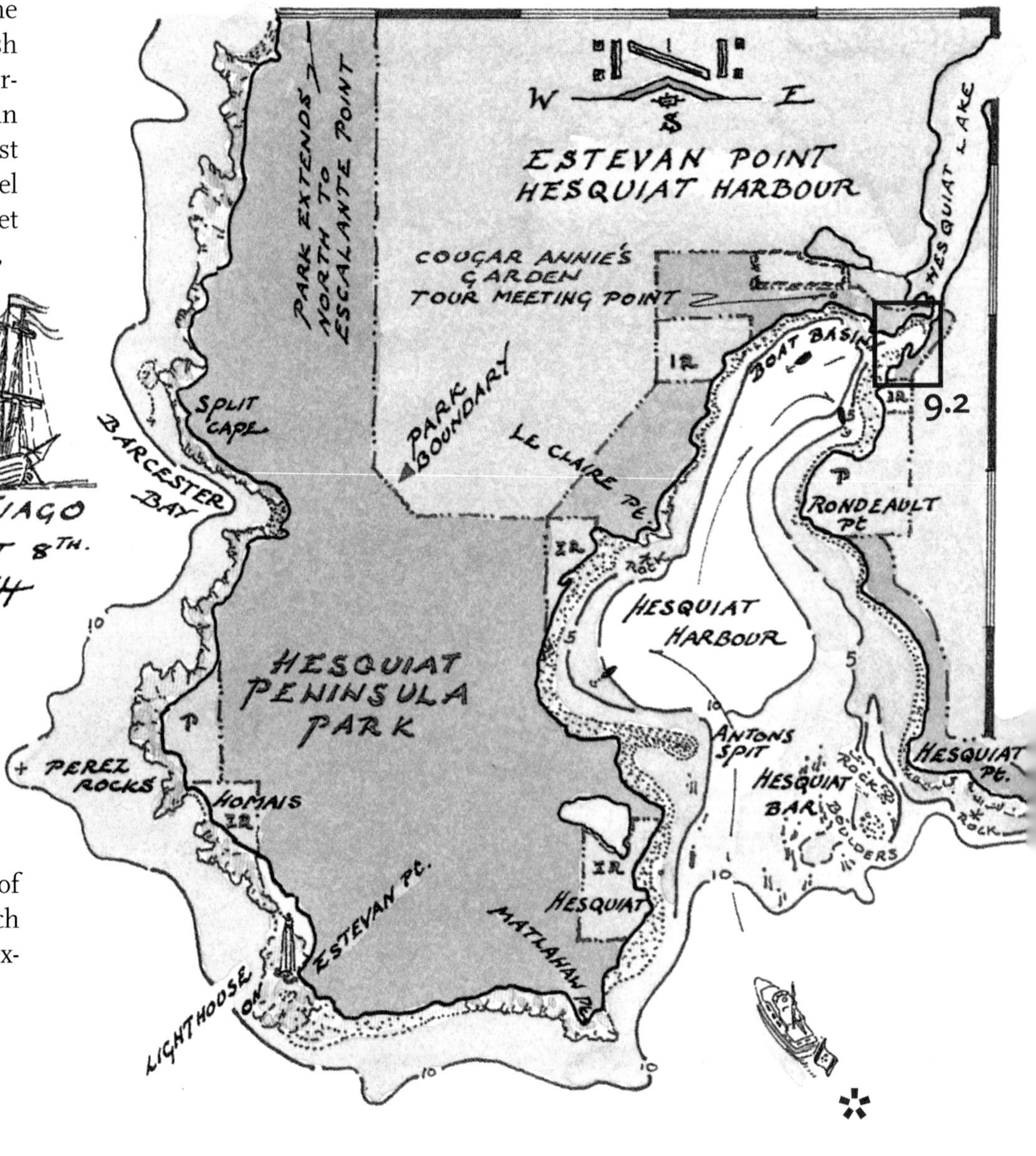

Not to be used for navigation. Depth contours are approximate and in metres.

CHART 3674.

APPROACH Rae Basin lies in the extreme NE portion of Hesquiat Harbour—approach from Boat Basin with caution.

ANCHOR The "Outer Basin" has room for two or three boats to anchor in 5–7 m (16–23 ft) with good holding on a mud bottom. The "Inner Basin" has better protection with room for two or three boats to anchor in 3–5 m (10–16 ft) with good holding in mud.

Note: Keelboats and deep-draft vessels are advised not to enter the "Inner Basin" because the entrance is shallow.

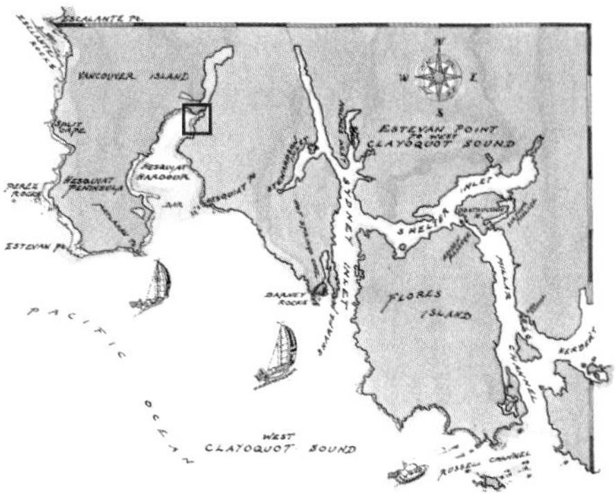

✲ 49°28.27'N 126°24.78'W

A pretty cove and a sandy beach backed by sun-bleached driftwood lie at the head of Rae Basin. The beach is ideal for landing your dinghy or kayak. Hesquiat River leads to Hesquiat Lake from here. In 1915, pioneer Ada Annie Rae-Arthur created a homestead in the wilderness of Boat Basin while raising her 11 children. "Cougar" Annie outlived four husbands and created a beautiful, five-acre garden in the rainforest. In summer months the Boat Basin Foundation welcomes drop-in visitors to Cougar Annie's Garden daily. Arrive at the beach at around 4:30 pm and the caretakers Katrina or Neil, or Peter Buckland will meet you. The meeting point, marked with a sign, is about 50 metres (165 ft) east of the beach cabin. Cost for the tour is a minimum $30 donation per person to the non-profit foundation. Donations are vital to its survival—they contribute to the upkeep of the garden and facilities, and support programs that will preserve this significant piece of West Coast history. For more information, visit www.boatbasin.org.

For an exhilarating day tour of the garden from Tofino, contact Ocean Outfitters Gift Gallery in Tofino: phone 1-877-906-2326 or visit www.oceanoutfitters.bc.ca.

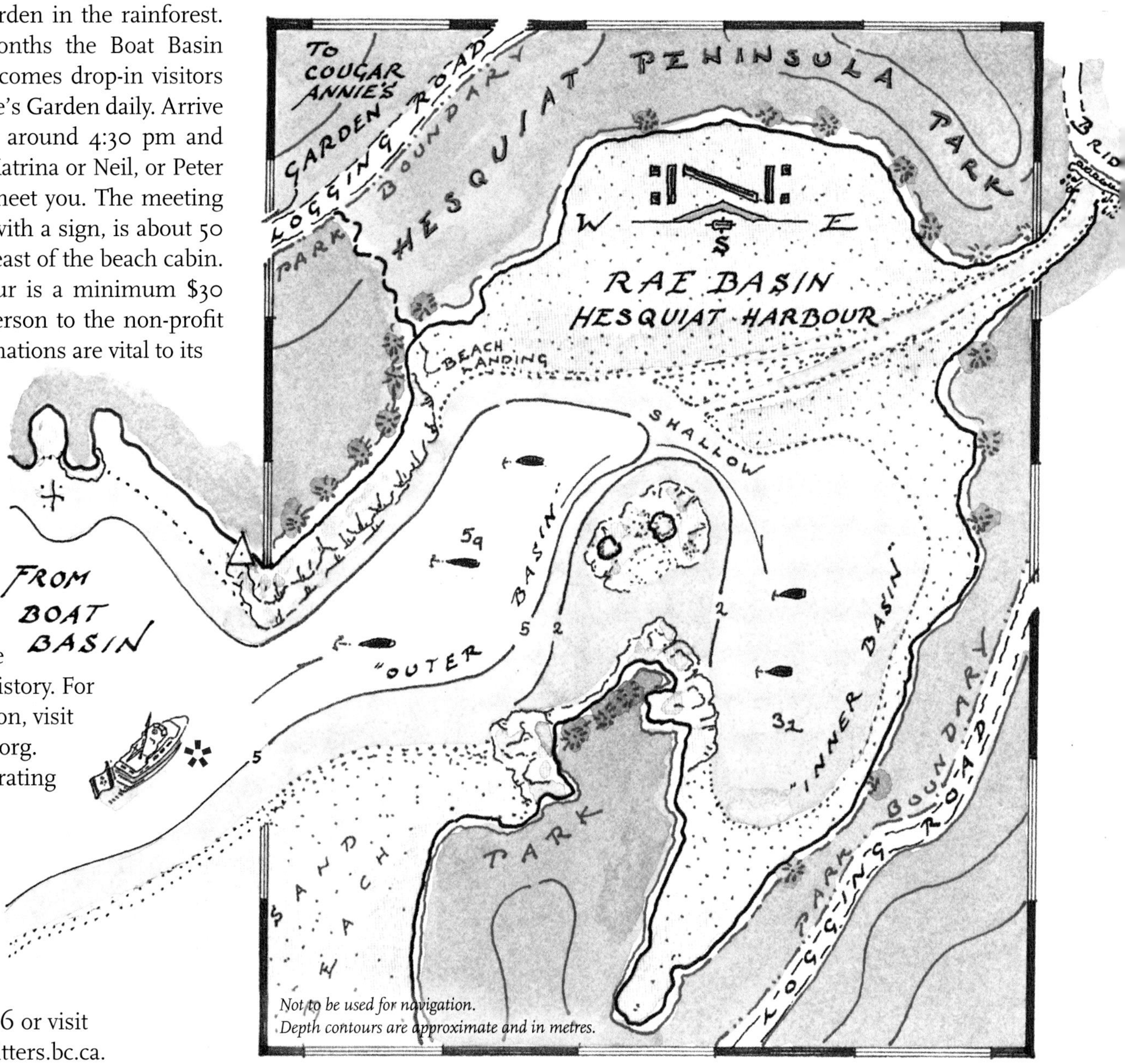

Not to be used for navigation.
Depth contours are approximate and in metres.

9.3 HOT SPRINGS COVE, MAQUINNA PROVINCIAL MARINE PARK

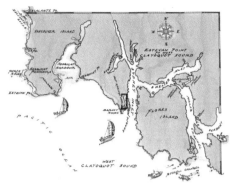

✦ 49°21.26'N 126°16.04'W

PUBLIC WHARF The wharf is very busy in summer months—the outside is used extensively by tour boats, water taxis and float planes. Room on the inside is limited.

Note: Anchoring out is far more desirable here. A campground is owned and operated by the Refuge Cove Band—their community is situated across the cove from the public wharf and they welcome visitors.

CHARTS 3674.

APPROACH Enter the cove from the S leaving Sharp Point and the light to the E. Favour the E shore as a rock lies off the beach on the W shore.

ANCHOR Off the public wharf or further N. The cove has good protection from moderate winds and swell conditions. Anchor in 4–8 m (13–26 ft) with good holding in mud and shell.

CAUTIONARY NOTE

At the entrance to the park a sign reads "In order to avoid offending other visitors ALL VISITORS MUST WEAR BATHING SUITS in and around the hot springs pools"—a big blow for those who come here to bathe in the traditional manner—*au naturel*. Visitors must pay a small fee before entering the park.

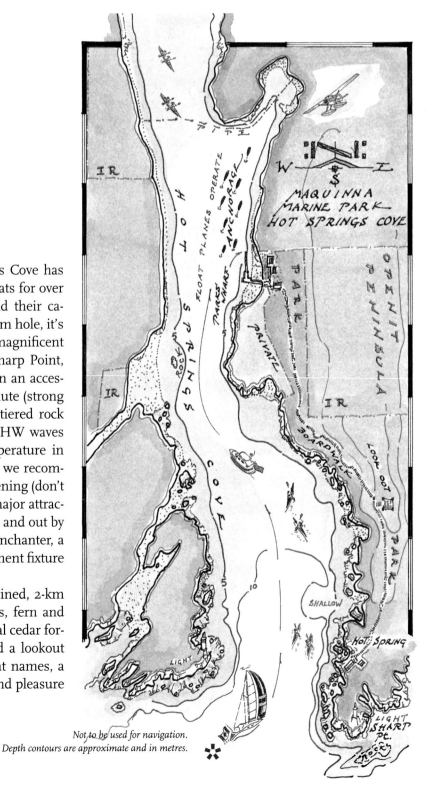

Not to be used for navigation.
Depth contours are approximate and in metres. ✦

Sheltered by Openit Peninsula, Hot Springs Cove has provided refuge for fishermen and their boats for over 100 years and for the Nuu-chah-nulth and their canoes for centuries. Not only is the cove a good storm hole, it's also home to Maquinna Provincial Park and the magnificent Ramsay Hot Spring. Tucked behind the tip of Sharp Point, this 50-degree C geothermal spring tumbles down an accessible waterfall at a rate of nearly 500 litres per minute (strong enough to wash off your swimsuit!), into three tiered rock pools neatly positioned to take advantage of the HW waves that sluice in, giving each pool a different temperature in which to soak. During the busy summer months we recommend visiting the pools in the early morning or evening (don't forget a flashlight), as the hot springs are now a major attraction, with large numbers of visitors transported in and out by boat and float plane—some staying at the The Innchanter, a floating B&B in an old power yacht that is a permanent fixture in the cove.

The trail to the pools consists of a well-maintained, 2-km (1.3-mile) wood boardwalk that snakes over moss, fern and skunk cabbage, and through the shade of a magical cedar forest. The walkway has a series of steep stairs and a lookout platform. Many of its planks are carved with boat names, a tradition started years ago by visiting fishermen and pleasure boaters.

One fine shower—Anne enjoys the sulphurous waters of Hot Springs Cove.

9.4 YOUNG BAY, SYDNEY INLET

CHARTS 3674.

APPROACH The bay lies on the E shore, at the junction of Holmes Inlet and Sydney Inlet. The entrance is clear.

Enter the anchorage by leaving the white rock and treed islet to the N.

ANCHOR This protected anchorage is large and relatively deep. Anchor in 8–14 m (26–46 ft) with a stern line ashore to limit swing. Holding is good in mud and sand.

Originally the location of an Ahousaht village, Young Bay was also the site of a pilchard reduction plant in the 1920s. Thanks to an unusual environmental incident, the warm Japanese current that usually passes hundreds of miles off Vancouver Island shifted to the island shoreline, bringing schools of pilchard into Clayoquot Sound—like herring, these fish were valuable because of their high oil content.

Cecilia Creek empties into the bay, providing fresh water for kayakers, boaters and wildlife. The cozy anchorage at the head of the bay is backed by old-growth forest and steep grassy bluffs, and there are rocks and islets to explore at leisure. A rough trail leads from the mouth of Cecilia Creek through the forest to the lake above. A mystery wreck about a kilometre (a half-mile) N of Young Bay is a designated heritage site.

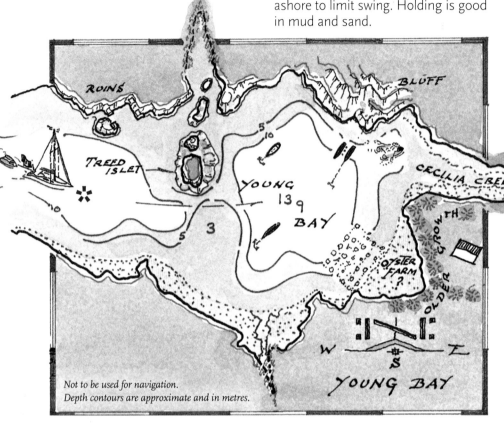

Not to be used for navigation.
Depth contours are approximate and in metres.

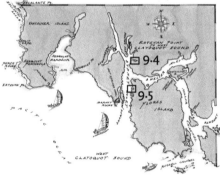

9.4 ✿ 49°25.71'N 126°13.73'W
9.5 ✿ 49°22.49'N 126°14.03'W

CHARTS 3674.

APPROACH This small bay lies on the Flores Island shore, at the entrance to Sydney Inlet. Leave the rock in the entrance to the S.

ANCHOR There is a one-boat spot between the rocks and another in the NE corner with good protection from the SE and moderate protection from the NW. Anchor in depths of 4–7 m (13–23 ft) with good holding in mud.

9.5 HOOTLA-KOOTLA BAY

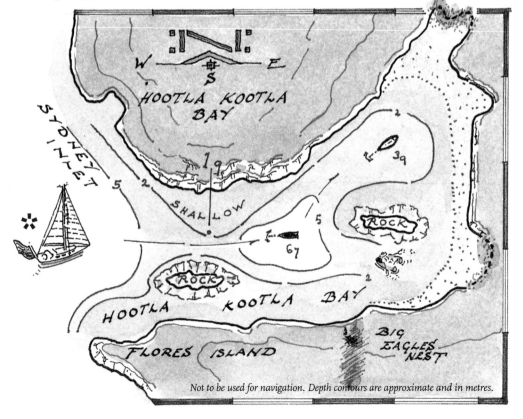

Not to be used for navigation. Depth contours are approximate and in metres.

A delightful hideaway, Hootla-Kootla Bay provides convenient anchorage for boaters travelling south on the outside of Flores Island. This was also a pilchard factory site.

BOTTLENECK COVE, HOLMES INLET 9.6

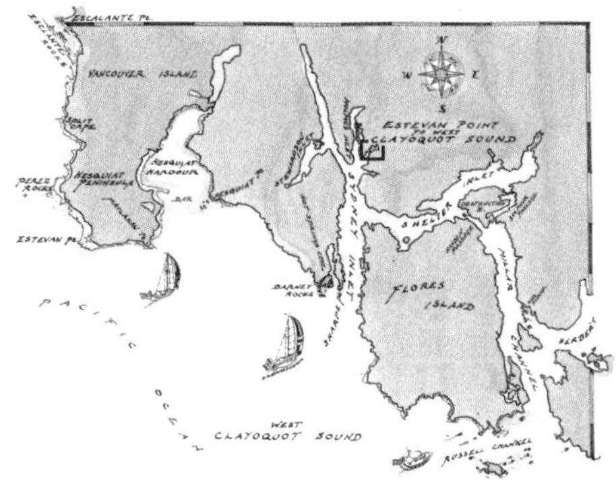

✲ 49°26.46'N 126°13.63'W

CHARTS 3674.

APPROACH The narrow (bottleneck) entrance lies to the E at the entrance to Holmes Inlet. Stay centre channel where the minimum charted depth is 7.3 m (24 ft).

ANCHOR The cove is more commodious than it appears on the chart and affords all-weather protection. Swing in 5–10 m (16–33 ft) with good holding in mud and shell.

Holmes Inlet leads north from Sydney Inlet at Adventure Point and ends at Ice River estuary. Lagoon-like Bottleneck Cove lies at the south end of the inlet and once housed a small village called Hasyukwis, where canoes were designed and carved. The well-protected anchorage is bigger than it looks on the chart and is surrounded by steep, grassy cliffs.

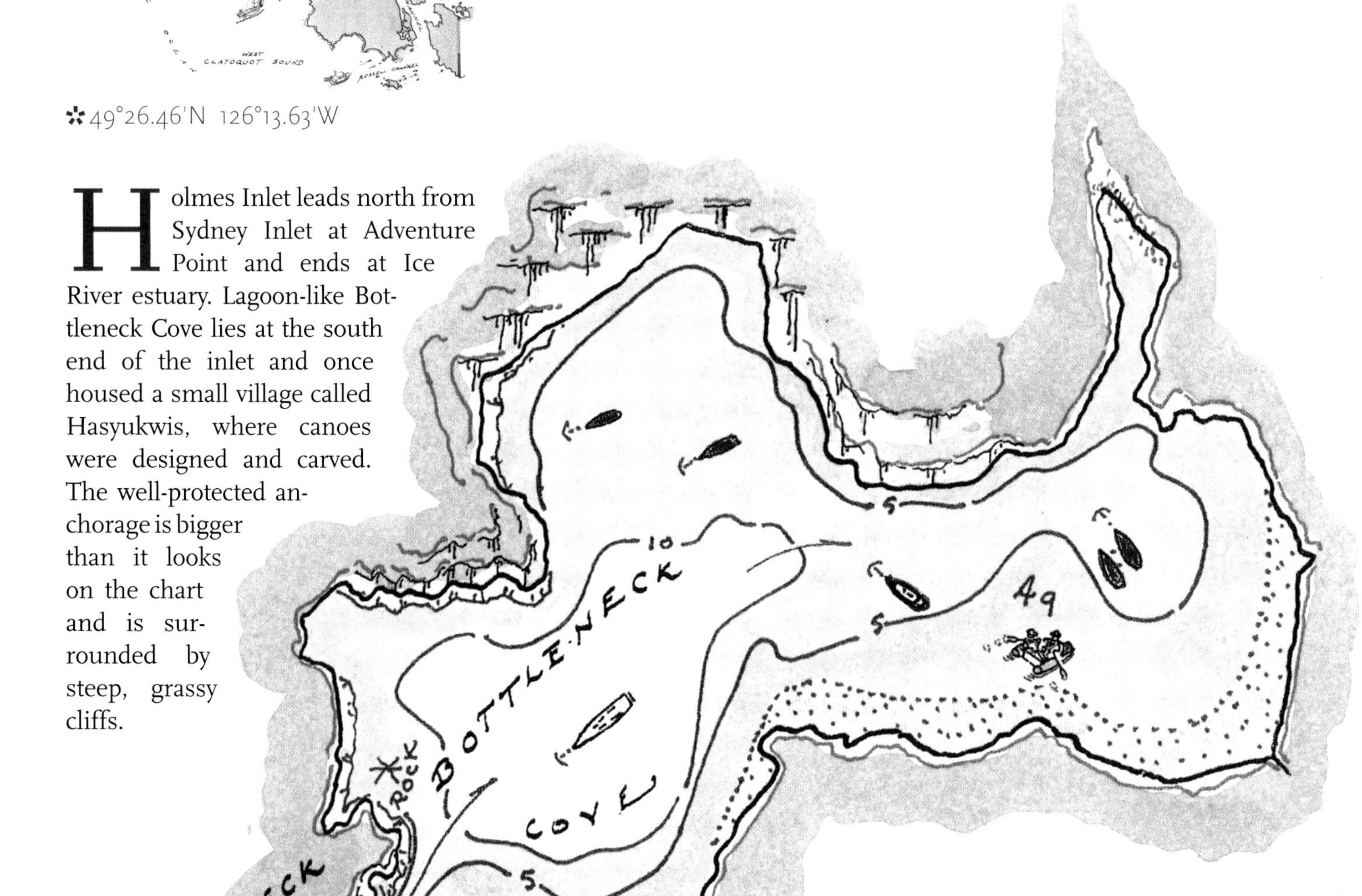
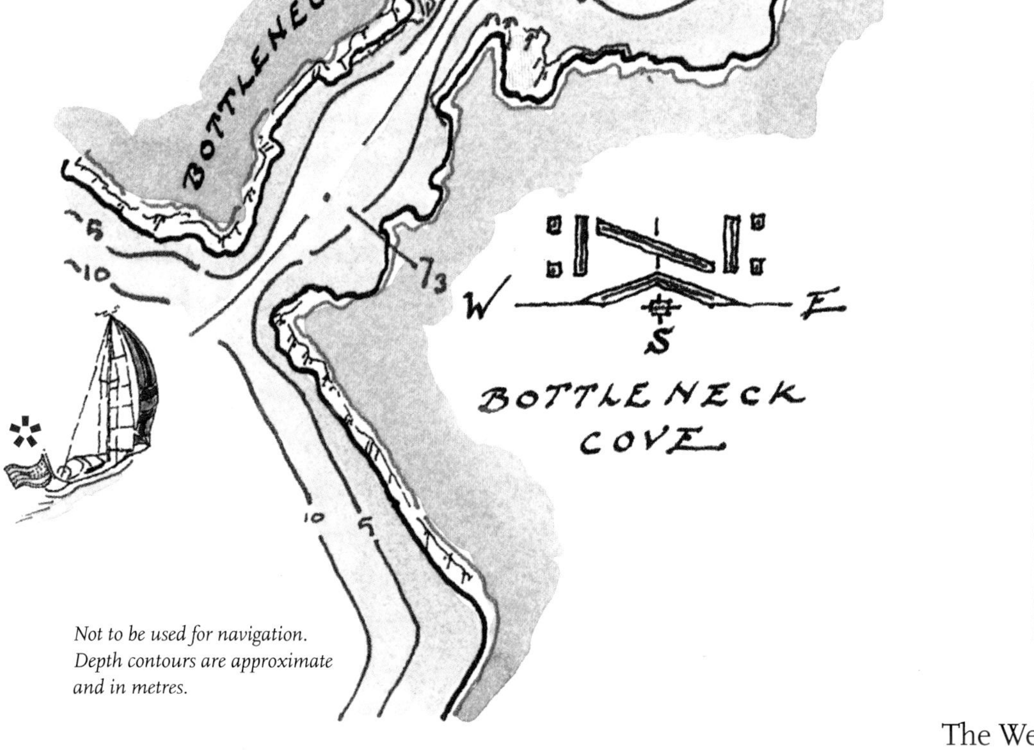

Not to be used for navigation. Depth contours are approximate and in metres.

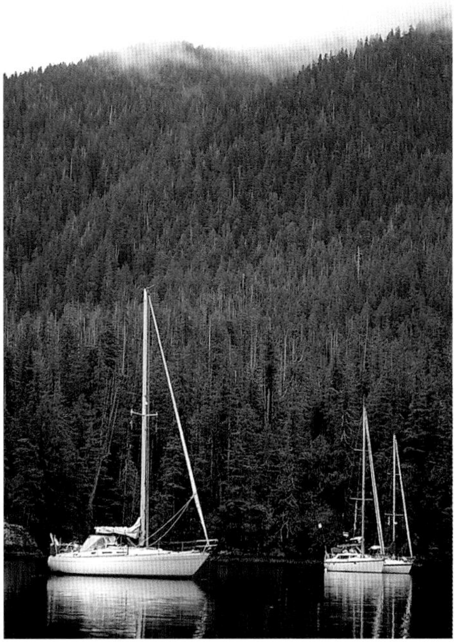

Friends "buddy-boat" as they cruise south.

9.7 MEGIN RIVER DELTA, SHELTER INLET

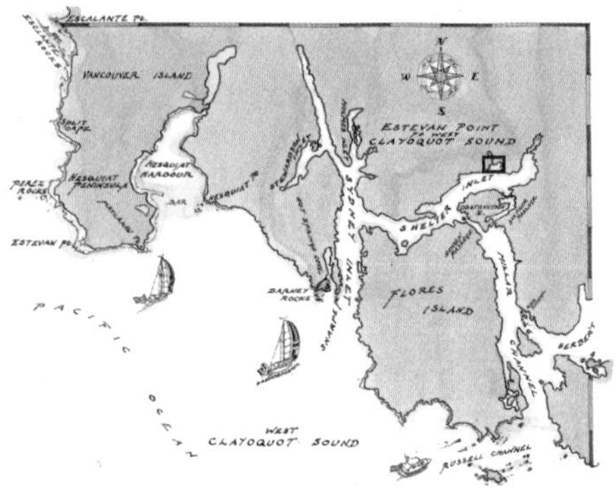

✲ 49°25.90'N 126°05.08'W

CHARTS 3674.

APPROACH

(A) At LW the rock-lined opening to the Megin River is quite conspicuous.

(B) Head for the beach NE of the islets and round up on the 10-m (33-ft) contour.

ANCHOR

(A) In the estuary where the current from the river stream will steady the boat. A temporary picnic spot with good holding in 4–8 m (13–26 ft) in mud and sand.

(B) Tuck in behind the three islets and anchor in 4–12 m (13–40 ft) with good holding in mud and gravel. Afternoon winds will create chop in this anchorage, but when the wind dies in the early evening it's a comfortable spot to overnight in.

A natural playground, Megin River Delta and nearby Bacchante Bay are two spots we would love to explore at leisure on a return visit. The area is part of the Strathcona Provincial Park Megin-Talbot Addition, and the Megin River Ecological Reserve protects old-growth Sitka spruce and western red cedar on the lower expanse of the river. The Megin River supports spawning salmon, and we learned from a party of kayakers that it is navigable (with a little hard work) to picturesque Megin Lake where freshwater mussels have been reported.

The second attraction worth investigating is a waterfall that tumbles down into an inviting pool. At HW the abovementioned kayakers paddled up one of the rivers to the main pool and beach for an excellent view from the edge of the waterfall.

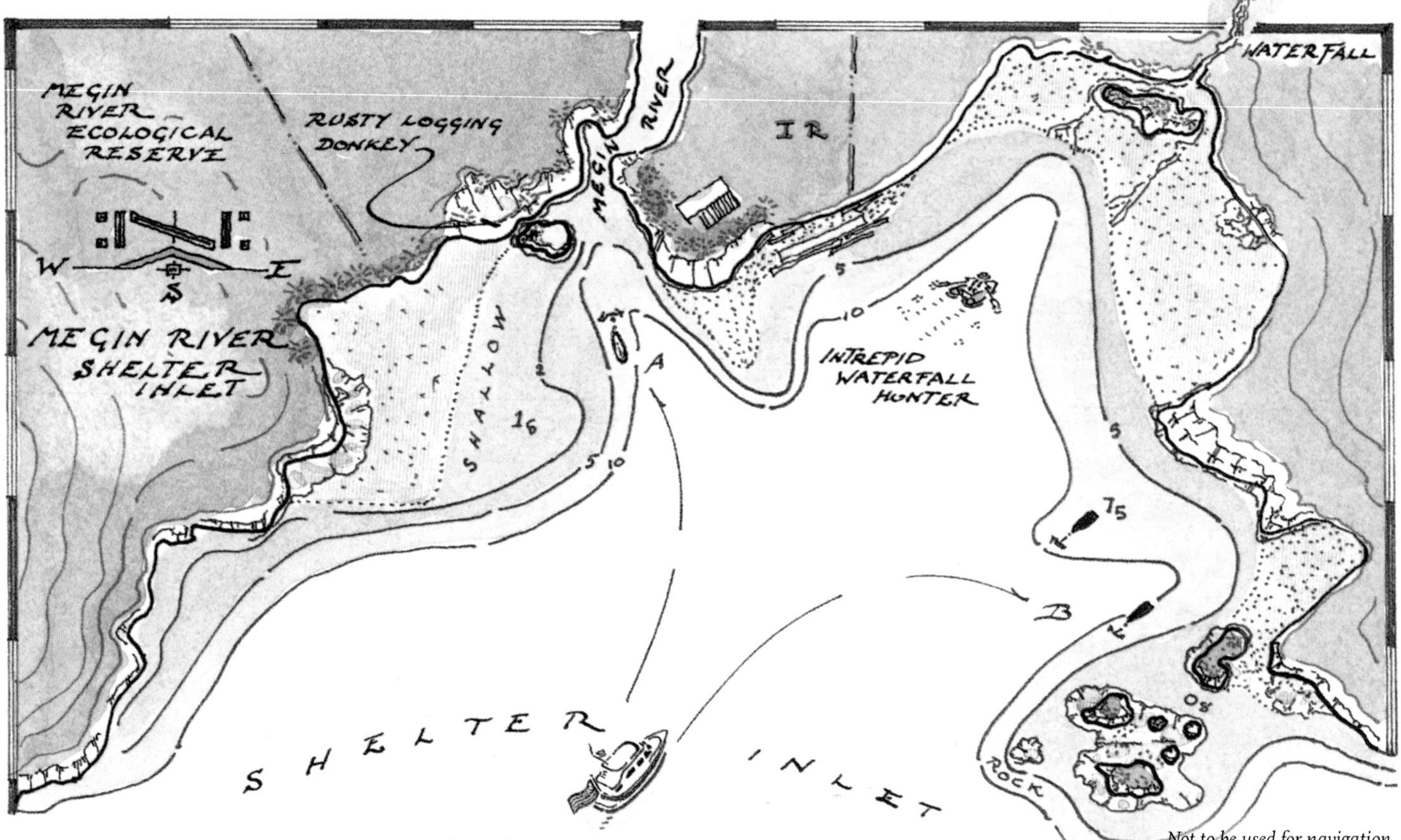

Not to be used for navigation.
Depth contours are approximate and in metres.

CHART 3674.

APPROACH From the N, from Shelter Inlet or from the S, from within Sulphur Passage. A string of rocks and islets appear to block the passage between Obstruction Island and Vancouver Island. However, there are two routes as indicated on the map. Proceed with caution and on a rising tide.

Note: Most boaters transit via the west route. Do not attempt to transit in fog, even if you have radar.

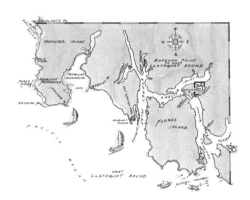

S ulphur Passage cuts through Sulphur Passage Provincial Park, which encompasses all of Obstruction Island, a portion of land to the east and a strip on the NW shore of Shelter Inlet. The passage is a maze of rocks and islets with current to 4 knots, transit with care.

Tucked in the southeast north of the islets.

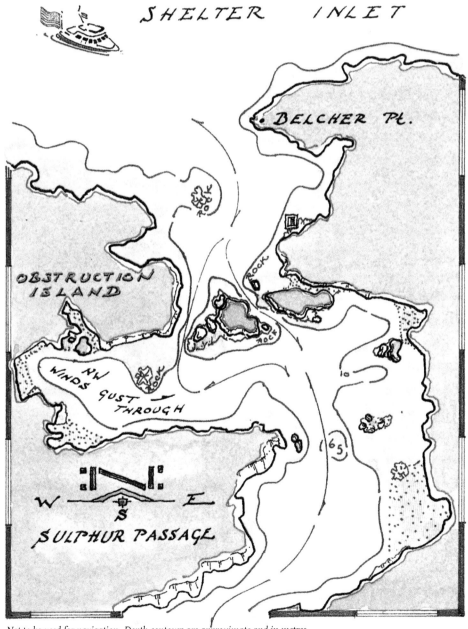

Not to be used for navigation. Depth contours are approximate and in metres.

9.9 BACCHANTE BAY, WATTA CREEK

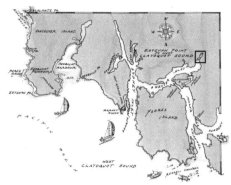

✽ 49°26.53'N 126°02.71'W

CHARTS 3674.

APPROACH The entrance lies NE of a one-tree rock at the head of Shelter Inlet. The centre channel is clear.

ANCHOR

(A) At the head of the commodious all-weather bay, off the grassy delta of Watta Creek. Good holding in sticky mud in 6–14 m (20–46 ft).

(B) NW of the entrance where rock shelves provide a great picnic spot with a lovely view.

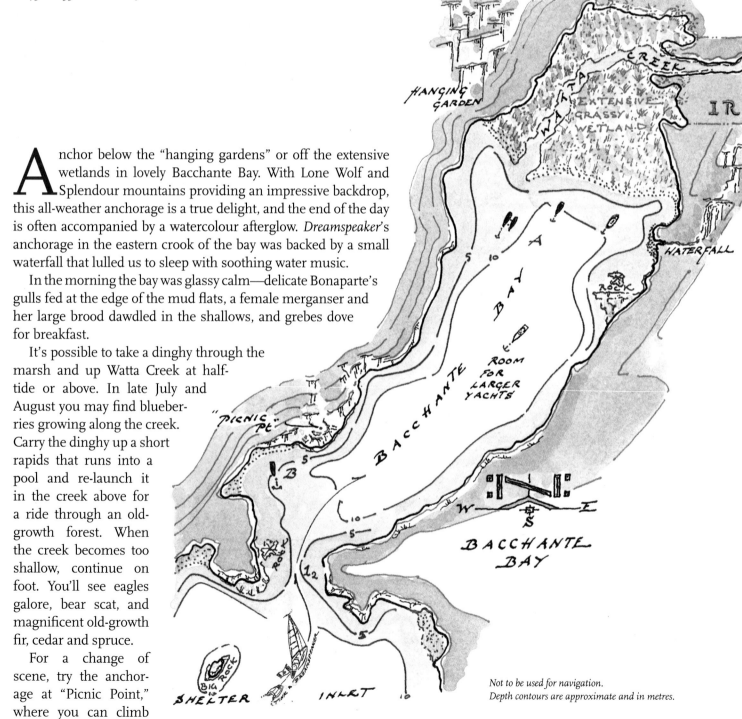

Not to be used for navigation.
Depth contours are approximate and in metres.

Anchor below the "hanging gardens" or off the extensive wetlands in lovely Bacchante Bay. With Lone Wolf and Splendour mountains providing an impressive backdrop, this all-weather anchorage is a true delight, and the end of the day is often accompanied by a watercolour afterglow. *Dreamspeaker's* anchorage in the eastern crook of the bay was backed by a small waterfall that lulled us to sleep with soothing water music.

In the morning the bay was glassy calm—delicate Bonaparte's gulls fed at the edge of the mud flats, a female merganser and her large brood dawdled in the shallows, and grebes dove for breakfast.

It's possible to take a dinghy through the marsh and up Watta Creek at half-tide or above. In late July and August you may find blueberries growing along the creek. Carry the dinghy up a short rapids that runs into a pool and re-launch it in the creek above for a ride through an old-growth forest. When the creek becomes too shallow, continue on foot. You'll see eagles galore, bear scat, and magnificent old-growth fir, cedar and spruce.

For a change of scene, try the anchorage at "Picnic Point," where you can climb the grassy ledges and investigate the small beach at low water.

Bacchante Bay, one of the West Coast's more dramatic anchorages.

9.10 "WEST" WHITE PINE COVE, HERBERT INLET

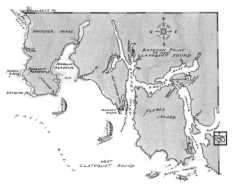

CHART 3674.

APPROACH From the NW, either side of an islet off the entrance. The passage in to the "Outer Cove" is free of obstruction. There is a bar at the entrance to the "Inner Cove" with a minimum depth of 0.5 m (1.7 ft)—time your entrance and exit to the state of the tide.

ANCHOR

"Outer Cove"—tuck in or swing as indicated in depths of 10–13 m (33–43 ft) in mud.

"Inner Cove"—room for two or three boats. Note the rock and surrounding shallows. Anchor in depths of 3–6 m (10–20 ft) in mud.

✣ 49°18.40'N 125°59.17'W

Not to be used for navigation. Depth contours are approximate and in metres.

Directly west of White Pine Cove (which offers little shelter) is an anchorage well protected from wind and swell. The still waters of the lagoon anchorage behind the centre islet provide a snug, land-locked sanctuary for three or four boats and the freshwater creek and small beach are worth investigating.

Spot the bald eagle's nest.

Not to be used for navigation. Depth contours are approximate and in metres.

CHARTS 3674 (see inset for detail).

APPROACH The entrance to Matilda Inlet lies between the N tip of McNeil Peninsula and a light off the Flores Island shore. Stay in centre channel to the Ahousat General Store wharf and head S to the anchorage.

ANCHOR At the head of the inlet (be aware of the eel grass boundary) or in the channel. The inlet experiences inflow winds in the afternoon and outflow winds at night. Keep a short scope and check your swing—the holding is very good in sticky mud in 4–8 m (13–26 ft).

MARINA The Ahousat General Store has temporary moorage for visitors to the store and café as well as overnight moorage. Water is available but there is only enough power for local, permanently moored boats. The marine ways can haul out boats up to 12 m (40 ft). The store's post office will hold mail if advised: General Delivery, Ahousat, BC

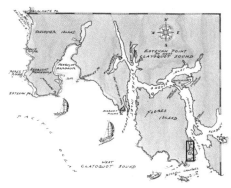

✤ 49°18.22'N 126°04.20'W
(Waypoint at entrance to Matilda Inlet)

VOR 1AO Canada. Call on VHF Channel 68 or 250-670-9575.

FUEL On the store float, gasoline, diesel and stove oil.

Note: The café is open from 9 am–8 pm in July and August, serving hearty breakfasts, burgers, fish and chips, and nightly specials. The store carries basic groceries, some fresh produce, frozen food, ice cream, snacks, hardware and fishing gear.

Matilda Inlet is known by the locals and fishermen as one of the most sheltered anchorages in Clayoquot Sound. It's close to the Ahousat General Store, café and fuel dock and a dinghy ride away from the First Nations community of Marktosis, which welcome visitors.

Gibson Provincial Marine Park begins at the head of the inlet. On the shaded SW shore the tepid waters of Ahousat Warm Springs (25 degrees C) feed a rectangular, man-made pool. Used regularly by local families and occasional boating and kayaking visitors, the sulphur spring is fed by the same kind of geothermal flow as Ramsay Hot Springs.

From here a muddy track follows the shoreline and joins a swampy 1-km (.5-mile) creekbed trail to the spectacular sweep of Whitesand Beach, which provides lovely views across Russell Channel to Clayoquot Sound. Be prepared for a tricky hike—wear boat boots and take everything needed for a day at the beach, including water. It took us a good hour and a half to hike both ways but the opportunity to explore the fine-sand beach made it worthwhile.

Moorage fronts the Ahousat store and restaurant.

A killer whale spyhops outside Clayoquot Sound. Adrian Dorst photo.

Chapter 10
EAST CLAYOQUOT SOUND

Chapter 10
EAST CLAYOQUOT SOUND

TIDES

Volume 6, *Canadian Tide and Current Tables*

Reference Port: Tofino

Secondary Ports: Kennedy Cove, Warn Bay, Cypress Bay

CURRENTS

No current station for this area. However, currents play a major role in navigation in this chapter.

Note: In the passes, currents around Tofino and Meares Island run at 2–5 knots.

WEATHER

Weather Channel VHF WX2 Nootka, 21B Mount Ozzard.

Areas—West Coast Vancouver Island South—listen for marine reports from Lennard Island lighthouse. Listen for La Pérouse Bank weather buoy for offshore conditions.

On a windy coast there's sometimes just not enough breeze to fill the sail.

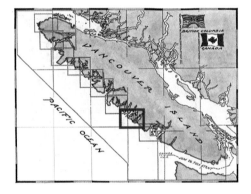

CAUTIONARY NOTES

The large-scale chart 3685 is a must for the detail required in this area. It is easy to run aground on the sandbars and mud flats, especially on the approach to Tofino, the entry into East Clayoquot Sound via Browning Passage, and Tsapee Narrows. The main channels are well marked and safe passage should be relatively easy.

Note: Extensive crab traps in Lemmens Inlet serve as good navigation markers— they have approximately 2–10 m (6.6– 33 ft) of water below the floating buoy.

Boats travelling offshore and SE from Hotsprings Cove around Flores Island might be tempted to extend their day's run and pass East Clayoquot Sound and Tofino to reach Barkley Sound and Ucluelet, a distance of 50 nautical miles. However, we recommend a stop in Tofino, a more manageable run of approximately 30 nautical miles.

Bustling Tofino is growing rapidly in its role as the economic, cultural and tourist centre of the west coast of Vancouver Island. The town's main development and downtown core occupy the southeastern tip of Esowista Peninsula.

A pleasant uphill walk from the public wharf on Fourth will bring you to Main and Campbell streets, where you will find a well-stocked co-op store, a library, banks and a vibrant medley of shops, art galleries, gift and bookstores, cafés, restaurants, pubs and ecotour operators.

Over thirty species of migrating birds rest and feed on the eelgrass beds of the Tofino Mud flats and the salt marshes that occupy both sides of Browning Passage, extending to 32 square km (12.3 square miles) in area at LW.

The Big Tree Trail on nearby Meares Island is easily accessed by dinghy, kayak and water taxi. A mossy boardwalk winds its way up and down steep stairs, and around magnificent spruce trees and huge cedars festooned with mosses and ferns.

Lemmens Inlet almost bisects Meares Island; on its inner NW shore. "God's Pocket" offers visiting boaters a cozy spot to anchor for the night. Adventure Cove, on the inlet's eastern shore, is the site of Fort Defiance, built by Captain Robert Gray of the American fur-trading ship *Columbia*. On the island's outer eastern shore, charming Dawley Passage and the provincial park that protects it lead to an anchorage in Windy Bay that is overlooked by tremendous sheer cliffs.

Farther E, the secluded hideaway at the head of Gunner Inlet is on *Dreamspeaker's* list of ideal anchorages. It offers excellent protection and good depth for two or three boats. Alternatively, anchor at the head of hushed Tranquil Inlet. A black granite cliff rises directly out of the warm waters of "East Nook" to command this one-boat cove.

While in Tofino Inlet, enjoy the all-weather protection of Kennedy Cove and Cannery Bay. In Cypress Bay, north of Meares Island, the commodious anchorage of Quait Bay is almost landlocked by the rainforest.

FEATURED DESTINATIONS

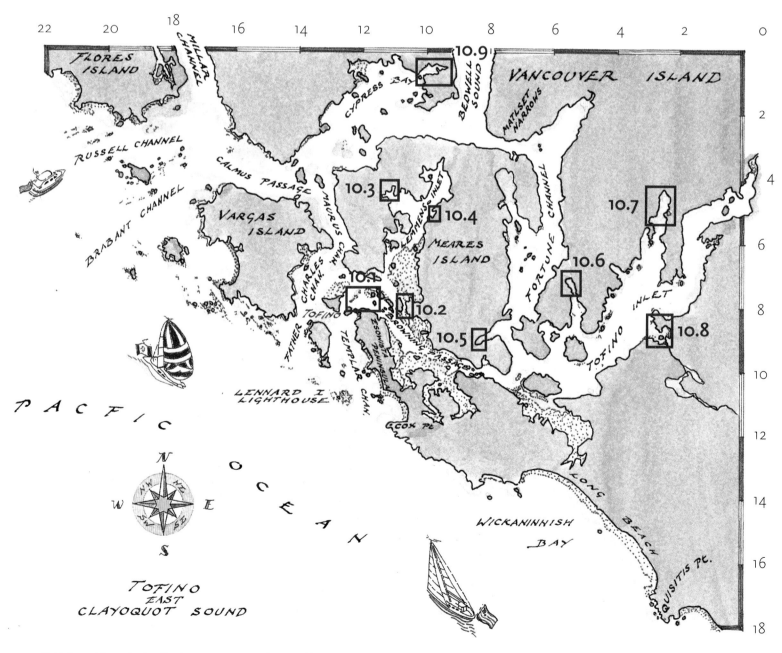

Not to be used for navigation. Depth contours are approximate and in metres.

10.1 TOFINO, DUFFIN PASSAGE

Strawberry Island from Fourth Street Wharf.

Fourth Street Wharf welcomes visiting boaters.

Whale-watching is Tofino's "big box" resource.

N amed in 1792 after the Spanish hydrographer Vicente Tofino de San Miguel, Tofino is also known as "Tuff City" by the locals and is a busy, bustling town. The village's main development and downtown core occupy the southeastern tip of Esowista Peninsula. Tofino is rapidly growing as the economic, cultural and tourist centre for the west coast of Vancouver Island because of its proximity to Long Beach and other Pacific Rim Park destinations (last population count 1,906).

Uphill from the public wharf on Fourth to Main and Campbell streets you will find the well-stocked co-op store with delivery to Fourth Street Wharf, a library, banks and a vibrant medley of shops, art galleries, gift and bookstores, cafés, restaurants, pubs and ecotour operators.

An outdoor public market opens each Saturday at 10 am in the summer months. Tofino has a great theatre that offers "Movie Nights," and you are never far from a home studio or spa that offers yoga classes, barefoot reflexology, shiatsu or hot stone massage.

While in Tofino, take some time off the boat to enjoy a guided birdwatching tour with Adrian Dorst, the renowned nature photographer (250-725-1243), rent a hybrid or electric bike (Tofino Cycles, 250-725-2453), or pack a picnic lunch and catch the local "Beach Bus" to Cox Bay and Long Beach to watch the surfing and walk the longest beach on Vancouver Island (1-866-986-3466). Or treat yourself, the skipper or the kids to surfing or skim-boarding lessons—Live to Surf (250-725-4464), Surf Sister Surf School (250-725-4456). Pick up the *Tofino Time*, a free magazine about events and activities in and around Tofino. There are many enterprises to visit in Tofino. Here are some that we tried:

• **Tofino Co-op (250-725-3226)** on First Street for groceries and other necessities; everything you might need—delivered to Fourth Street Wharf for $1! • **Wildside Seafoods (250-725-3244)**—freshly caught prawns and salmon directly from the fish boats. • **Common Loaf Bake Shop (250-725-3915)** on First Street—fresh bread, pastries, coffee, sandwiches and more. • **Raincoast Interpretive Centre (250-725-2560)** on Main Street—a must for the whole family. • **Eagle Aerie Gallery (250-725-3235)** on Campbell Street—a traditional longhouse featuring the work of Tsimshian artist Roy Vickers. • **House of Himwitsa (250-725-2017)** on Main Street—First Nations-owned gallery, exhibits include work by master carver Sanford Williams of Yuquot, Friendly Cove.

CHARTS 3685.

APPROACH Duffin Pass lies off Tofino's waterfront—approach from the N out of Deadmans Pass—stay in centre channel. Approach from the SW by rounding Grice Point out of Templar Channel, or from the SE by rounding Usatzes Point, from Browning Passage.

ANCHOR NW of Strawberry Island within the 10-m (33-ft) contour. Moderate protection from SE and NW outflow winds from Lemmens Inlet. No protection from the sightseeing boats that rocket through the passage and float planes taking off and landing. Currents are strong here and boats can swirl when the wind blows against the current—allow ample swinging room. It's not advisable to row ashore as dinghies can be easily swept downstream.

PUBLIC WHARF Tofino wharfs W-E. Wingen Lane Float has a depth of 1 m (3.3 ft) and can accommodate small boats with shallow draft. Convenient dinghy access. Fourth Street Wharf has a minimum depth of 2.7 m (9 ft) throughout except for the northeast corner, which is shallower. Shoaling has been reported off the docks and sailboats may ground at low tide. Visiting boaters are welcome although rafting is expected. Call ahead on VHF Channel 66A or 250-725-4441 for assistance. Showers, laundry facilities, internet, garbage disposal and power. Water is always available at $1 per 15 minute (approximately 150 gallons). Strictly two hours' free moorage—go overtime and you'll be charged for half-day moorage. Crab Dock has a depth of 6 m (20 ft) off the W end of the float—visitors welcome.

MARINA Weigh West Marine Resort has some transient moorage by reservation only—call 250-725-3277.

FUEL Method Marine fuel dock has gas, water and propane and a well-stocked marine store at the top of the ramp.

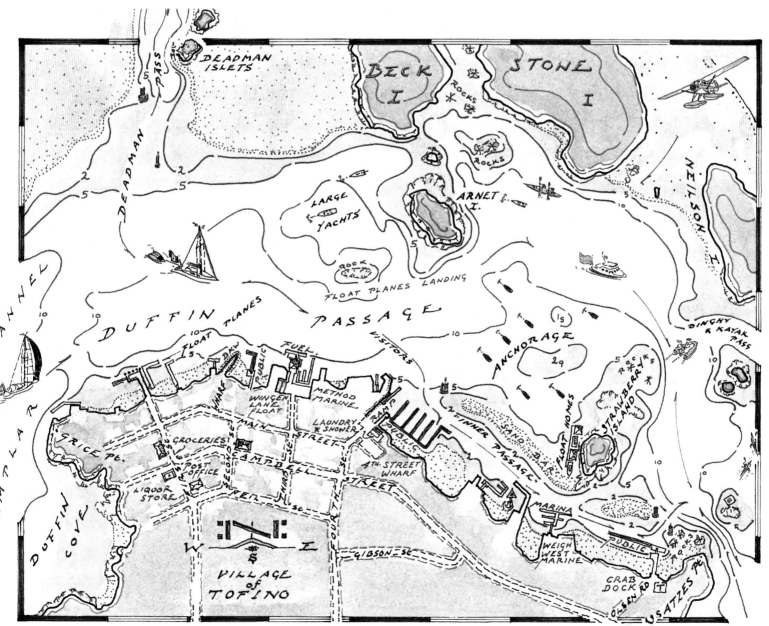

Not to be used for navigation. Depth contours are approximate and in metres.

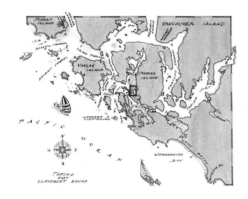

CHART 3685.

APPROACH Best accessed by dinghy with an outboard or by water taxi from the Fourth Street public wharf—call 1-877-726-5485.

ANCHOR Temporary anchorage is possible as indicated—best approached at LW slack due to swift currents. Anchor in 3–5 m (10–16 ft) in sticky mud.

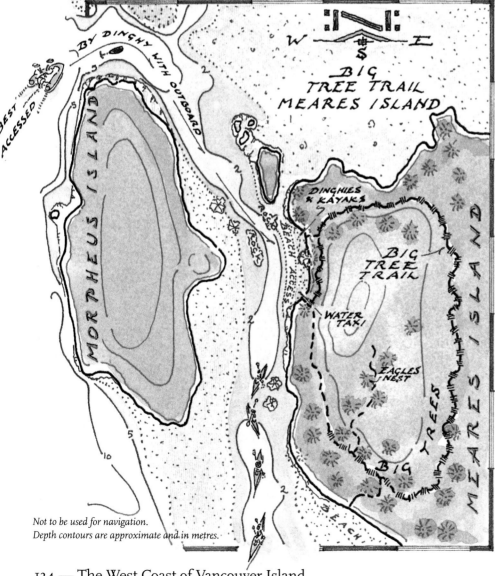

Not to be used for navigation.
Depth contours are approximate and in metres.

Meares Island is home to some of the world's largest cedar trees and Tofino's only source of fresh water. Two decades ago, the hard work and determination of environmental protesters and the Tla-o-qui-aht and Ahousaht First Nations foiled plans to log the island's ancient old-growth forests. Meares Island is now a Tla-o-qui-aht Tribal Park, and both First Nations bands have pledged to preserve the island and its water supply, while granting recreational access to all visitors.

Easily accessed by dinghy, kayak, water taxi or, with care, by larger boats, the Big Tree Trail leads from the beach to a moss-covered, half-kilometre (quarter-mile) boardwalk that winds its way up and down steep stairs and around magnificent spruce and huge cedar trees festooned with trailing mosses and ferns. Look for the beautiful Hanging Garden Tree that is said to be about fifteen hundred years old and the fourth-largest western red cedar in British Columbia.

A variety of wildlife resides in this hushed temperate rainforest—from petite Pacific tree frogs and western red-backed salamanders to wolves, bears and cougars.

The authors marvel at a big tree on Meares Island. Richard A. Jensen photo.

10.3 "GOD'S POCKET," MEARES ISLAND, LEMMENS INLET

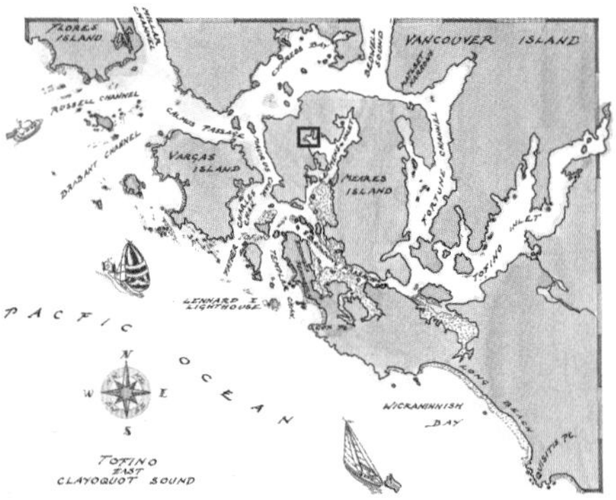

✲ 49°12.58'N 125°53.21'W

CHARTS 3673.

APPROACH From the SE. A large oyster farm straddles an islet in the entrance—leave it to the NE.

ANCHOR

(A) In the NW pocket.

(B) In the bight to the W of the oyster farm. Good protection from the NW and outflow winds. Moderate protection from the SE. Good holding in 6–8 m (20–26 ft) in soft mud—confirm the set of your anchor.

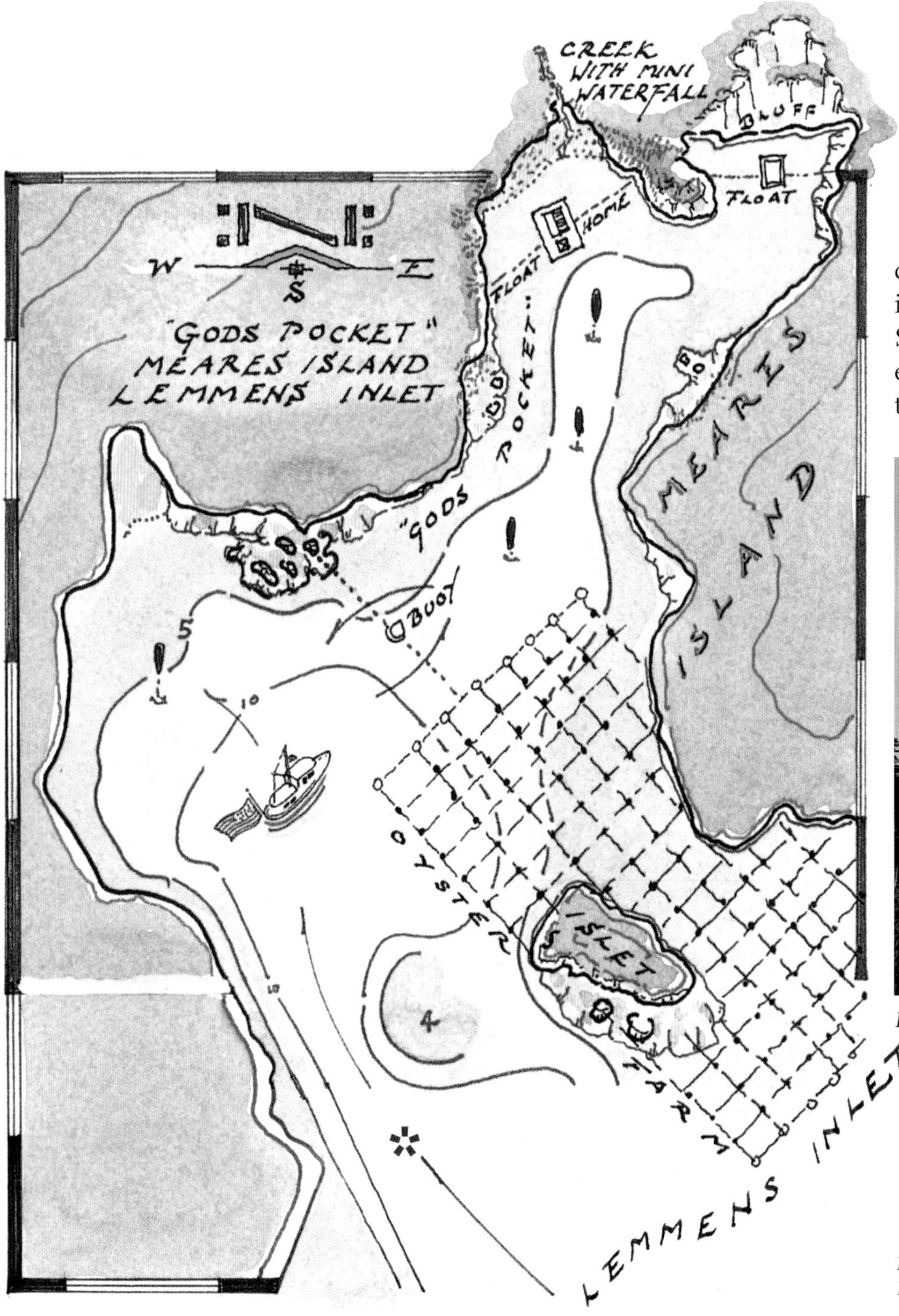

Locally named, this sheltered pocket of paradise off Lemmens Inlet offers visiting boaters a cozy spot to anchor for the night. Laze in the cockpit with a good book (see Selected Reading page 190), surrounded by lush rainforest and soothed by the sound of a small waterfall.

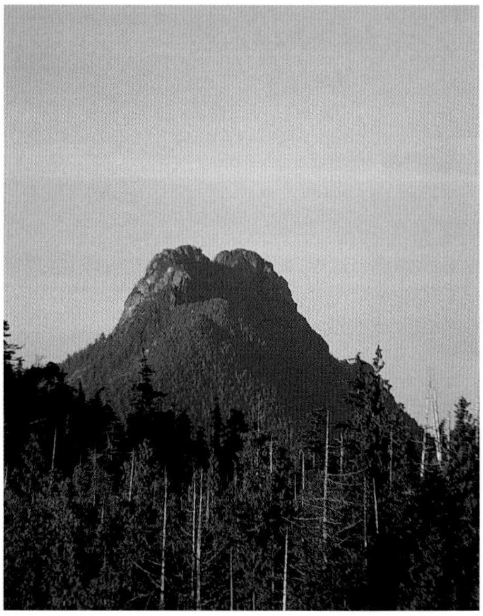

Lone Cone is the highest point on Meares Island.

Not to be used for navigation.
Depth contours are approximate and in metres.

ADVENTURE COVE, MEARES ISLAND, 10.4
LEMMENS INLET

A snug refuge that holds the setting sun longest can be found tucked into Meares Island, off Lemmens Inlet. Adventure Cove is the site of Fort Defiance, built by Captain Robert Gray of the American fur-trading ship *Columbia*. The partially excavated site is a provincial historic landmark. While wintering here in 1791–1792, the crew of the *Columbia* built the sloop *Adventure*. Before leaving in 1792, Gray ordered the destruction of the First Nations village of Opitsat in reaction to rumours of an attack that never materialized, demolishing 200 magnificent longhouses and their carvings.

The Tla-o-qui-aht village of Opitsat has a 5,000-year history, was the winter home of the noted Chief Wickaninnish, and today has a thriving community of more than 200 residents living along the waterfront.

✤ 49°12.23'N 125°51.30'W

CHARTS 3673.

APPROACH From the W, leaving Columbia Islet to the S.

ANCHOR One or two boats can share the cove with the two float homes. Good protection from all quarters, especially from SE winds. Anchor in 3–5 m (10–16 ft) with good holding in mud.

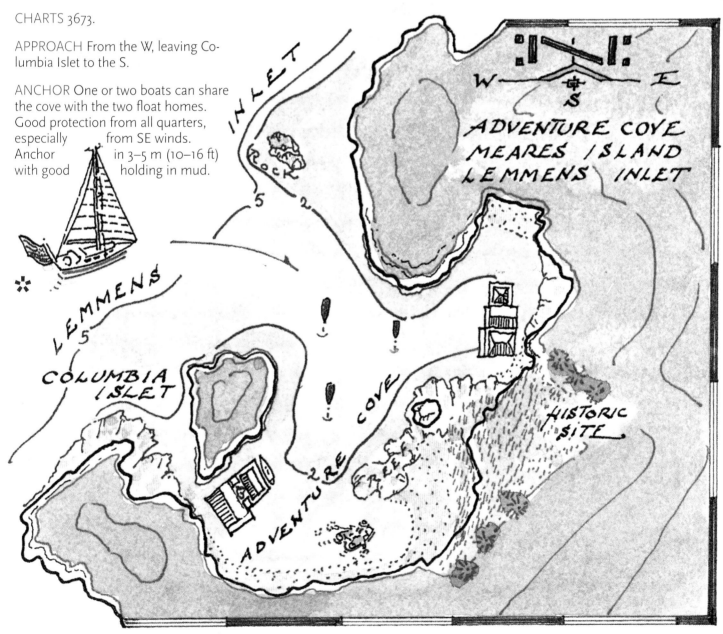

Not to be used for navigation. Depth contours are approximate and in metres.

10.5 WINDY BAY, MEARES ISLAND

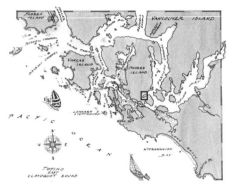

CHARTS 3685 and 3673.

APPROACH From the NE out of Dawley Passage. The approach is clear.

ANCHOR In 8–12 m (26–40 ft) below the cliffs that rise vertically from the water to form the Sea Peak dome. Protected from all winds except NE outflow. However, as the bay's name implies, winds can whistle across the low saddle at its head. Good holding in mud.

✲ 49°08.50'N 125°48.45'W

"Pyramid Rock."

Charming Dawley Passage and provincial park lead into peaceful Windy Bay. Overlooked by tremendous sheer cliffs that rise steeply to the 387-m (1,277-ft) Sea Peak dome, the anchorage has a small beach and creek at its head with a perfectly shaped "pyramid rock" amid the bleached driftwood. The bay will hold three boats quite comfortably and is an ideal spot to simply unwind.

Two alternative anchorages can be found off Fortune Channel: Mosquito Harbour and Heelboom Bay. Fronted by a small beach, the original cabin that was used as a base for the Meares Island logging protest still sits in good repair at Heelboom Bay.

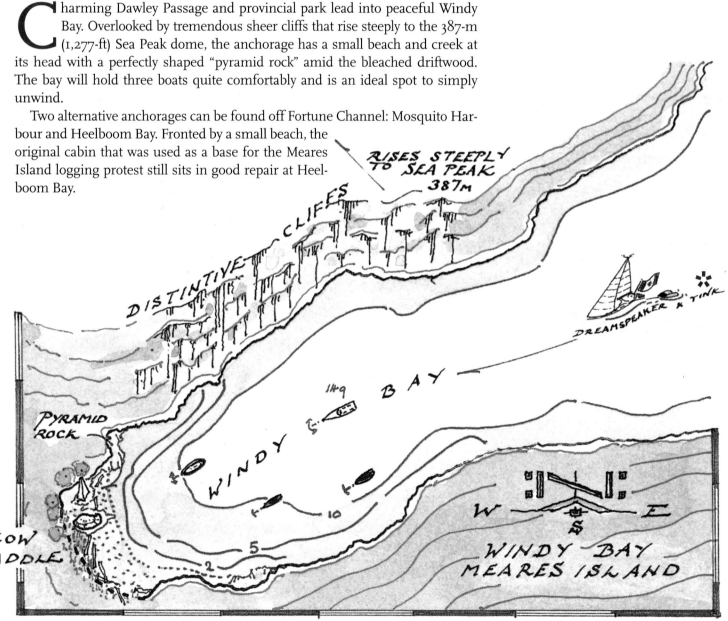

Not to be used for navigation. Depth contours are approximate and in metres.

HEAD OF GUNNER INLET 10.6

CHARTS 3673.

APPROACH At LW from the south—locate the rocks in the entrance before proceeding N. Keep clear of the two charted rocks midway up Gunner Inlet. On entering the narrows, favour the W shore. The run in from the approach waypoint is centre channel—favour the E shore.

ANCHOR At the head of the inlet in depths of 4–6 m (13–20 ft) with good protection from the NW and moderate protection from the SE. Good holding in sand and mud.

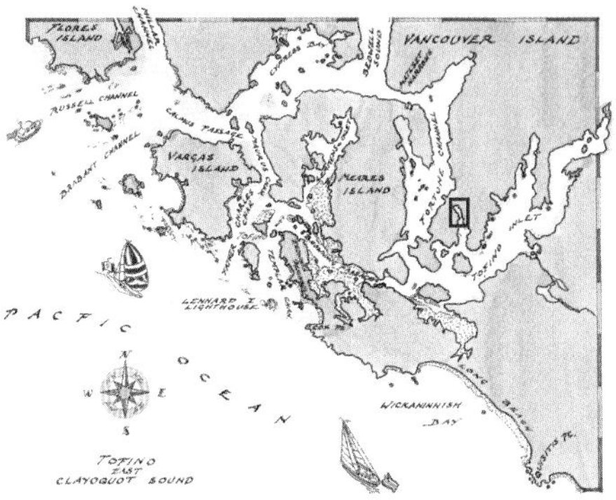

✲ 49°09.54'N 125°44.48'W

Windy Bay and the secluded hideaway at the head of Gunner Inlet are on *Dreamspeaker's* list of ideal anchorages. Navigate your way past the entrance rocks to find a slim, finger-like passage bordered by soft grassy shallows. Gunner Inlet offers excellent protection and good depth for two or three boats to anchor. High water creates a lovely basin at the head of the inlet that's ideal for a little rowing exercise—you'll also find a wrecked fishboat and a large boulder to investigate.

While enjoying sundowners in the cockpit we spied a lone bear poking under the rocks for tasty morsels and munching on berries in the shrubbery behind the foreshore.

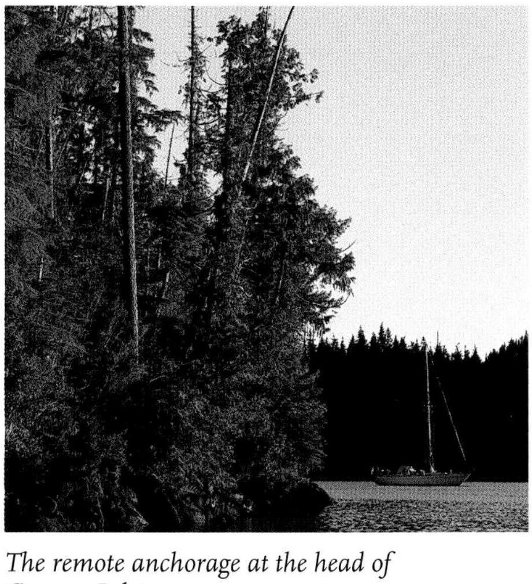

The remote anchorage at the head of Gunner Inlet.

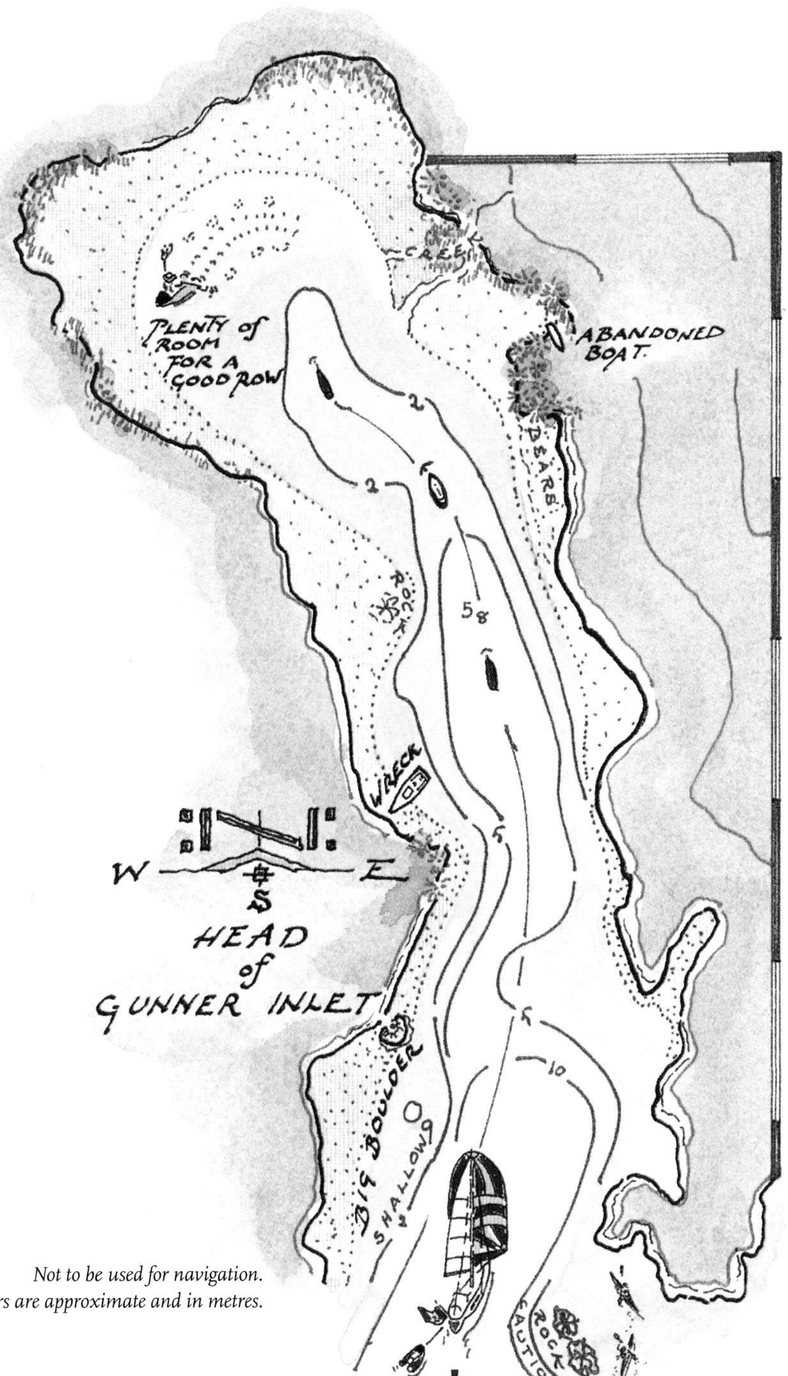

Not to be used for navigation.
Depth contours are approximate and in metres.

10.7 HEAD OF TRANQUIL INLET

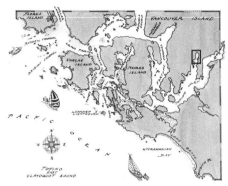

✴ 49°11.90'N 125°40.45'W

CHARTS 3673.

APPROACH Rankin Rocks lie to the W of the entrance to Tranquil Inlet. The approach is clear, leaving the shallows over the charted rock to the E.

ANCHOR

(A) "East Nook"—a cozy cove that is protected from all quarters except the NE. Plenty of room for one boat to swing in depths of 5–7 m (16–23 ft) with good holding in mud and sand.

(B) "West Nook"—a less intimate anchorage with plenty of room to swing in depths of 6–12 m (20–40 ft). Good holding in gravel and mud.

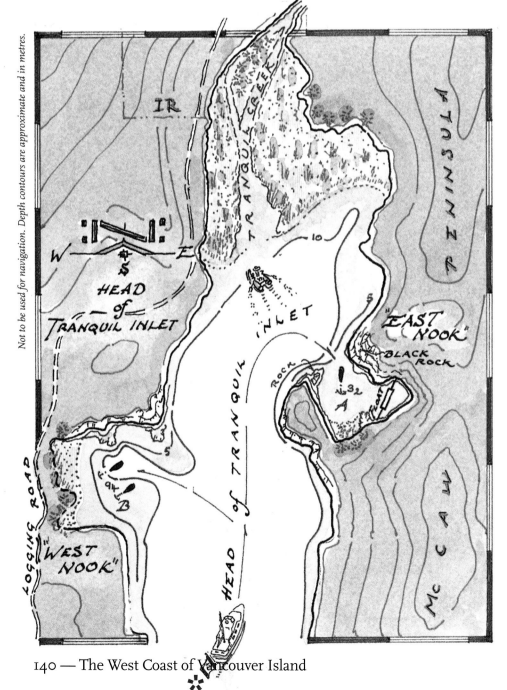

Not to be used for navigation. Depth contours are approximate and in metres.

A logging road runs along the west side of Tranquil Inlet; it is hidden by trees and the occasional truck passed by with very little disturbance.

A black granite cliff rises directly out of the warm waters of "East Nook" to command this one-boat cove. It was sunny and clear the day we visited, and Laurence celebrated our find by diving in and swimming to touch the smooth black rock before circumnavigating *Dreamspeaker*, then dashing up the boat ladder.

"West Nook" is a little less private but offers room to swing off a beautiful little beach backed by soft grasses.

A slab of black granite dives deep into the east nook.

KENNEDY COVE AND CANNERY BAY, TOFINO INLET 10.8

CHARTS 3673.

APPROACH

(A) The entrance to Kennedy Cove lies between "Cannery Island" and a treed islet.

(B) Cannery Bay has a clear, open entrance—take care to round-up before you reach the mud flats.

ANCHOR

(A) Near the head of the cove in the stream from the river. Good all-weather protection in 4–8 m (13–26 ft) with good holding in sand.

(B) The large bay provides good protection from the SE but is somewhat exposed to the W. Anchor in 4–8 m (13–26 ft) with good holding in sand.

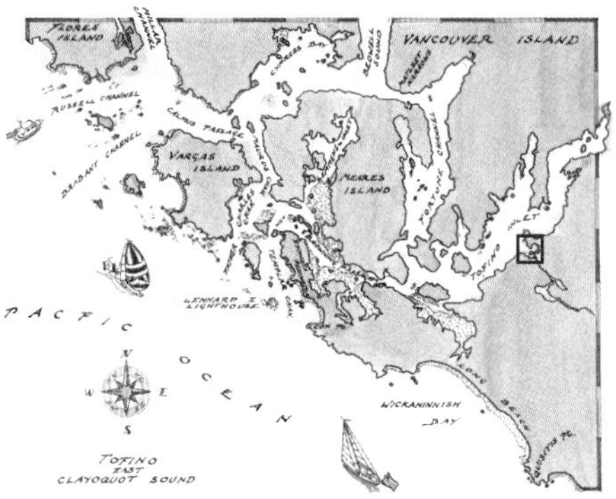

(A) 49°08.58'N 125°40.55'W

Kennedy River runs from one of Vancouver Island's largest lakes into the all-weather protection of Kennedy Cove. As we quietly entered the cove a great blue heron stood like a sentinel, waiting for the right moment to stab its prey. Our appearance didn't interrupt his mission.

Kennfalls Creek flows into Cannery Bay, creating a grassy marsh that attracts the local wildlife and migrating birds. This pleasant, open anchorage offers room to swing while you catch up on odd jobs on the boat or take a leisurely row to the "special rock" at the NW head of the bay.

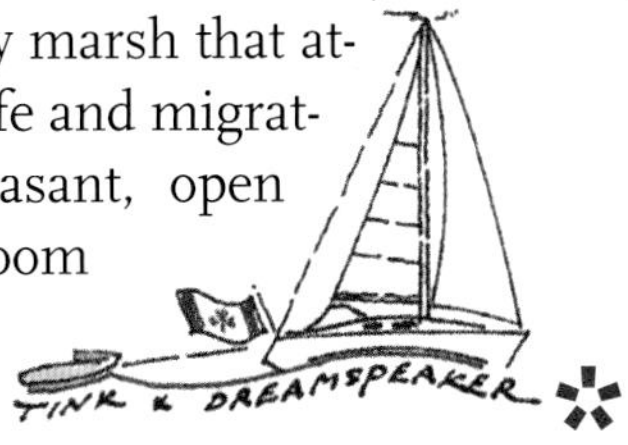

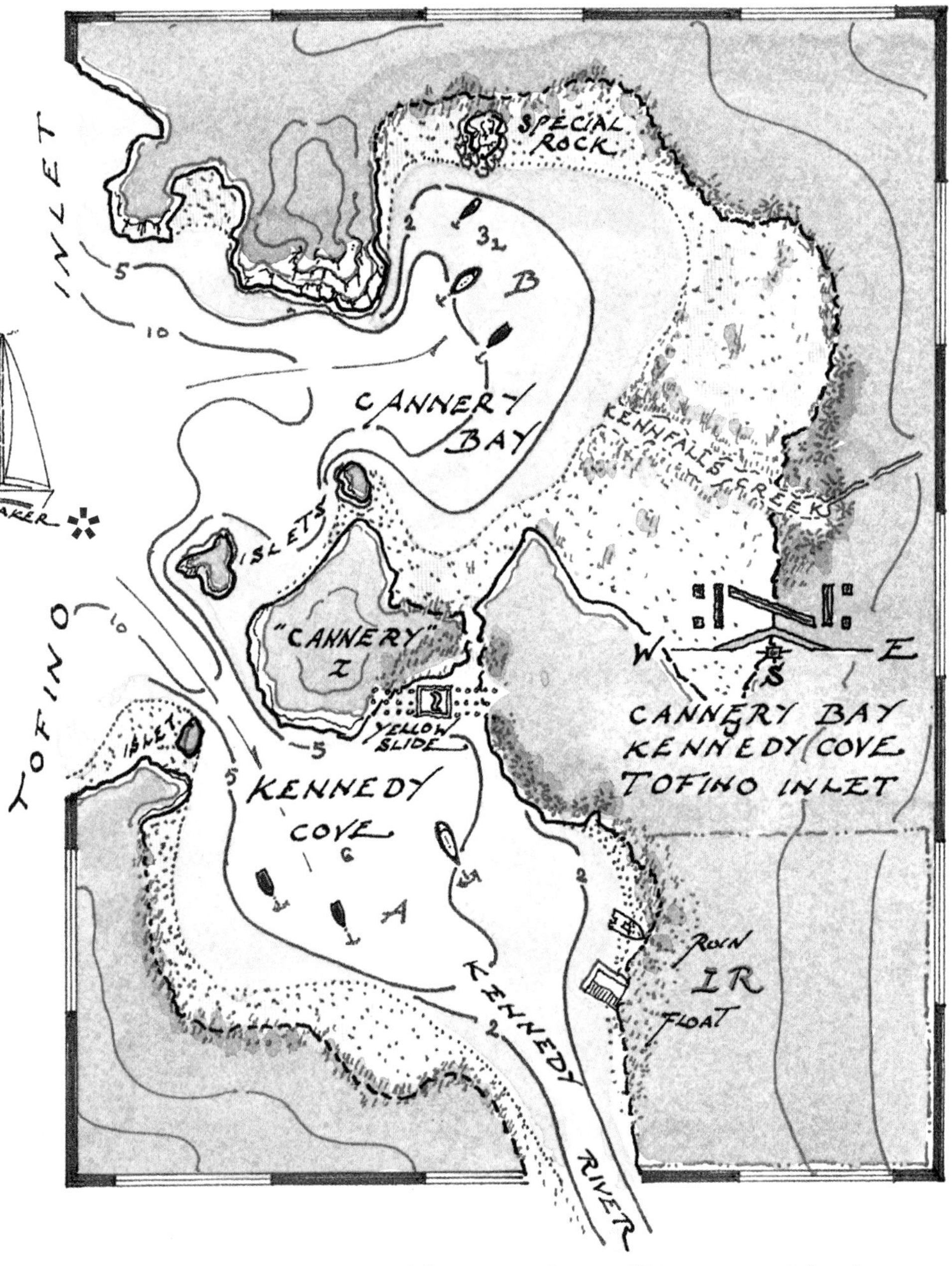

Not to be used for navigation. Depth contours are approximate and in metres.

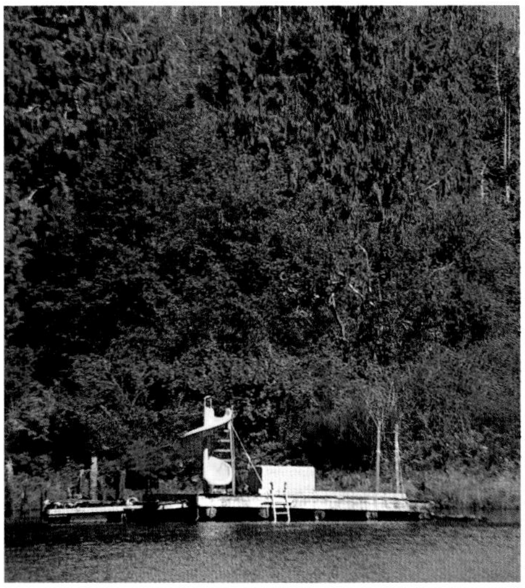

A waterslide waits for the local weekend crowd.

The spectacular mountain backdrop of Quait Bay.

QUAIT BAY, CYPRESS BAY 10.9

CHARTS 3673.

APPROACH The entrance to Quait Bay lies in the NW corner of Cypress Bay. There is a minimum charted depth of 4 m (13 ft) in the channel, which lies NW off the rocks and islet. Favour the W side on entering and exiting. Once through the channel the run in is clear.

ANCHOR The virtually landlocked bay offers a commodious anchorage with protection from all quarters. Anchor in 8–10 m (26–33 ft) with excellent holding in mud.

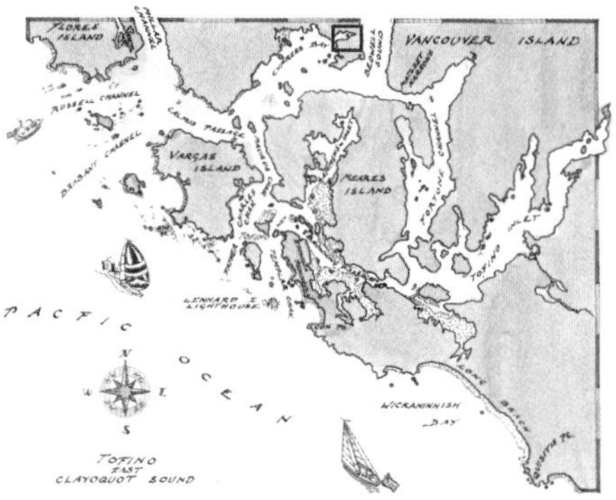

✲49°16.35'N 125°52.01'W

Almost landlocked by the rainforest, Quait Bay offers a commodious anchorage with plenty of room for boats to swing. The former Quait Bay Lodge and surrounding land, including the trail to the lake and waterfall, are now private.

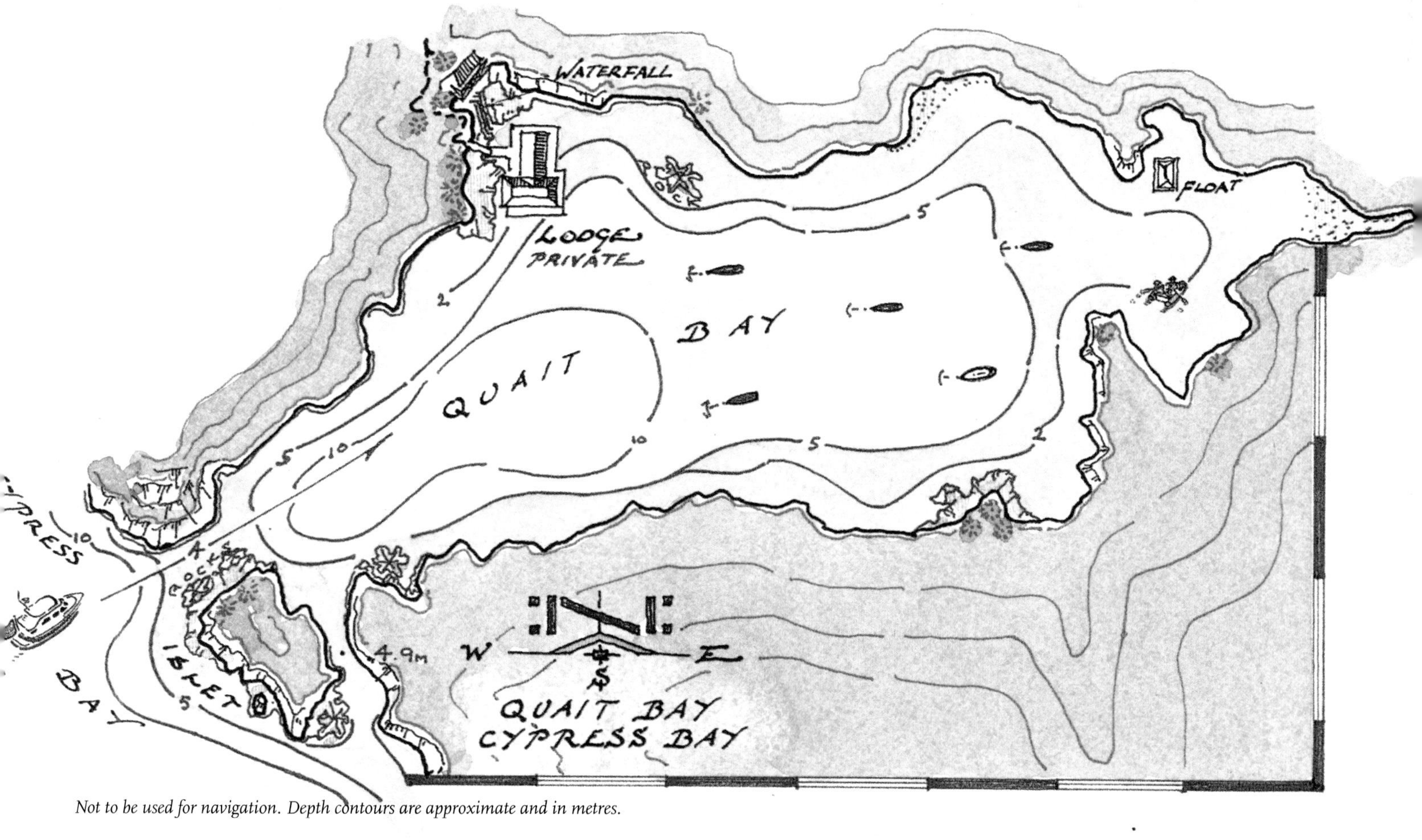

Not to be used for navigation. Depth contours are approximate and in metres.

Chapter II

BARKLEY SOUND

MV Lady Rose, approaching the Bamfield wharfhead, is a familiar sight in Barkley Sound.

Chapter 11
BARKLEY SOUND

TIDES

Volume 6, Canadian Tide and Current Tables

Reference Port: Tofino

Secondary Ports: Ucluelet, Bamfield, Stopper Islands

Reference Port: Port Alberni (for Port Alberni)

CURRENTS

No current station for this area. However, if transiting Alberni Inlet to Port Alberni, currents run at 2–4 knots on the ebb and flood, depending on the size of the tide.

WEATHER

Weather Channel VHF WX 2 Nootka, WX 2 Alberni, 21 B Mount Ozzard.

Areas: West Coast Vancouver Island South—for conditions in Barkley Sound listen for marine reporting stations at Amphitrite Point and Cape Beale lighthouse. Listen for La Pérouse Bank weather buoy for offshore conditions.

Note: Barkley Sound is more open to the ocean than sounds and inlets farther north, and experiences more frequent and longer-lasting fog than those inlets. August can be especially foggy.

Downtown Ucluelet—a fish boat high and dry!

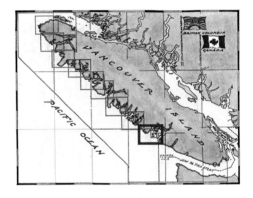

CAUTIONARY NOTES

Barkley Sound is big and poor visibility due to fog is a major hazard.

Our advice is never to venture out in fog.

If caught underway, seek shelter immediately when possible.

Keep a sharp lookout for vessels running in fog, waypoint to waypoint.

The other danger is the extent of commercial traffic.

Transiting the Broken Group and its plethora of rocks is dealt with in Chapter 12, page 162.

Its entrance spanning 16 nautical miles from Amphitrite Point to Cape Beale, Barkley Sound is the most expansive sound on the West Coast. Ucluelet, Bamfield and Port Alberni are the major communities of the sound; clustered at its centre is Pacific Rim National Park and the Broken Group islands (see Chapter 12).

This chapter explores Barkley Sound's periphery, beginning in Ucluelet Inlet. Ucluelet offers a quiet, funky alternative to Tofino. Fuel and a well-run public wharf are available here, and provisioning couldn't be easier.

To the NE, scenic Pipestem Inlet is narrow and gorge-like where it passes between the steep slopes of Broughton Peaks to the S and Black Peaks to the N. The only possible anchorage inside the inlet is "Cataract Cove," close to the delightful waterfall at Lucky Creek.

The Pinkerton Islands, N of the Broken Group, offer a peaceful archipelago to explore by dinghy or kayak. Anchorage can be found among the islands or in a quiet cove bordered by pastoral meadows.

Alberni Inlet, the principal inlet off Barkley Sound, branches north from Trevor Channel for a scenic 18 nautical miles before it reaches Port Alberni at its head. A historic port and mill town with a large fishing fleet, this is the largest community on the West Coast, with direct road access to the major population centres of Vancouver Island.

Bamfield lies on the W and E sides of Bamfield Inlet, within easy reach of the islands and islets of the Broken and Deer groups. Fuel, moorage and anchorage are available here. East Bamfield is the commercial centre, with road access. Charming West Bamfield has no road access.

Robbers Passage offers a scenic anchorage, and the Port Alberni Yacht Club outstation on Fleming Island welcomes visitors.

Sheltered by Fry Island, the anchorage of Marble Cove provides a convenient lunch or overnight stop. Just N of Marble Cove, picturesque "Tzartus Cove" is a quiet base for exploring the sea caves found along the Tzartus Island shoreline,

Snugly protected from the surf pounding on the outside of Sandford Island, the fair-weather anchorage between Fleming and Sandford islands has a windswept feel, with exquisite ocean and mountain vistas. Dodger Channel, the most westerly anchorage of the Deer Group, is a convenient departure point for the passage east through Juan de Fuca Strait.

FEATURED DESTINATIONS

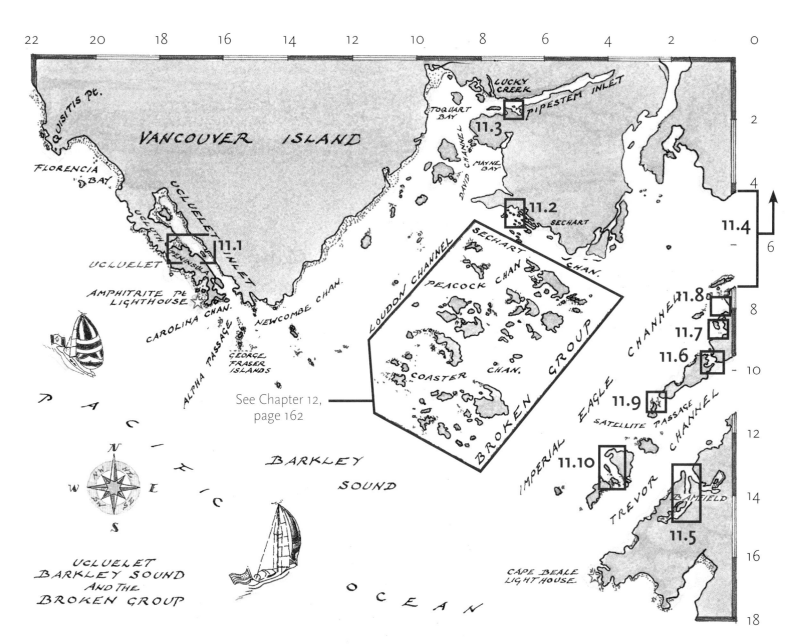

Not to be used for navigation. Depth contours are approximate and in metres.

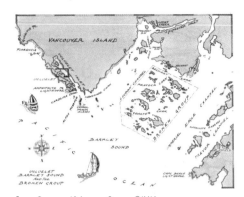

✳ 45°55.30'N 125°31.08'W
at the entrance to the inlet

The Ucluelet commercial fishing fleet is still very active.

A touch of the tropical.

Ex-hydrographic vessel restored and renamed the
Canadian Princess.

Ucluelet ("yoo cloo' let"), situated on the southern end of Ucluth Peninsula, translates as "safe harbour" in the Nuu-chah-nulth language, a fitting name for this protected village that is officially known as the District of Ucluelet. Long, narrow Ucluelet Inlet is the sea channel for Port Albion, Ucluelet and the Itatsoo Indian Reserve farther north—it is busy with traffic in the summer months, especially on weekends. Watch out for fleets of charter fishing vessels leaving *en masse* in the early morning and returning in the afternoon.

With a charm of its own, Ucluelet is a great place to walk and discover the new enterprises that pop up each year as the community grows to offer a quiet, funky alternative to Tofino. We were welcomed into the harbour by raucous barking from a group of hefty sea lions on the western shore, and were lucky to find space at the public dock, where *Dreamspeaker* provided a rafting platform for a smaller vessel that evening.

Power and water are available on the docks, and toilet facilities and a very knowledgeable harbour master can be found on shore. Showers are available at the West Coast Motel and laundry facilities in the mall on Peninsula Road, the street where it all happens: shops, gift stores, cottage artisans, cafés and restaurants, an excellent fish bistro, a bakery and deli and the well-stocked Co-op, which will deliver to your boat for a small charge.

A much larger town than Bamfield, Ucluelet is the best place in Barkley Sound for provisioning for a trip northward. It is still an active fishing port—Pioneer Boatworks serves the local fishing fleet and carries machinery parts and other small items that may be of use to recreational boats.

Phase one of the Wild Pacific Trail is a 2.7-km (1.7-mile) loop that provides a pleasant forty-minute hike to Amphitrite Point Lighthouse. Many other trails are accessible from Peninsula Road and will take you to Big Beach, past Little Beach, and on to Terrace Beach and He-Tin-Kis Park and boardwalk.

Note: Friends told us the Canadian Princess Resort (aboard a former hydrographic vessel) at the head of the Boat Basin has a first-rate restaurant that is open to visitors who are not guests of the resort.

CHARTS 3646.

APPROACH Approach Ucluelet Inlet leaving Francis Island Light to the W. The channel is well marked.

CUSTOMS For those who need to report to customs (year-round clearance for permit holders, clearance for non-permit holders is available from June 1–Sept 30), tie up at the Otter Street Float, a public dock known locally as the "52 Steps Dock"—there is a payphone just up from the dock.

ANCHOR The southern anchorage in Spring Cove and the upper reaches of Ucluelet Inlet are not convenient to the Village of Ucluelet and its amenities. Some boats anchor immediately to the north of the Small Craft Harbour entrance.

PUBLIC WHARF The well-managed and friendly Ucluelet Small Craft Harbour in Boat Basin has visitor moorage on docks C, D and E. Call 250-726-4241. If they are full, the alternative is the Otter Street Float. Whiskey Dock is used primarily by commercial vessels but if space permits can be used for temporary moorage when making a quick run into town.

MARINA Island West Fishing Resort offers transient moorage for boats up to 12 m (40 ft). Call ahead to reserve a berth: 250-726-7515

FUEL Eagle Marine: 250-726-4262. Water is available and the small store stocks hardware, lubricants, ice and bait.

LAUNCH At Island West Fishing Resort

Note: Strong winds funnel up and down Ucluelet Inlet especially in late afternoon. A pump-out station is proposed for the outer basin in 2008.

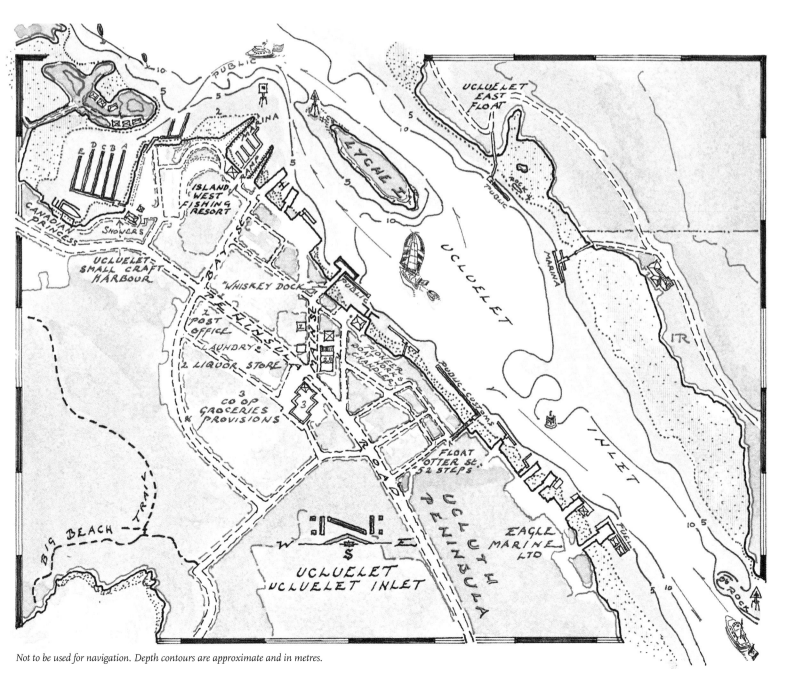

Not to be used for navigation. Depth contours are approximate and in metres.

11.2 PINKERTON ISLANDS

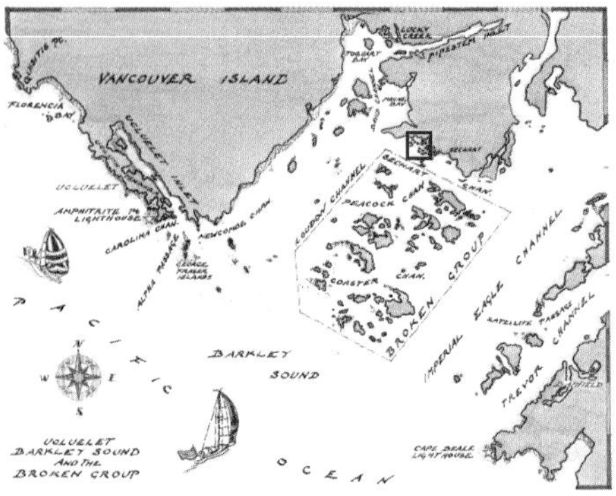

48°57.66'N 125°17.22'W

CHARTS 3670.

APPROACH From the SW between a rock and an islet. The run in is a backward "S." Round up off the creek estuary and mud flats.

ANCHOR Swing between the islands, islets and rocks or take a stern line to one of the two rings. Good holding in 4–8 m (13–26 ft) in mud and sand.

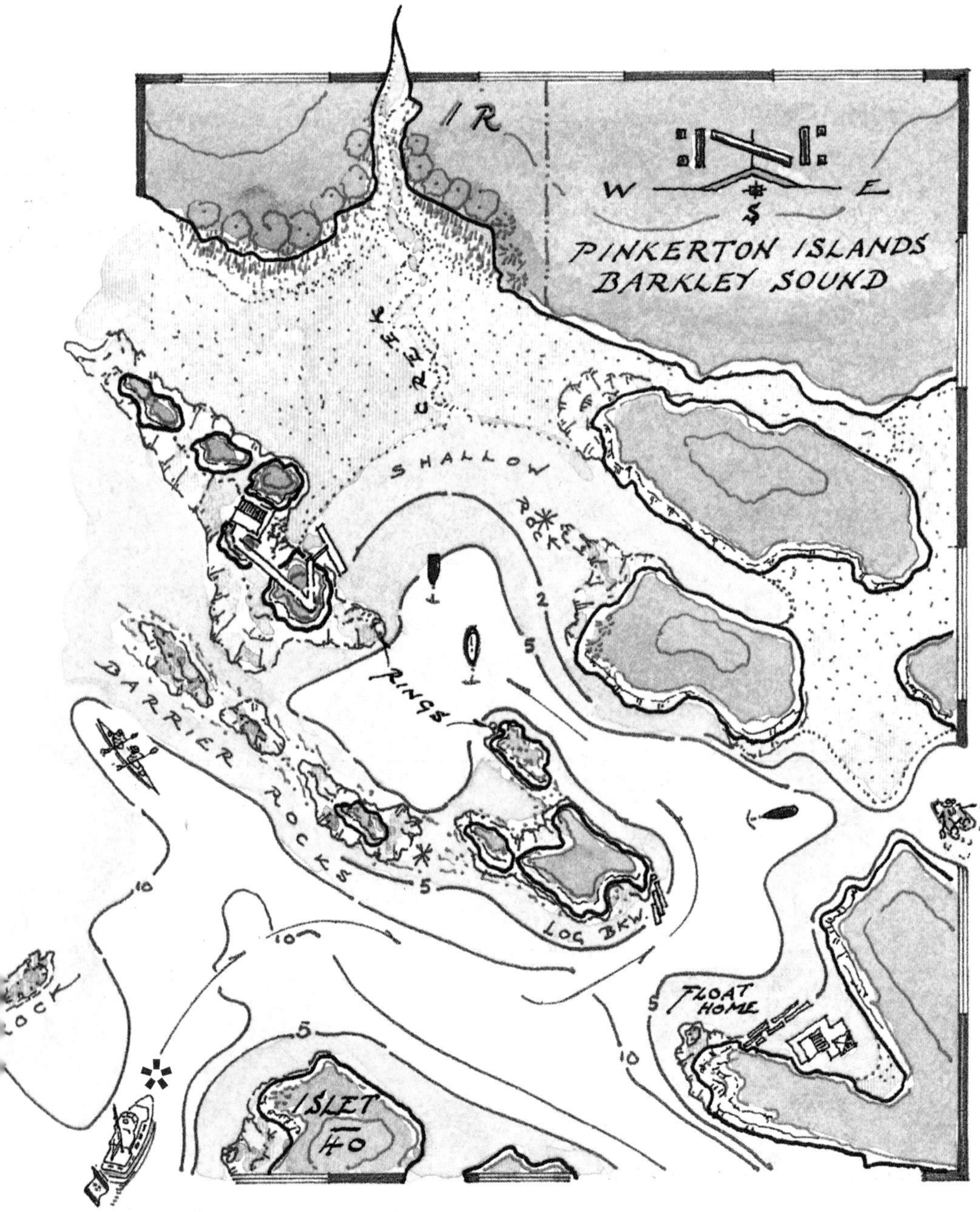

An archipelago of their own, and popular with kayakers, the Pinkerton Islands lie N of the Broken Group. After investigating the islands, islets, channels and nooks within the group, we chose to anchor inside the Barrier Rocks in a cove bordered by pastoral meadows and grassy banks lined with deciduous trees. Although there are a few holiday cabins on the waterfront, this was a pleasant spot to while away a Sunday reading in the cockpit and exploring in *Tink*. Equis Indian Reserve was the Tseshaht people's winter village in the early 1800s and was used for the "Wolf Ritual"—a Nuu-chah-nulth rite for young men.

NE of the Pinkerton Islands is Sechart Lodge. Built on a former whaling station on the mainland, it is the primary pick-up and drop-off location for kayakers travelling on the MV *Lady Rose* to begin or end their adventures in Barkley Sound and the Broken Group. The lodge (1-800-663-7192) has accommodation, showers and a dining room that serves hearty meals.

Not to be used for navigation.
Depth contours are approximate and in metres.

“CATARACT COVE,” PIPESTEM INLET 11.3

CHARTS 3670.

APPROACH From the NW. A group of small islands and islets form two small basins suitable for anchoring.

ANCHOR In 5–7 m (17–23 ft) over an uncertain kelp and rock bottom. Stern anchors or stern lines are recommended because swinging room is limited, especially in the E basin. Good protection from light NW winds that don’t reach this far up the inlet. When strong NW winds funnel between the steep peaks, this becomes unsuitable as an anchorage.

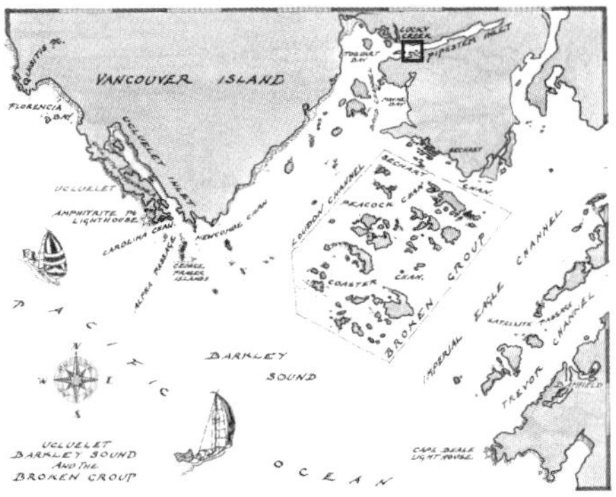

✣ 49°01.28'N 125°17.13'W

Scenic and peaceful, Pipestem Inlet is long, narrow and gorge-like in certain sections as it passes between the steep mountain slopes of Broughton Peaks to the south and Black Peaks to the north. The inlet has the warmest recorded water temperature on the west coast of Vancouver Island (21 degrees C or 70 degrees F). The only possible anchorage in the inlet itself is in “Cataract Cove” where Cataract Creek flows into the inlet. This is a charming spot to anchor and explore the surrounding islands, islets and lagoon—or just stay the night. If Cataract Cove is full or not to your liking, you can also anchor north of Refuge Island, near the entrance to the inlet.

Whether you anchor in Cataract Cove or at Refuge Island, be sure to take your motorized dinghy or kayak to visit the lovely waterfall at Lucky Creek on the north side of the inlet. The shaded channel twists through dense forest to the head of the creek, where a trail leads up the west side of the falls to a series of blissful bathing pools. Enter and exit the creek an hour before and after HW because the entrance is very shallow at low water. Note that at the height of summer the nearby lodges transport their guests by dinghy to visit the falls.

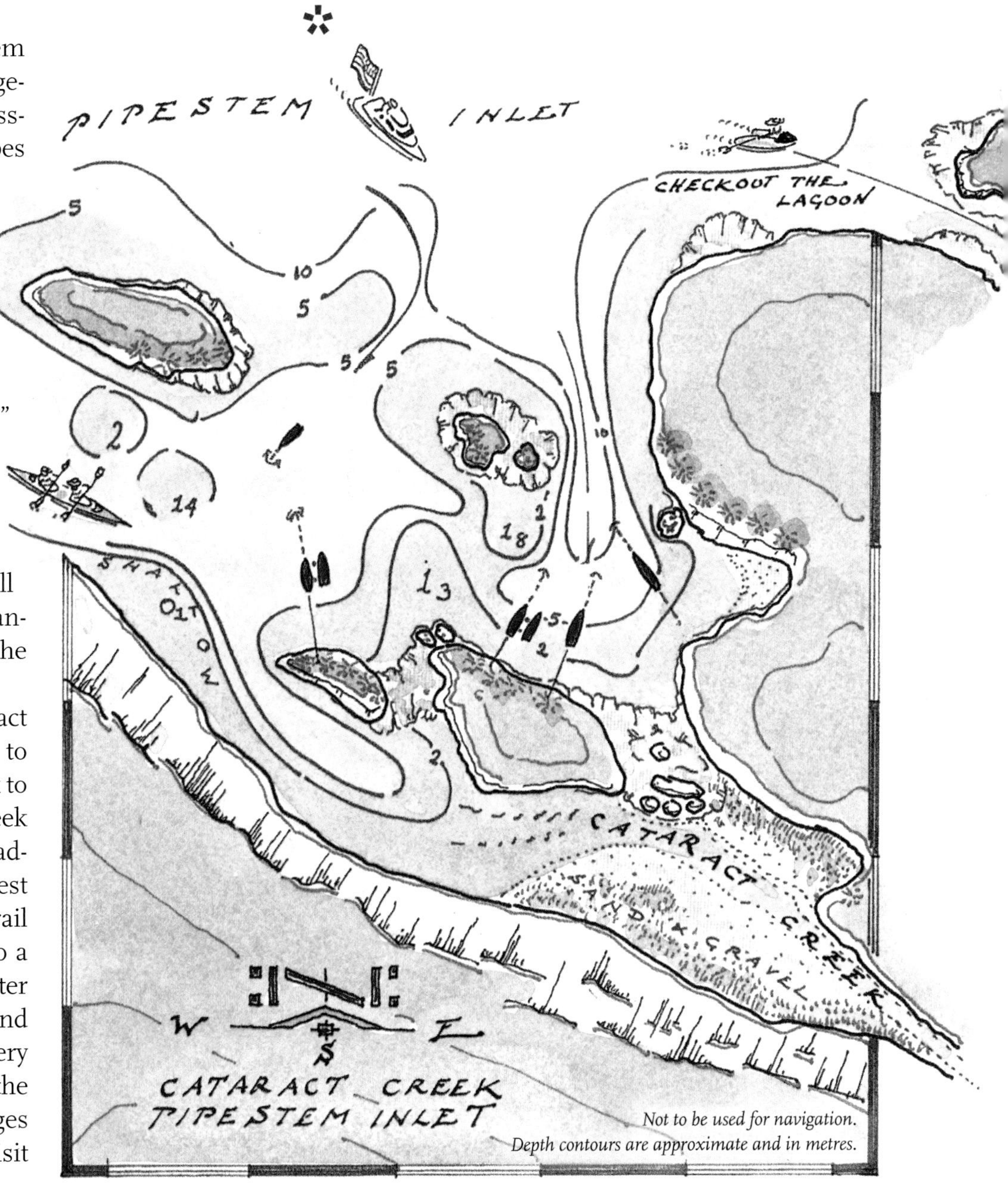

Not to be used for navigation.
Depth contours are approximate and in metres.

PORT ALBERNI & ALBERNI INLET

11.4A

The city of Port Alberni lies on the eastern shore of the head of Alberni Inlet. The port extends 20 nautical miles from Alberni Inlet's entrance, the confluence of Trevor Channel and Junction Passage. Mountains rise steeply on both sides of the inlet, funnelling afternoon inflow winds that can reach up to 30 knots or more. Currents are not as strong as one would expect in the inlet, a maximum of 1 knot on the flood and 1.5 knots on the ebb, but wind blowing in the same direction can accelerate the surface current three times.

When going N toward Port Alberni, take advantage of the flooding current and afternoon inflow winds; likewise, when returning S ride the ebbing current and early morning outflow winds. Anchorages en route to Port Alberni are scarce as the waters of the inlet are very deep. Temporary anchorage can be found on the western shore at Hook Bay and on the eastern shore south of the spit at China Creek. There is no designated small craft anchorage at the head of the inlet.

11.4B

Port Alberni's four marinas are operated by the Port of Port Alberni Authority. Most visiting boaters find moorage at Harbour Quay Marina (11.4-E), the newest facility. The other three marinas do offer some visitor moorage; however, China Creek Marina (11.4-D) and Clutesi Haven Marina (11.4-F) cater mainly to sport fishing boats. Fishermen's Harbour is for fishing and commercial vessels.

Port Alberni is a popular location to launch trailerable boats for access to the West Coast. It has an extensive revitalized downtown and Harbour Quay. This is a convenient spot to provision, relax and see the sights—the area is bustling with stores, restaurants, bistros, gift shops and excellent First Nations art galleries. The quay is also home port to the regularly scheduled cargo and passenger ships *Lady Rose* and *Francis Barkley*, which serve the scattered communities of Barkley Sound and the West Coast. The local forestry museum displays fascinating heavy logging equipment, and visits to active logging and mill operations are available from the forestry visitor centre.

Suitable overnight anchorages are at the entrance to Alberni Inlet (Chart 3668).

11.4A SAN MATEO BAY

APPROACH Tuck into the small cove inside Bernard Point.

ANCHOR Good protection in 6–10 m (20–33 ft) with good holding in gravel and mud.

11.4B SNUG BASIN

APPROACH South from Uchucklesit Inlet—the entrance is clear of obstructions.

ANCHOR In the S portion of the basin in 14–18 m (46–60 ft) or, for deeper water and room to swing, in the northern portion of the basin. Good protection and holding in mud.

11.4C LIMESTONE BAY

APPROACH From the SW of Alberni Inlet, keeping the light to starboard; the run in to the bay is clear.

ANCHOR Excellent protection at the head of the bay in 4–6 m (13–20 ft). Good holding in mud and sand.

11.4C

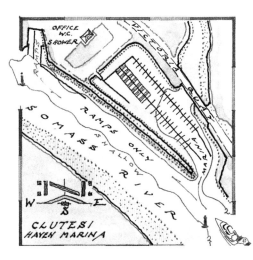

11.4-F CLUTESI HAVEN MARINA

Clutesi Haven Marina is approximately 1.5 nautical miles up the Somass River from Port Alberni. VHF channel 66A. 250-724-6837.

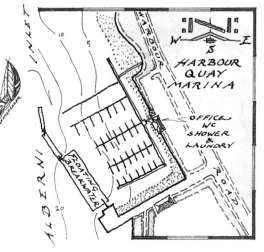

11.4-E HARBOUR QUAY MARINA

Harbour Quay Marina is at the head of Alberni Inlet, in downtown Port Alberni. VHF channel 06. 250-723-1413.

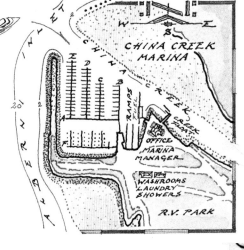

11.4-D CHINA CREEK MARINA

China Creek Marina and Campground is approximately 5 nautical miles S of Port Alberni at the mouth of China Creek. VHF channel 66A. 250-732-1413.

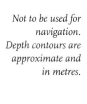

Not to be used for navigation. Depth contours are approximate and in metres.

11.5 BAMFIELD, BAMFIELD INLET

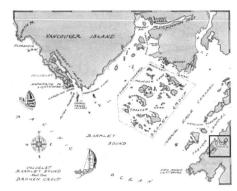

✴ 48°50.45'N 125°08.44'W

The approach to Bamfield Inlet off Aguilar Point with Bamfield Marine Science Centre on the east shore.

Bamfield and Anne's outfit make a colourful match.

Brady's Beach is well worth the hike.

The Bamfield area is the long-standing territory of the Huu-Ay-Aht Nation, whose history extends back ten thousand years. It is also home to many pioneering families who braved the wild West Coast in the early part of the 20th century. Bamfield was the western terminus of the trans-Pacific telegraph cable, which closed in 1959 and now houses the Bamfield Marine Sciences Centre. Bamfield is also the western terminus of the legendary West Coast Trail, originally built to aid shipwreck survivors.

Bamfield provides easy access to the islands and islets of the Broken and Deer groups and offers protected anchorage—the most popular location is "downtown" between the W and E public wharves. A more secluded area, available to those without tall masts, lies past Burlo and Range islands, in the upper end of Bamfield Inlet. A third anchorage is in Grappler Inlet. During fishing season in August, Bamfield Inlet bustles with sport fishing boats.

The community of Bamfield lies on both the W and E sides of Bamfield Inlet. Charming West Bamfield is located on Mills Peninsula with no road access and a well-maintained 1-km (.5-mile) wooden boardwalk that begins at the public wharf and meanders past colourful cabins. The Netloft Gallery is also the tourist information centre and offers an excellent selection of local art, books and homemade preserves.

Next is the post office and Bamfield General Store with a BC Liquor outlet. The store keeps a fair selection of fresh produce, groceries and some local specialty items—its dock is reserved for visiting shoppers. Then it's on to the wharfhead where the freighters *Lady Rose* and *Francis Barkley* load and unload provisions, hardware, appliances, tourists and kayakers daily in the summer months (www.ladyrosemarine.com). The Canadian Coast Guard's RHIOT training school is located at the Bamfield coast guard station.

East Bamfield is the commercial centre, with a small grocery store, café, hotel, pub, marine store, fishing lodges, the Red Cross Outpost Hospital, and road access.

Don't miss the 20-minute hike to spectacular Brady's Beach. The sand has a soft, flaxen hue and the water is surprisingly warm, sometimes reaching 17 degrees C (63 degrees F) at the surface.

CHARTS 3646.

APPROACH From Trevor Channel by rounding Aguilar Point. The inlet is deep except for a well-marked rock that extends out from the W shore near the West Bamfield public wharf.

ANCHOR S of the rock and off the E shore, near the public wharf. Good holding in mud in 5–15 m (16–50 ft). Setting the anchor in deeper locations can be difficult.

PUBLIC WHARF The public wharves on the E and W shorelines welcome visiting boaters. No water on the docks. Shower and laundry facilities are available at the Trail Lodge on Grappler Road, East Bamfield.

FUEL Gas, diesel, water and ice available from Bamfield Kingfisher Marina, which is open in summer months 6 am–9 pm but will never turn away any boater who requires fuel.

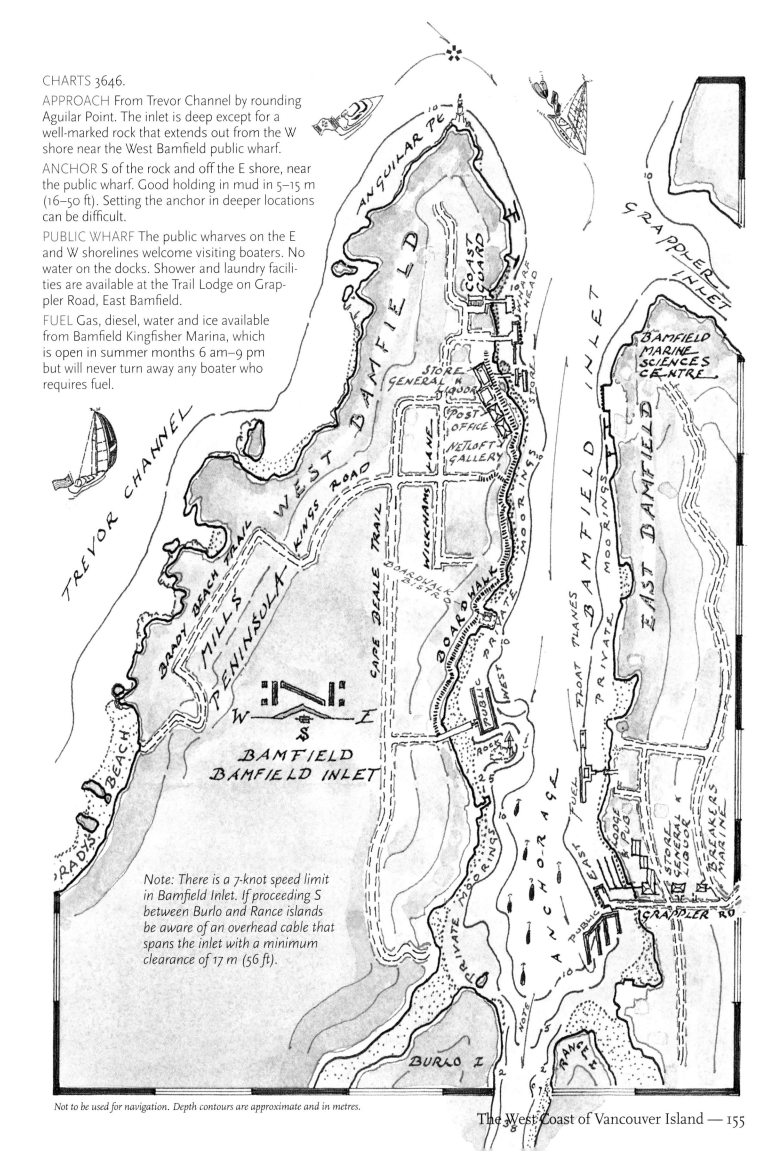

Note: There is a 7-knot speed limit in Bamfield Inlet. If proceeding S between Burlo and Rance islands be aware of an overhead cable that spans the inlet with a minimum clearance of 17 m (56 ft).

Not to be used for navigation. Depth contours are approximate and in metres.

11.6 ROBBERS PASSAGE, DEER GROUP

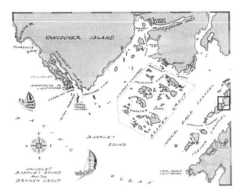

✣ 48°53.50'N 125°06.50'W

CHARTS 3671. 3668 (Inset).

APPROACH The channel is between Tzartus Island and Fleming Island. From the S out of Trevor Channel. Stay close to the starboard-hand (red) marker. From the N out of Imperial Eagle Channel.

ANCHOR All-round protection (slightly less at HW) can be found N of the Port Alberni Yacht Club docks or in the NW corner off the beach. Anchor in 5–10 m (16–33 ft) with good holding in mud and shell.

MARINA The Port Alberni Yacht Club outstation welcomes visiting boaters when space is available. Power and water are limited. They are usually full over Canada Day (July 1) and Labour Day weekends. See the caretaker.

Note: The passage is traversed by sport fishing boats—some skippers slow down and some don't.

Robbers Passage offers a scenic anchorage with a pocket sand-and-gravel beach, and rocks overlooking the passage to explore. The two holiday float houses add a homey touch, and the small oyster farm is marked with buoys. The Port Alberni Yacht Club outstation on Fleming Island is usually full over Canada Day (July 1) and Labour Day weekends, but at any other time they welcome visitors to tie up for the night and make use of their shaded hiking trails, picnic sites and shower. A large cave can be found on the western side of the bay, in the middle of the island.

Sea caves are an accessible feature in Barkley Sound.

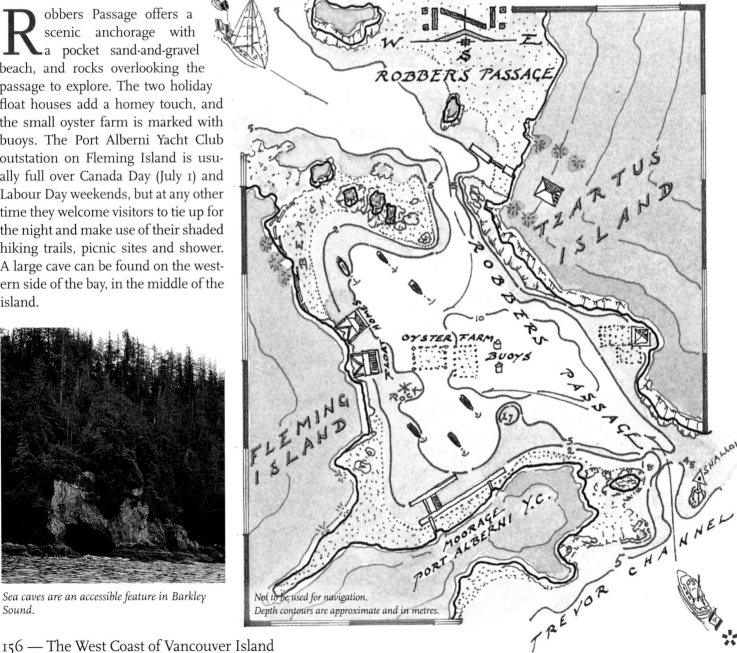

Not to be used for navigation.
Depth contours are approximate and in metres.

CHARTS 3671.

APPROACH From Imperial Eagle Channel—beware of off-lying rocks and reefs. The run in is clear.

ANCHOR Good holding in gravel and sand in 6–8 m (20–26 ft). Good protection from the SE but open to the W.

Note: A running swell will break on the outer rocks but is minimal at the head of the cove.

Just N of Marble Cove, picturesque "Tzartus Cove" provides a quiet base for exploring the impressive sea caves found along the Tzartus Island shoreline, or just lazing in the cockpit sheltered from a southeasterly.

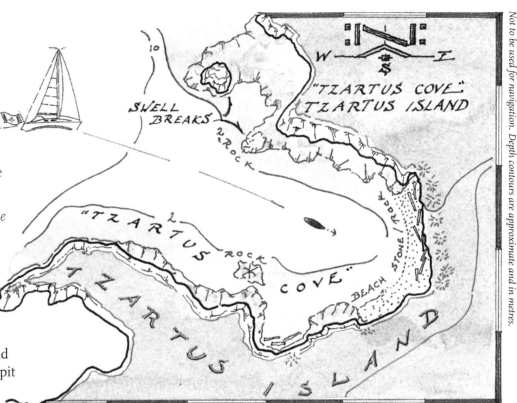

MARBLE COVE, 11.8
TZARTUS ISLAND

CHARTS 3671.

APPROACH By rounding the southern tip of Fry Island into the bay between Fry and Tzartus islands.

ANCHOR Behind Fry Island. Moderate protection from SE and westerly winds in depths of 4–8 m (13–26 ft). Moderate holding in kelp and a mixed bottom. A private fishing lodge, the Canadian King Lodge, is located in the cove.

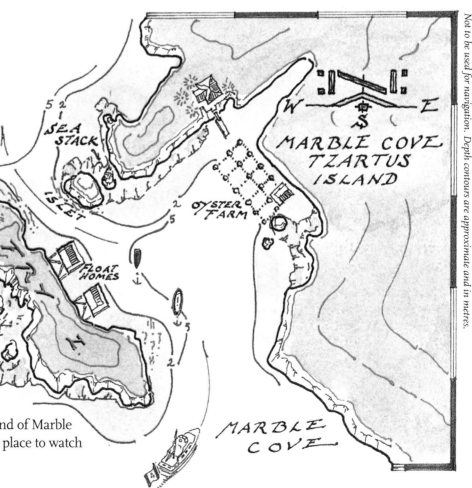

Sheltered by Fry Island, the anchorage of Marble Cove provides a convenient lunch spot or overnight stop. A magnificent extended arch or sea cave can be found at the south end of Marble Cove on Fry Island. This is also an excellent place to watch for sea life at low tide.

Not to be used for navigation. Depth contours are approximate and in metres.

11.9 SANFORD AND FLEMING ISLANDS "PASS"

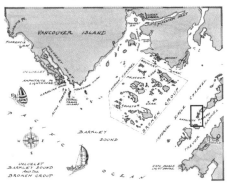

CHARTS 3671.

APPROACH

(A) Out of Imperial Eagle Channel between the distinctive "Two-Tree Islet" and Fleming Island.

(B) Out of Trevor Channel between Sandford Island and Ross Islets.

ANCHOR Between Sandford Island and Ross Islets as indicated. Here the boat is out of the swell and moderately protected from westerly winds but open to all other quarters. Anchor in 4–8 m (13–26 ft) in mud, sand and shell.

✤ (A) 48°52.61'N 125°09.89'W
✤ (B) 48°52.00'N 125°09.74'W

S nugly protected from the dramatic surf pounding on the outside of Sandford Island, but open to the views and winds over the low-lying rocks and islets surrounding it, the fair-weather anchorage in the rocky pass between Fleming and Sanford islands has a windswept, truly West Coast feel, with exquisite ocean and mountain vistas. Exploring the islets and rocks by dinghy or kayak at LW is great fun; a delightful sand-and-shell beach can be found at Ross Islets.

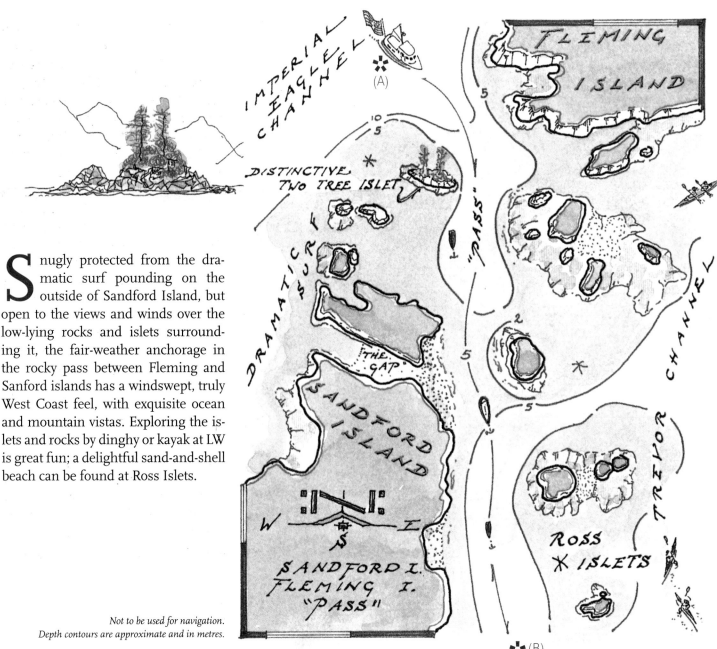

Not to be used for navigation.
Depth contours are approximate and in metres.

✤ (B)

CHARTS 3671.

APPROACH The channel lies between Diana and Haines islands.

(A) From the N—the run in is clear.

(B) From the S between Voss Point and Taylor Islet. The run in is relatively narrow with a minimum depth of 2.8 m (9.2 ft). This entrance is best approached at better than half-tide. Sport fishermen roar through here and at LW a deep-draft boat could bump the bottom in their wake.

ANCHOR In the channel N or E of Haines Island. Good protection from swell, SE and W winds. Moderate protection from the NW. Anchor in 4–8 m (13–26 ft) with good holding in mud, sand and shell.

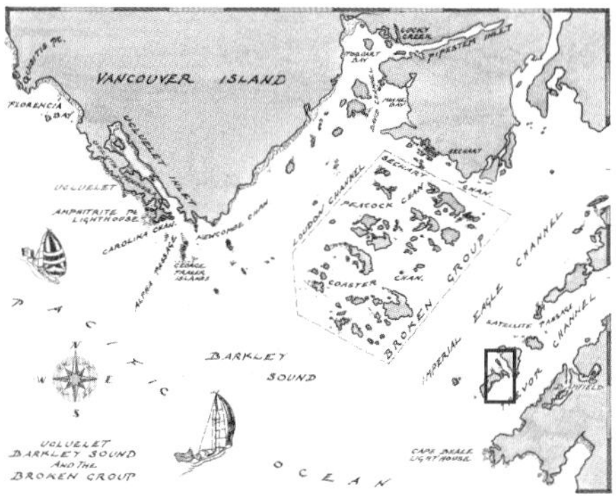

✲ (A) 48°50.67'N 125°12.52'W

✲ (B) 48°49.71'N 125°11.66'W

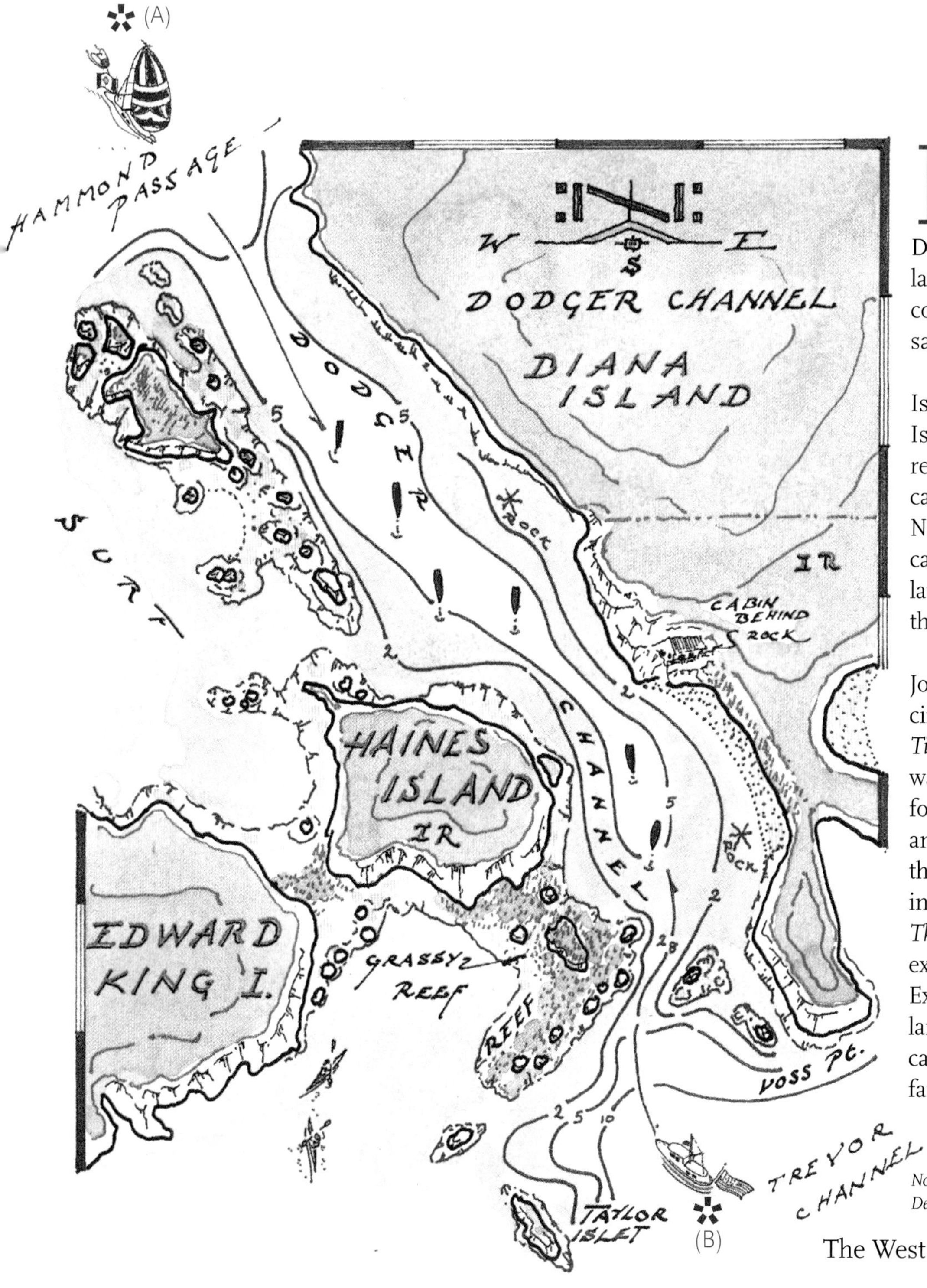

Protected Dodger Channel provides an enticing long, narrow anchorage that is sheltered by Diana, Haines and Edward King islands. Dodger Channel also provides a convenient departure point for the passage east through Juan de Fuca Strait.

The north and south ends of Diana Island are Indian Reserves, as is Haines Island, which has a fascinating grassy reef at its southern end. Archaeological research suggests that a large First Nations village, named Ooheh, was located here for several centuries. In the late 1800s the island was named after the 87-ton steam schooner *Diana*.

Voss Point acknowledges Captain John Voss who stopped here on his circumnavigation in the dugout canoe *Tilikum*. Beautiful Edward King Island was named after Captain Edward King, founder of the *New Westminster Times* and the *Victoria Gazette*. King died on the island in 1861 during a deer hunting trip (see Selected reading page 190: *The Wild Coast* by John Kimantas—an excellent resource to the West Coast). Exposed to the Pacific Ocean, the island shoreline offers a variety of sea caves and sea pillars to investigate in fair weather.

Not to be used for navigation.
Depth contours are approximate and in metres.

Alone at anchor on the Pacific Rim — for Larry and Tipperary, this is as good as it gets.

Chapter 12

BROKEN GROUP,
PACIFIC RIM
NATIONAL PARK

Chapter 12
BROKEN GROUP, PACIFIC RIM NATIONAL PARK

TIDES

Volume 6, Canadian Tide and Current Tables
Reference Port: Tofino, Secondary Port: Effingham Bay

CURRENTS

No current station for this area. Expect moderate currents in the passages between the islands and islets.

The park is a haven for boats and a kayaker's paradise.

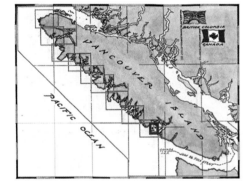

WEATHER

Weather Channel VHF WX 2 Nootka. WX 2 Alberni. 21B Mount Ozzard.

Areas: West Coast Vancouver Island South—for conditions in Barkley Sound listen for marine reporting stations Amphitrite Point and Cape Beale lighthouses. Listen for La Pérouse Bank for offshore conditions.

CAUTIONARY NOTES

Chart 3670 (Broken Group): This large-scale chart is a must when cruising in the Broken Group. Exploration at LW—when the countless rocks and reefs are visible—is strongly advised. Fog is more common in late July and August—unless you have to venture out, stay put and relax until it lifts.

Chart 3670 (Broken Group, Scale 1:20,000) is essential for the recreational boater attempting to navigate the Broken Group.
Chart 3671 (Barkley Sound) is not of adequate scale for safe navigation of the maze of islands, islets, rocks and reefs that make up the Broken Group.

Note: Eyeball navigation, rather than over-reliance on GPS and chart plotters, is advised when exploring the Broken Group. Plan to enter or leave these anchorages at LW, except 12.5 "Jaques-Jarvis Lagoon."

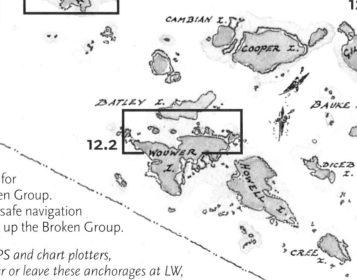

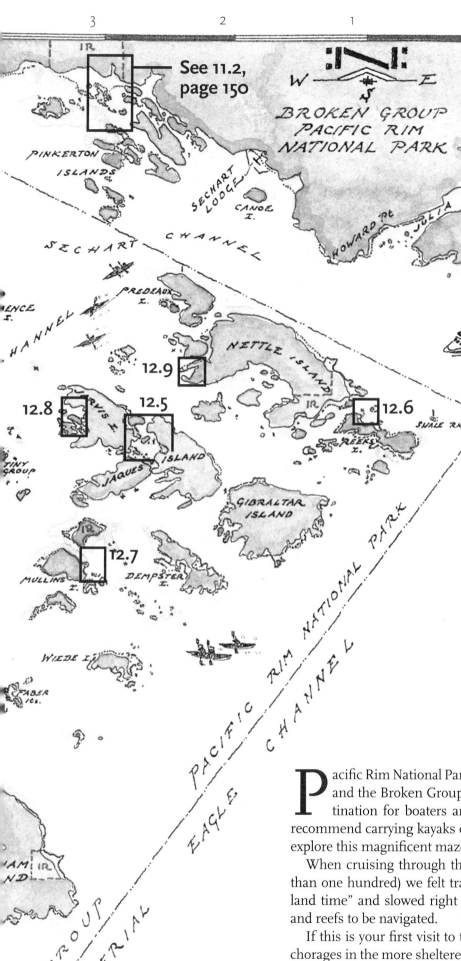

See 11.2,
page 150

FEATURED DESTINATIONS

P acific Rim National Park is comprised of the West Coast Trail, Long Beach, and the Broken Group, which has become the favourite West Coast destination for boaters and kayakers from BC and Washington State. We recommend carrying kayaks onboard because they offer one of the best ways to explore this magnificent maze of islands and islets.

When cruising through the multitude of low-lying islands and islets (more than one hundred) we felt transported into another world. We switched to "island time" and slowed right down—a sensible reaction given the many rocks and reefs to be navigated.

If this is your first visit to the Broken Group, it might be wise to explore anchorages in the more sheltered waters before graduating to the open and rugged outer islands, where you will discover sea caves, steaming blow holes and wave-sculpted rocks.

The Broken Group is also home to more than two hundred species of birds and a variety of wildlife. Those who stay a little longer into the season may be rewarded with an abundance of chanterelle mushrooms, or so we've read.

Not to be used for navigation.
Depth contours are approximate and in metres.

✤ 48°53.15'N 125°22.26'W

CHARTS 3670.

APPROACH From the W via the marked channel between Clarke and Benson islands or from the E out of Coaster Channel. Best entered at LW.

ANCHOR

(A) In the NE off the Clarke Island shore or in the wind line between Clarke and Owen islands to keep the boat steady. Anchor in depths of 4–8 m (13–26 ft) in sand and mud.

(B) In a bight off Benson Island's E shore with protection from NW winds for two boats on short scope. A stern anchor is advised if staying overnight. Anchor in depths of 4–8 m (13–26 ft) in sand and gravel.

Note: Both anchorages are exposed to some swell at HW, when the surrounding rocks are awash.

Not to be used for navigation.
Depth contours are approximate and in metres.

The anchorage between Clark and Owen islands affords views of the setting sun to the NW. The sand beach on Clark Island's NE shore is one of the loveliest in the Broken Group and popular with kayaking groups. The site of one of the many summer villages of the Tseshaht First Nations, Benson Island's anchorage, off the delightful white sand-and-shell beach, proved to be a real treat. Huge Pacific blue mussels cling to the rocks and the tide pools are filled with fascinating sea life, including pulsating, emerald green "giant sea anemones."

Well-kept trails lead through a grassy meadow where a hotel and summer residence were once located to a second beach, then over the top of the island. Convenient root-steps between the salal bushes provide access to the windy W side, which is exposed to the full brunt of the open Pacific. Here a steep cliff overlooks a rock-and-stone beach where heavy surf can be seen surging and breaking on the jagged boulders.

BATLEY AND WOUWER ISLANDS 12.2

CHARTS 3670.

APPROACH From the E between Batley and Wouwer islands. A group of islets and rocks form a nook off the Wouwer Island shore.

ANCHOR

(A) In the nook with a stern anchor or stern line ashore. Westerly winds can blow through the gap.

(B) In a bight between the reef and rocks and the shore.

Note: These anchorages afford moderate protection from the NW and SE and should be considered temporary spots in anything other than settled conditions. Anchor in 3–8 m (10–26 ft).

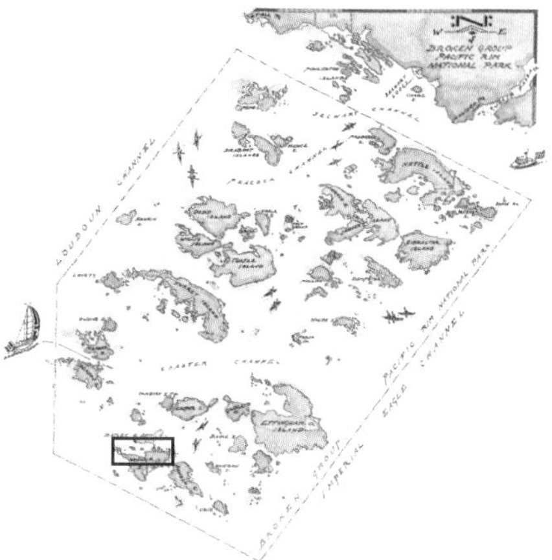

✲ 48°52.00'N 125°21.09'W

Two small but convenient anchorages can be found between the rocks and reefs of windswept Batley and Wouwer islands—one of the best spots to observe the large sea lion rookery from a safe distance. On our exploratory row to observe the rookery, used by a mix of Steller's and California sea lions, we were fascinated to find that they come in a variety of colours, from shiny black and charcoal to brown and ginger. Mothers with pups lazed and sunned on the smooth lower rocks, while majestic bulls struck regal poses on prominent rocky platforms. Their full-throated barking travels easily across water so be prepared for a noisy—and sometimes smelly—stay.

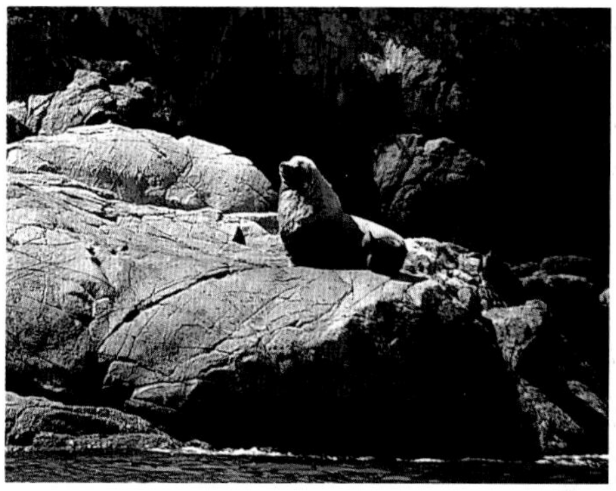

A majestic sea lion offers a full-throated bark.

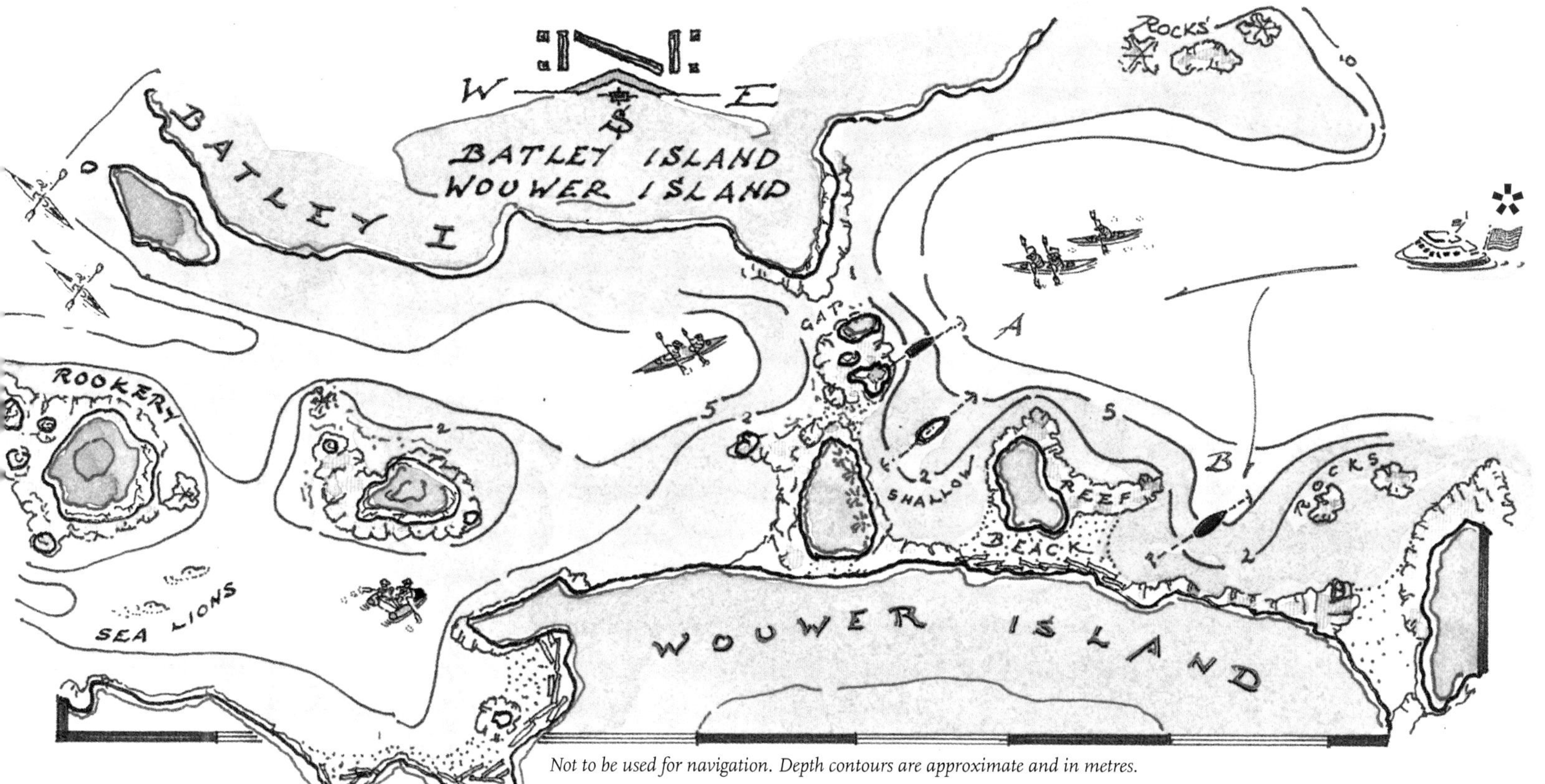

Not to be used for navigation. Depth contours are approximate and in metres.

Cruisers find Effingham Bay a pleasant spot to drop the hook.

CHARTS 3670.

APPROACH

(A) From the E out of Coaster Channel.

(B) From the S between Gilbert Island and a reef off Effingham Island with a minimum charted depth of 3 m (10 ft). The passage in lies midway between an islet and the Effingham Island shore.

ANCHOR In 8–16 m (26–53 ft) with good holding in mud and gravel. This commodious bay can accommodate a number of boats in good depths with ample swinging room. Open to winds and light swell from the W, although good protection from the SE.

✶ 48°52.63'N 125°19.07'W

Effingham Bay is a pleasant, protected spot to drop the hook and use as a base for exploring neighbouring islands and islets in the Broken Group. It has become a favourite destination for cruisers and kayakers exploring the West Coast of Vancouver Island.

Effingham Island is the largest in the Broken Group with cliffs as high as 100 m (330 ft) at Meares Bluff. Below the bluff is a sea arch and on the southern shore of the island a sea cave— both are navigable by dinghy or kayak. A 20-minute trail across the island begins at the SE end of the bay. The trail leads to a large midden near the centre of the island's eastern shore.

Not to be used for navigation. Depth contours are approximate and in metres.

12.4 JOES BAY ANCHORAGE

CHARTS 3670.

APPROACH (A) From the N between Dodd and Chalk islands at LW.

(B) From the E between Chalk and Turtle islands at LW. Watch for the rocks that extend off Walsh Island.

ANCHOR Protected by Dodd, Chalk, Turtle, Willis and Walsh islands, this commodious anchorage provides all-weather protection and plenty of swinging room in depths of 5–10 m (16–33 ft) with good holding in sand and mud.

Note: Strong winds will blow across the anchorage but chop does not build up.

✳ (A) 48°55.45'N 125°19.24'W

The morning dawns mirror-calm.

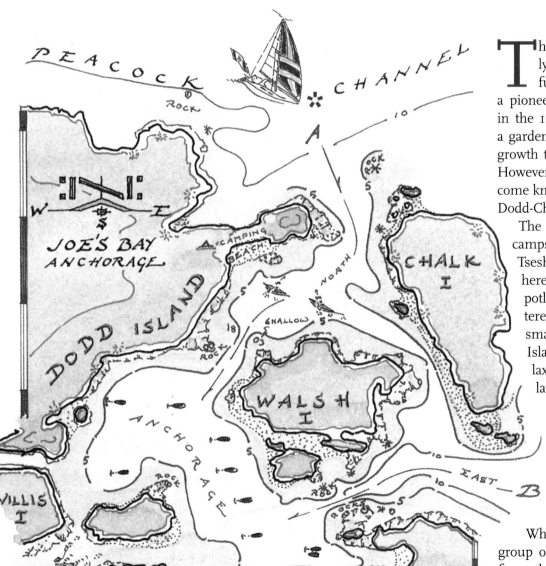

The small bay to the SE is officially named Joes Bay after colourful "Salal Joe" (Joe Wilkowski), a pioneer who lived on Dodd Island in the 1960s and 1970s and created a garden among the magnificent old-growth trees that is still visible today. However, the entire anchorage has become known as Joes Bay anchorage or Dodd-Chalk islands anchorage.

The impressive midden near the campsite was a key village site and Tseshaht Wolf Rituals were held here; later it became a site for potlatch ceremonies. The sheltered campground is fronted by a small shell beach that faces Turtle Island—a wonderful setting to relax and contemplate the intricate layers of West Coast history.

While at anchor we witnessed a group of sea lions and seals feeding from the many "herring balls" they were creating.

Not to be used for navigation.
Depth contours are approximate and in metres.

"JAQUES-JARVIS LAGOON" 12.5

CHARTS 3670.

APPROACH With caution as a bar with a minimum depth of approximately 1 m (3.3 ft) lies in the entrance. (With 2 m (6.6 ft) of draft, we found plenty of room to enter and exit two hours before and after HW.) Proceed to the inner basin leaving the rocks to the W.

ANCHOR In 4–6 m (13–20 ft) with good holding in black, sticky mud. All-weather protection for two or three boats on short scope.

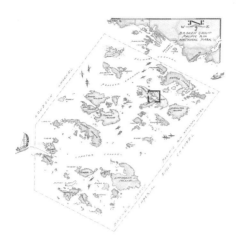

✽ (48°55.59'N 125°16.64'W

Encircled by lush forest with branches tipping the water's edge, Jaques and Jarvis islands safeguard a beautifully protected lagoon that is rich in intertidal life and Native history. Stone-ring fish traps are still visible in the "Pool" between the islands. Although the anchorage is landlocked, a breeze from the W or SE makes this a pleasant spot to drop the hook on a hot, sunny day and explore the lagoon by dinghy or kayak. Tranquility at its best!

Tranquility at its best.

12.6 REEKS ISLAND

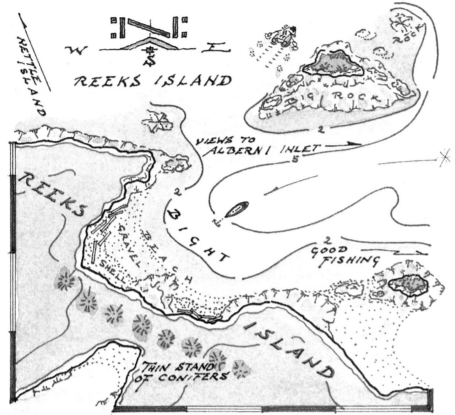

Not to be used for navigation. Depth contours are approximate and in metres.

CHARTS 3670.

APPROACH At LW from the E—round up carefully off the beach, between the rocks.

ANCHOR A one-boat bight with a thin line of conifers giving good protection from the W and moderate protection from the SE. Anchor in 4–8 m (13–26 ft) in sand and mud. The bight is exposed to some residual swell and wake from boats zipping through Sechart Channel.

The northeasternmost island in the Broken Group, club-shaped Reeks Island provides anchorage in a small bight and is ideal as a lunch or tea stop. Overnighting in settled weather is also possible. Good fishing can be found near Swale Rock and the views out to Alberni Inlet are lovely.

12.6 ✽ 48°55.56'N 125°13.96
12.7 ✽ 48°54.48'N 125°17.19'W

12.7 MULLINS ISLAND

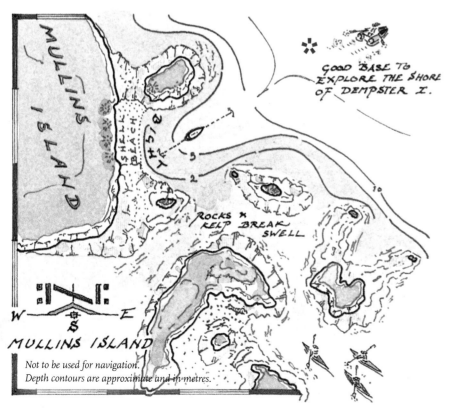

Not to be used for navigation. Depth contours are approximate and in metres.

CHARTS 3670.

APPROACH The passage into the anchorage should be navigated with caution at LW.

ANCHOR A one-boat picnic nook with good holding in 6–8 m (20–26 ft) in gravel and mud, with moderate protection from the W. If staying overnight in settled weather, drop a stern anchor or take a stern line to shore.

This cozy one-boat nook tucked between rocks and kelp provides a handy base for exploring Dempster Island by dinghy or kayak. Anchored off the shell beach, *Dreamspeaker* was protected from swell by the extensive kelp beds that surround the rocks.

JARVIS ISLAND 12.8

CHARTS 3670.

APPROACH At LW—the anchorage is bigger than the chart suggests.

ANCHOR In depths of 6–8 m (20–26 ft) with good holding in gravel and shell. If staying the night, this one-boat nook requires a stern line to a convenient tree. Good protection from the SW and moderate protection from the W.

Asecluded haven for just one boat, the narrow nook on Jarvis Island's W offers all the essentials—good holding, a convenient tree to tie a stern line, and a short trail to the neighbouring cove and grassy marsh where we picked crisp sea asparagus that added zest to our seafood salad.

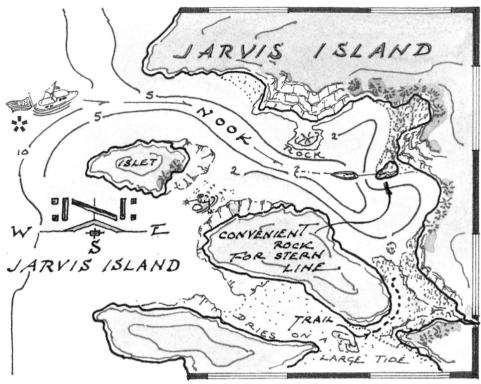

Not to be used for navigation. Depth contours are approximate and in metres.

12.8 ✿ 49°55.62'N 125°17.62'W
12.9 ✿ 48°55.85'N 125°16.31'W

NETTLE ISLAND 12.9

CHARTS 3670.

APPROACH From the W at LW. Enter between the islet and rock that extends N from the tip of Nettle Island.

ANCHOR In 6–8 m (20–26 ft) with good holding in mud and sand. The nook is protected from southeasterlies but will also be protected in light W to NW winds. If overnighting in settled weather a stern line to the large rock is advised.

Tucked into the western tip of Nettle Island and sheltered by an islet and rocky outcrop, "Nettle Nook" offers peace and protection with pleasant views of the mountains that rim Barkley Sound. The island is the largest of a group that includes Reeks, Erin and Prideaux islands. Until the 1940s, the reserve to the SE was a Tseshaht village that was used while its people fished for salmon and cod.

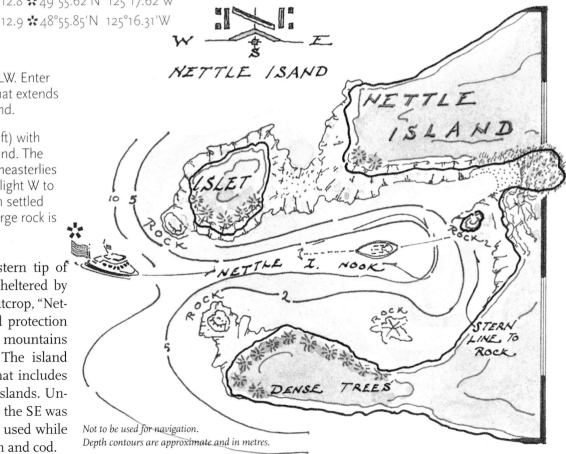

Not to be used for navigation. Depth contours are approximate and in metres.

12.10 TURRET ISLAND

CHARTS 3670.

APPROACH Best approached at LW from the SE or NW as indicated.

ANCHOR There is a selection of picnic spots between Lovett and Turret islands, and an overnight anchorage E of Nantes Island with moderate protection from the N and S. Fair holding in depths of 4–8 m (13–26 ft) in sand and mud.

A haven for kayakers and a picnic or overnight anchorage for boaters in fair weather, Turret, Trickett and Lovett islands form a landlocked and protected crescent of islets and reefs at LW. Turret Island supports old-growth Sitka spruce trees, with an especially magnificent example at its S end.

Parks information keeps visitors in the know.

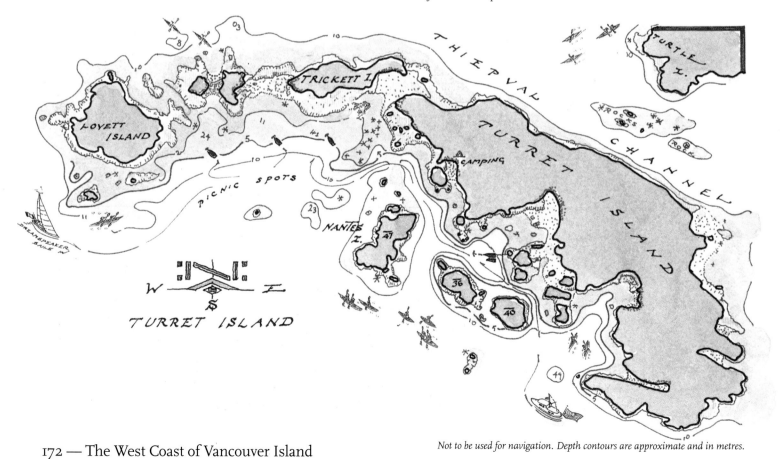

Not to be used for navigation. Depth contours are approximate and in metres.

Sailing in Coaster Channel.

12.11 "MENCE-BRABANT ISLANDS CHANNEL"

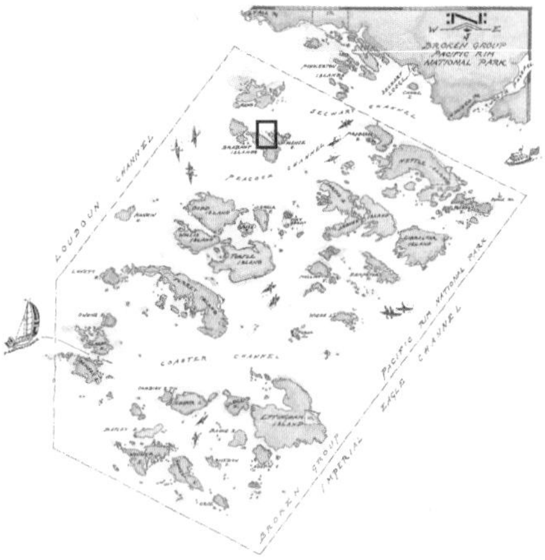

48°56.49'N 125°18.95'W

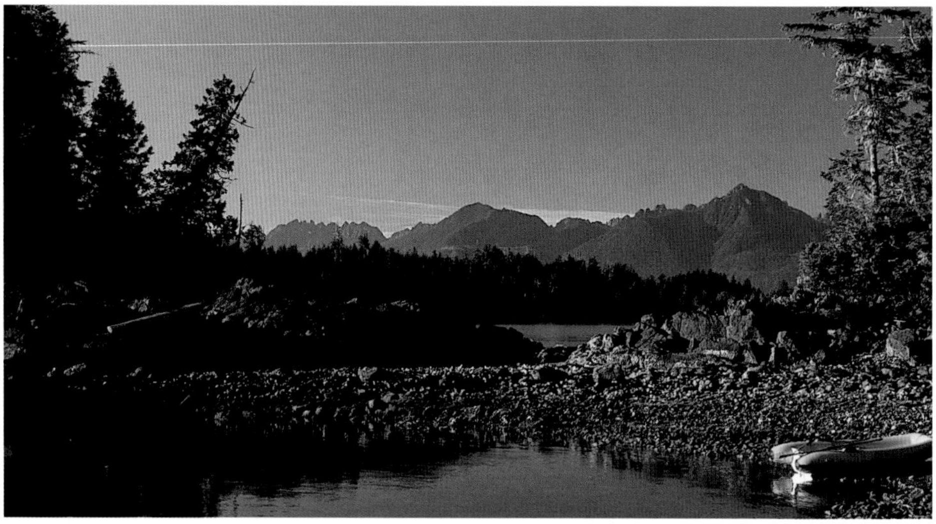

Looking toward Pipestem Inlet on a crisp, clear evening.

CHARTS 3670.

APPROACH From the W—round up adjacent to Mence Island and the rocky islet.

ANCHOR In the channel between the islands in 4–10 m (13–33 ft) with good holding in sand, shell and mud. Good protection from the SE and moderate protection from the NW. A stern anchor is advised.

Anchoring overnight in this magical spot completed our remarkable cruise through the Broken Group. While investigating the curved sand-and-shell beach, we discovered a man-made stone canoe launch, a large rock fish trap and the makings of a "clam garden." Oysters of various sizes grew in a cleared area that was divided into smaller sections by rows of large stones.

Our day here ended with a watercolour sunset while we munched on warm, freshly picked salal berries.

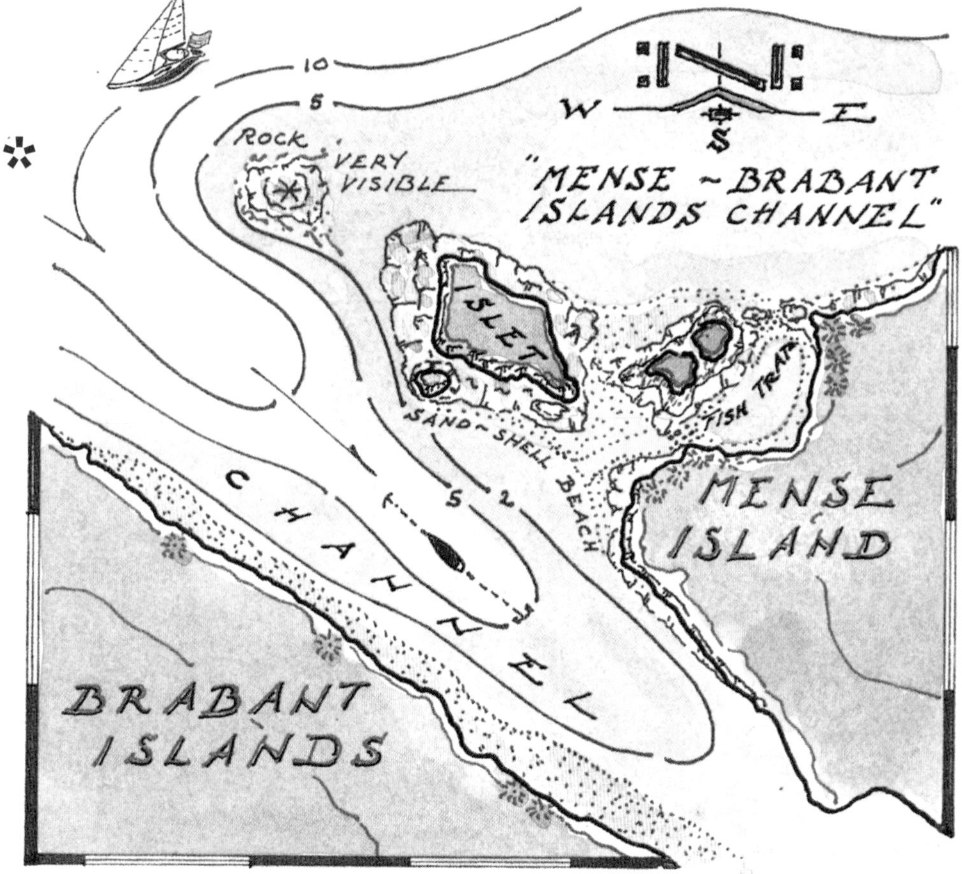

Not to be used for navigation. Depth contours are approximate and in metres.

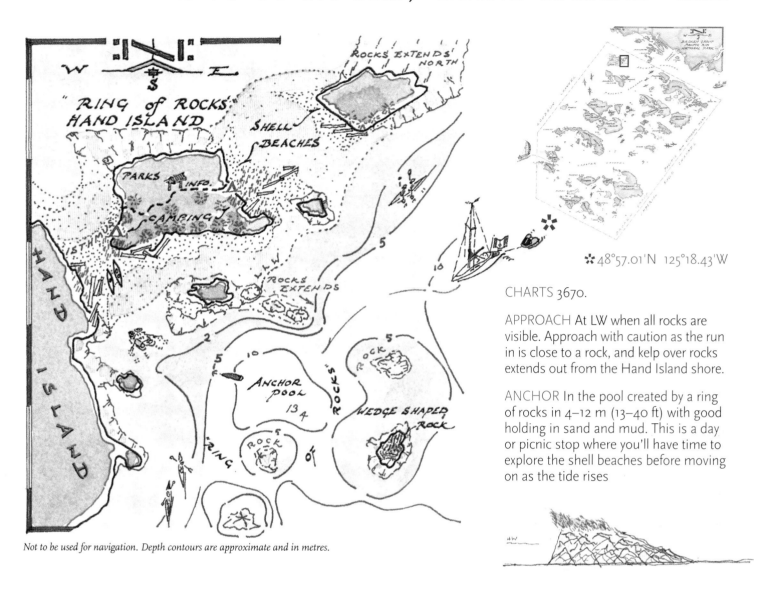

Not to be used for navigation. Depth contours are approximate and in metres.

✻ 48°57.01'N 125°18.43'W

CHARTS 3670.

APPROACH At LW when all rocks are visible. Approach with caution as the run in is close to a rock, and kelp over rocks extends out from the Hand Island shore.

ANCHOR In the pool created by a ring of rocks in 4–12 m (13–40 ft) with good holding in sand and mud. This is a day or picnic stop where you'll have time to explore the shell beaches before moving on as the tide rises

Misty morning surrounded by rocks.

Rocky Hand Island has a lagoon and beach on the N side and a midden on the small island off the NE corner—the remains of a former village site. It's hard to believe that in the early 1800s the island was home to a small summer trading post and a pioneering family. An un-maintained trail snakes through the middle of the island.

Popular with kayakers, the campsite is the closest for paddlers launching from Toquart Bay on the mainland and is usually dotted with multicoloured tents and kayaks. Spend a peaceful few hours exploring the rocks and inviting shell beaches, and celebrate your time in this magnificent Broken Group of islands and islets.

Chapter 13

JUAN DE FUCA STRAIT

The fog lifts and the sea sparkles—western approaches, Juan de Fuca Strait.

Sheringham Point—eastbound and nearly home.

Chapter 13
JUAN DE FUCA STRAIT

TIDES

Volume 5 and 6, Canadian Tide and Current Tables (for the W entrance).

Reference Ports: Port Renfrew, Sooke and Victoria

Secondary Ports: Neah Bay, on Port Renfrew; Becher Bay, on Sooke; Port Angeles WA, on Sooke

CURRENTS

Reference Stations: Juan de Fuca—West (for the W entrance), Juan de Fuca—East (for E entrance), Race Passage

WEATHER

Weather Channel VHF WX 3 Mt. Helmcken.

Areas: Juan de Fuca Strait. For coastal conditions listen for the reports from Pachena Point, Carmanah Point, Cape Flattery, Sheringham Point and Race Rocks.

Note: The W entrance is between Carmanah Point and Cape Flattery. The E entrance is between Race Rocks and Angeles Point. Due to the funnelling effect, the strength of the wind at the entrances is usually the forecast maximum.

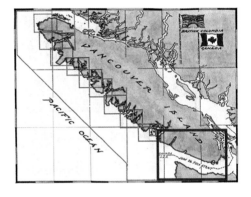

CAUTIONARY NOTES

Timing is key for a smooth transit E or W in Juan de Fuca Strait. Go with the current; avoid wind-against-current situations, which can produce potentially dangerous short, steep seas. Stay clear of the heavily-used major shipping lanes. Avoid travelling when fog is predicted.

The Vancouver Island shoreline of Juan de Fuca Strait and the strait's western approaches make up the West Coast's longest stretch of unbroken coastline, where safe shelter is scarce. The five lighthouses in the 75 nautical miles between Cape Beale and Race Rocks attest to the potential dangers here.

In the summer months the challenges on this passage are time, distance and a suitable weather window. Most boaters plan the passage from Bamfield to Sooke in one day. Bamfield (11.5) is a popular departure point with convenient fuel, provisions and communications.

If the forecast is for W to NW winds, consider a dawn departure from Bamfield, exiting Barkley Sound via Trevor Channel and aiming to round Cape Beale at HW. Ride the six hours of the ebbing coastal current SE to Juan de Fuca Strait's western entrance. As the W wind builds, you are now positioned to take advantage of the eastward-flooding current.

When these conditions align, you can expect a memorable Juan de Fuca passage because everything is in your favour. By late afternoon the westerly wind should have built considerably at Sheringham Point—and it's time to prepare for the run NE into Sooke Harbour (13.3). Anchor or find moorage at the public wharf or marina.

Alternatively, anchor in Becher Bay (13.4) before rounding Race Rocks en route to Victoria (13.5) where there is an array of options for downtown moorage.

On our journey E we departed mid-morning from the northern entrance to Dodger Channel (11.10), planning a two-day passage to Sooke. The NW winds were light and the fog closed in and, by following the depth contours on our chart, we found safe anchorage for the night at Port San Juan (13.1). The next morning, with the eastward-flooding current in our favour and the westerly wind building by noon, we surfed past Sheringham Point and sailed into Sooke Harbour.

Note: Travelling W to explore Barkley Sound and the Broken Group.

Early a.m., leaving Port Angeles (13.8) on an ebbing current in Juan de Fuca Strait and, ideally, an easterly wind. The 45 nautical miles to Neah Bay (13.6) should be an easy run. If a westerly wind does build, Pillar Point (13.7) will provide temporary shelter.

Neah Bay has moorage and a good anchorage. Explore its cultural attractions while waiting for favourable conditions for the 65-nautical mile hop to Ucluelet—the official customs port of entry on the west coast of Vancouver Island.

FEATURED DESTINATIONS

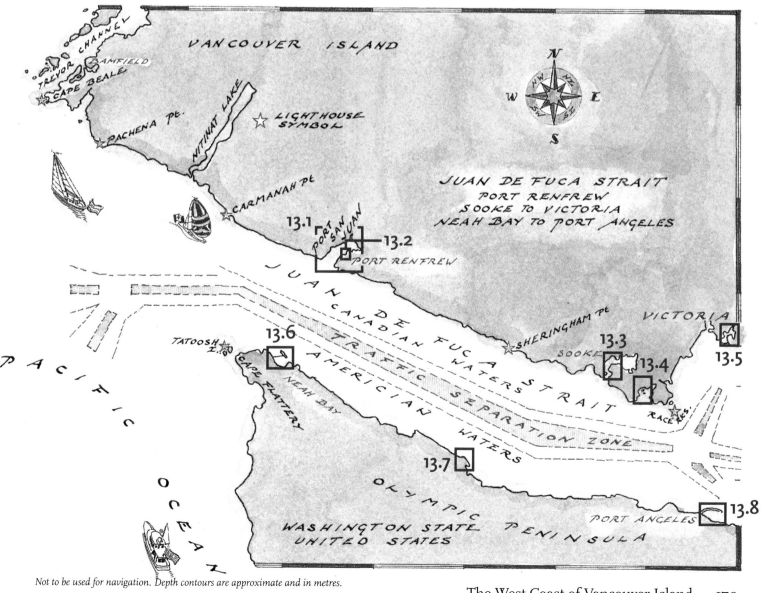

Not to be used for navigation. Depth contours are approximate and in metres.

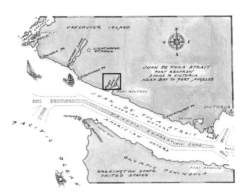

✤ 48°32.00'N 124°29.21'W

CHARTS 3647.

APPROACH On either side of the fairway buoy—give the rock- and kelp-strewn shoreline a wide berth.

ANCHOR Thrasher Cove—off a small sand and shell beach. Woods Nose—tuck into the NE nook. Seasonal rafts and floats limit swinging room. Snuggery Cove—see detail 13.2.

MARINA Browns Creek Marina, as marked on chart 3647, is in the NW corner at the head of the port and is suitable only for small, shallow-draft sport fishing boats.

Hammond Rocks loom out of the fog.

More of an inlet than a port, Port San Juan is open to SW winds and swells from Juan de Fuca Strait, but has a few spots to anchor in moderate weather. Our choice is the small anchorage off Thrasher Cove's sandy beach, which is sheltered for landing your dinghy or kayak. The West Coast Trail passes through the cove and during the busy summer evenings, this strip of sand is occupied by an array of multicoloured tents. Hikers are up early to begin their West Coast trek or complete their adventure and return to Port Renfrew, leaving you alone (with the kayakers) to explore the many sea caves, the finest one located just north of Owen Point, behind Kellet Rock.

Note: Port San Juan is open to the SW and has only moderate holding in dead kelp over mud and sand.

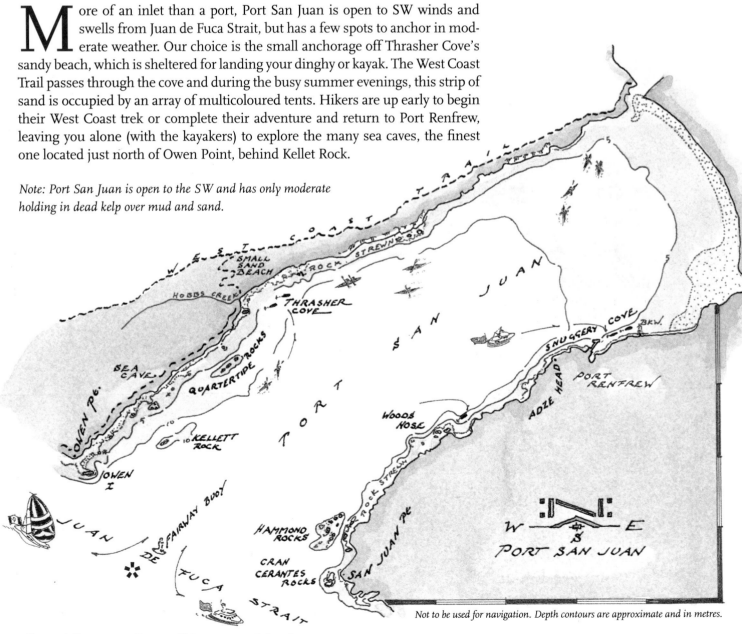

Not to be used for navigation. Depth contours are approximate and in metres.

PORT RENFREW
(SNUGGERY COVE)

CHARTS 3647.

APPROACH Snuggery Cove lies NE of Adze Head—the wharfhead is conspicuous.

ANCHOR Tuck in E of the wharfhead, parallel to the shoreline in 4–6 m (13–20 ft). Holding is moderate in a dead kelp, sand and mud bottom. Subject to swell.

MARINA Seasonal private floats lie south of the wharfhead in the cove.

✳ 48°33.38'N 124°25.36'W

The locally carved totem pole at Port Renfrew Hotel.

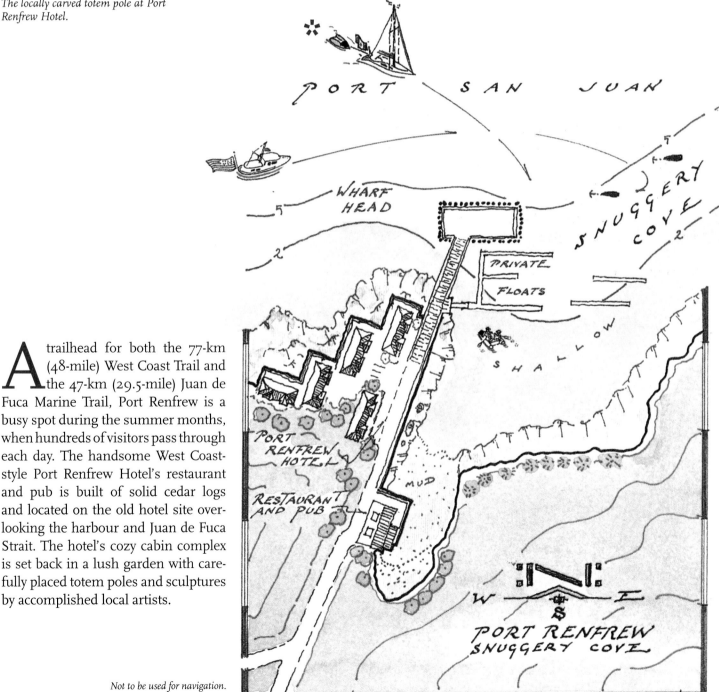

A trailhead for both the 77-km (48-mile) West Coast Trail and the 47-km (29.5-mile) Juan de Fuca Marine Trail, Port Renfrew is a busy spot during the summer months, when hundreds of visitors pass through each day. The handsome West Coast-style Port Renfrew Hotel's restaurant and pub is built of solid cedar logs and located on the old hotel site overlooking the harbour and Juan de Fuca Strait. The hotel's cozy cabin complex is set back in a lush garden with carefully placed totem poles and sculptures by accomplished local artists.

Not to be used for navigation.
Depth contours are approximate and in metres.

13.3 SOOKE HARBOUR—OUTER BASIN

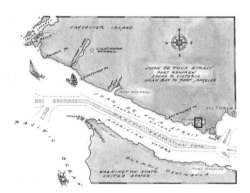

✿ 48°21.00'N 123°43.40'W

CHARTS 3411.

APPROACH Align the Outer Range (leading marks) to the W of Simpson Point. The light at the tip of Whiffin Spit is conspicuous. When the Inner Range (leading marks) is aligned, round the spit to port and head NW. A channel between the buoys leads to the marina and public wharf.

ANCHOR North of Whiffin Spit in 4–6 m (13–20 ft) with good holding in mud.

PUBLIC WHARF The public wharf provides extensive moorage and welcomes visitors– the wharfinger visits every evening to collect moorage fees.

MARINA Sooke Harbour Marina welcomes visitors but it is wise to pre-book: call 250-642-3236.

Note: On a large tide a current of up to 4 kts on both the ebb and flood swirls around the tip of the spit. Caution is required when entering or departing, especially at LW. The least depth over the bar between Simpson and Parsons points is 4.3 m (14 ft) but is subject to change.

S ooke Harbour has a tricky entrance and alignment of the Outer Range is crucial. When the Whiffin Spit light is abeam, make a hard turn to port to align the Inner Range and clear Grant Rocks. Protected anchorage can be found to the N of Whiffin Spit. This beautiful natural spit, with a light at its tip, protects Sooke Harbour from southerly and westerly winds, and separates it from Sooke Inlet. The harbour has extensive shallows, and care should be taken to stay within the marked channels while approaching the marina and public wharf.

Sooke Harbour Marina has a convenient visitor float on the outside. The channel leads NE from the marina to the public wharf, with its two sets of floats. Nearby Sooke town centre offers banks, supermarkets, a post office and a liquor store. Markus Wharfside Restaurant, just up from the public wharf, serves delicious Mediterranean cuisine and is a favourite with locals– reservations are recommended (250-642-3596).

Sooke Harbour House is an upscale choice for dinner—call 250-642-3421 if your boat budget permits.

Not to be used for navigation.
Depth contours are approximate and in metres.

CHARTS 3410.

APPROACH From the SE off Creyke Point. Campbell Cove and Wolf Island lie in the NW corner of Becher Bay. The channel between Lamb and Wolf islands is deep and free of obstructions.

ANCHOR In Campbell Cove N of Creyke Point. Stay clear of a rock in the centre of the bay. Better anchorage is available in Murder Bay, W of Wolf Island or in the cove on the NE shore of the island. Campbell Cove is exposed to the east. Of the three anchorages, the cove to the NE of Wolf Island is the most protected. Good holding in sand and mud in 2–5 m (6.5–16 ft).

MARINA Becher Bay Marina (250-642-3816) has limited guest moorage, maximum length 12 m (40 ft). Reservations a must. The marina has a café, washrooms and shower facilities.

LAUNCH At the marina.

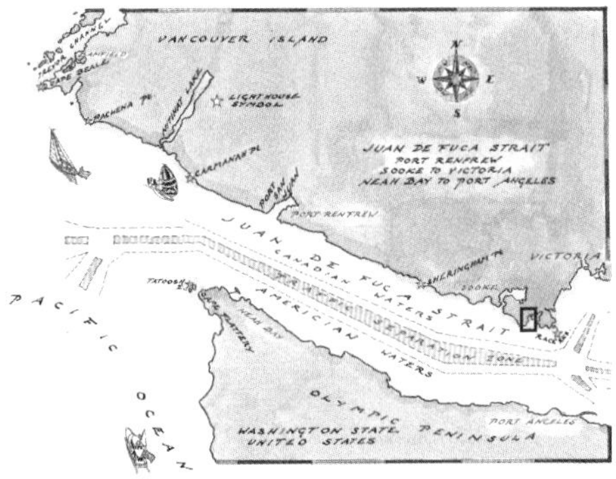

48°19.51'N 123°27.79'W

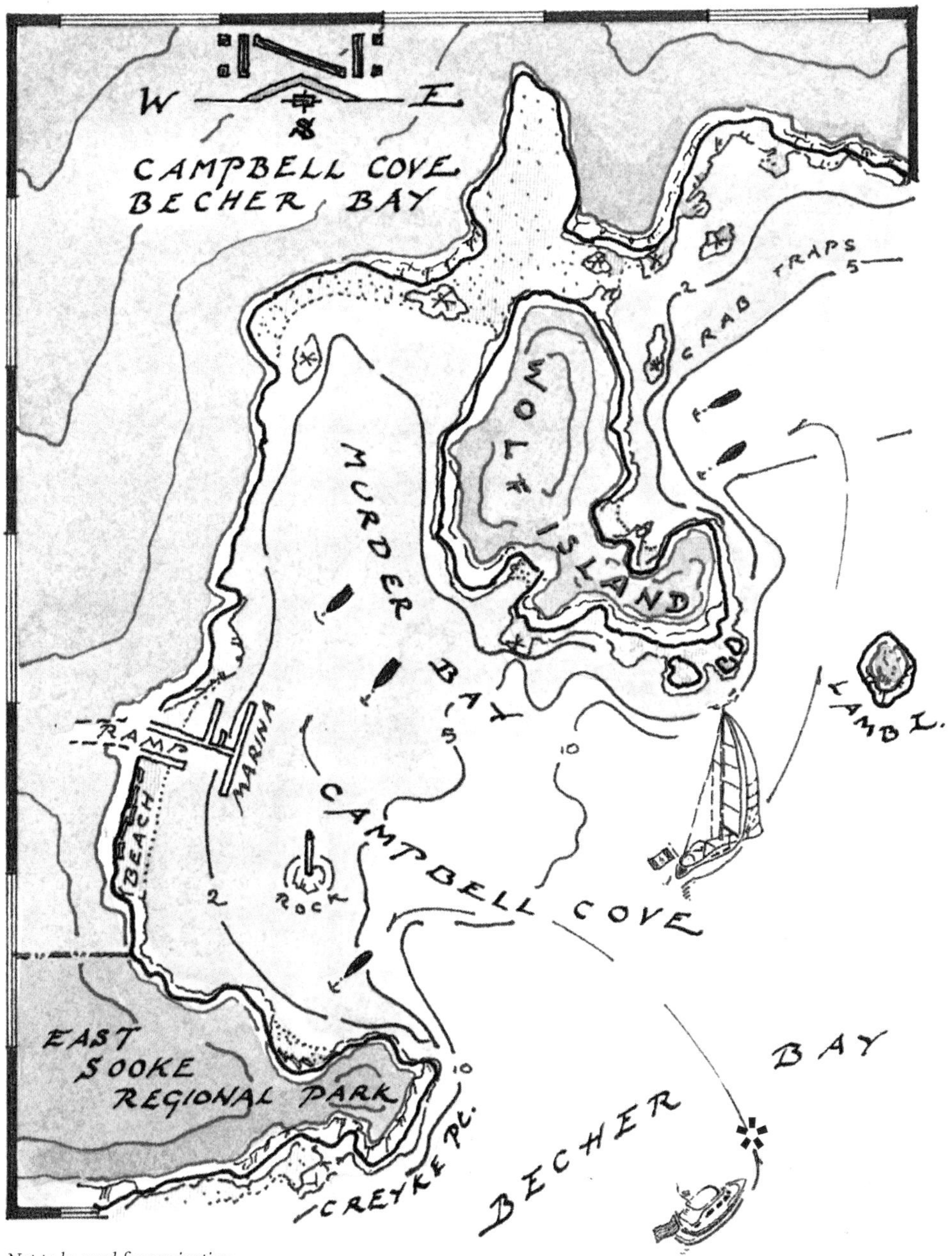

Not to be used for navigation.
Depth contours are approximate and in metres.

Becher Bay is less challenging to enter than Sooke Harbour, especially in foggy weather. Boaters looking for an easy overnight anchorage while en route to or from the West Coast of Vancouver Island may prefer Becher Bay to Sooke Harbour. Anchorage in Campbell Cove is protected from prevailing westerlies, but watch for the large drying rock (sometimes marked) in the middle of the bay. There are also underwater obstructions south of the bay. You can dinghy over to the pocket beach at Creyke Point, where you can reach the Aylard Farm entrance to East Sooke Regional Park.

Murder Bay, west of Wolf Island, affords a good anchorage, although the swell from Juan de Fuca Strait can make it very uncomfortable. A safe and secluded two-boat anchorage can be found in an unnamed cove behind Wolf Island. This is a truly peaceful anchorage frequently used by boats returning from Barkley Sound.

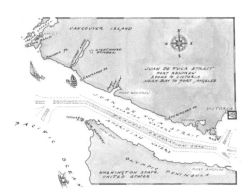

✵ 48°24.73'N 123°27.79'W

The Seattle Express *approaches Ogden Point.*

Dreamspeaker, Tink *and* Anne *below the Empress Hotel.*

Float plane activity is constant.

Your welcoming sign at the entrance to Victoria Harbour will be a classic-style light on the Ogden Point breakwater, often backed by an imposing cruise liner. The outer portion of the harbour serves as a commercial seaport, with the McLoughlin fuel terminal to port and the big ship docks and warehouses to starboard. West Bay opens to the northwest.

Beyond Shoal Point the Inner Harbour extends eastward, revealing comfortable urban surroundings. A floatplane operation zone extends from Shoal Point to Laurel Point, and planes take off and land regularly. The extensive public wharf at Erie Street has a fuel jetty, and floats and houseboats extend along the southern shore.

Once through the passage between Songhees and Laurel points, boaters enter James Bay and the majestic old harbour of Victoria. The harbour extends north beyond the twin lifting road/rail bridges at Johnson Street, allowing commercial and local pleasure craft into the Upper Harbour.

Victoria, British Columbia's capital and oldest city, is a wonderful mix of English charm and West Coast style. The BC Legislature Buildings lend a gothic air to the southern end of James Bay. Here you will find the Empress Wharf, opposite the famous, ivy-covered Fairmont Empress Hotel.

The Alpine Florist and Food Market at Fort and Blanshard streets offers a good selection of basic groceries, fruits and vegetables, as well as hot snacks and lunches to take out. The BC Liquor Store is located in the Bay Centre. Thrifty Foods, a full supermarket, is a good 20-minute walk away at Simcoe and Menzies streets. Victoria has a wonderful selection of mouthwatering bakeries, cafés and bistros and restaurants for every palette. Both Market and Bastion Squares are worth visiting for their mix of interesting shops and craft vendors. Charts are sold at Crown Publications on Ontario Street and at Bosun's Locker on Johnson Street, which also offers a yacht chandlery. Stock your on-board library at Munro's Books on Government Street.

Pick up the "Kids' Guide to Victoria" and "Gardens of the Pacific" at the visitor information centre on the corner of Wharf and Government streets; a visit to the Royal BC Museum is a must. Your stay in Victoria might not feel complete without an afternoon tea experience. The Fairmont Empress Tea Lobby serves traditional teatime fare, while Point Ellice House is a 15-minute ferry ride from the Inner Harbour and offers high tea and light lunches on the croquet lawn.

CHARTS 3412.

APPROACH A patrolled traffic separation scheme is in place between the Outer and Inner Harbour. Enter the Outer Harbour between the Ogden Point breakwater and Macaulay Point. The Middle Harbour extends E from Shoal Point and the Inner Harbour E of Laurel Point. The Upper Harbour lies N of Johnson Street Bridge, a lift bridge. The bridge monitors VHF channel 12—9:00 a.m. to 4:00 p.m. and 6:00 p.m. to midnight.

PUBLIC WHARF Extensive public moorage is available at Fisherman's Wharf in the Outer Harbour, and at the Empress Wharf and Wharf Street public wharf in the Inner Harbour. You'll find friendly staff, ice, showers and laundry facilities located south of the Wharf Street floats.

CUSTOMS A designated customs float is situated below the wharf manager's office at the Wharf Street public dock with 21 m (70 ft) of moorage on either side. There is a direct phone line to Canada Border Services Agency on the float.

Notes: A float plane operation zone lies between Shoal and Laurel points. A strobe beacon on Berens Island is activated when an aircraft is intending to land or take off. Victoria Harbour Ferry operates a fleet of tour and transportation ferries and monitors VHF channel 67. Anchoring is prohibited inside the Ogden Point breakwater unless directed by the harbour master. If you require information or assistance, harbour patrol monitors VHF channel 66A and is available to guide you to an appropriate berth.

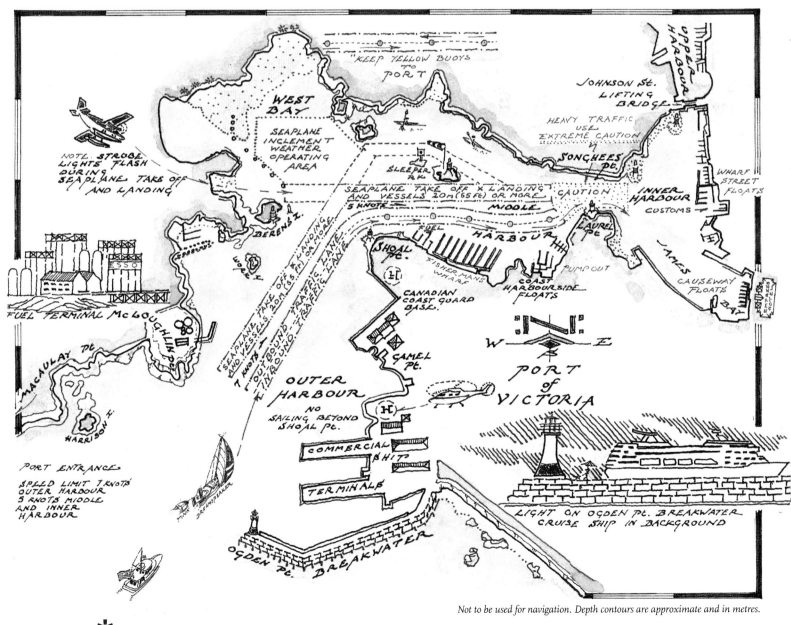

Not to be used for navigation. Depth contours are approximate and in metres.

The shipping lanes in Juan de Fuca Strait are heavily used—stay clear!

NEAH BAY, WASHINGTON STATE 13.6

CHARTS 3606. 18484 US (detail).

APPROACH N of the lighted port-hand (green) buoy. Enter mid-channel between Baadah Point and Waadah Island. The marina breakwater and community are conspicuous along the shoreline.

ANCHOR W of the breakwater. Holding good in sand and mud in depths of 6–12 m (20–40 ft). Protected from all weather except E-NE winds which are rare in summer.

MARINA Makah Marina (260-645-3012). Guest moorage is managed by the Big Salmon Resort April 1–September 30 (260-645-2374). They also monitor VHF 68. Power and water on the docks. Showers are available.

CUSTOMS Neah Bay is not a US customs port of entry but US boaters with I-68s or Nexus cards can call in from Neah Bay.

FUEL Gas and diesel available at the marina fuel dock.

N eah Bay is the most westerly sheltered anchorage in Juan de Fuca Strait. The highlight of a stop at Neah Bay, besides the well-maintained marina and grocery store, is the Makah Cultural and Research Center, which is housed in a long wooden building with a wide sloping roof. Recognized as the Makah Nation's finest tribal museum, the centre welcomes visitors to experience the life of the Makah people as it was more than five hundred years ago. The collection of some sixty thousand artifacts was uncovered from an archeological dig at Ozette, south of Neah Bay, where a mudslide destroyed a village, preserving everything it covered. The museum's notable Ozette exhibit shows only a small portion of artifacts from the dig and includes whaling, sealing and fishing gear, carvings, basketry and other tools. It also houses a full-sized replica longhouse and four cedar dugout canoes.

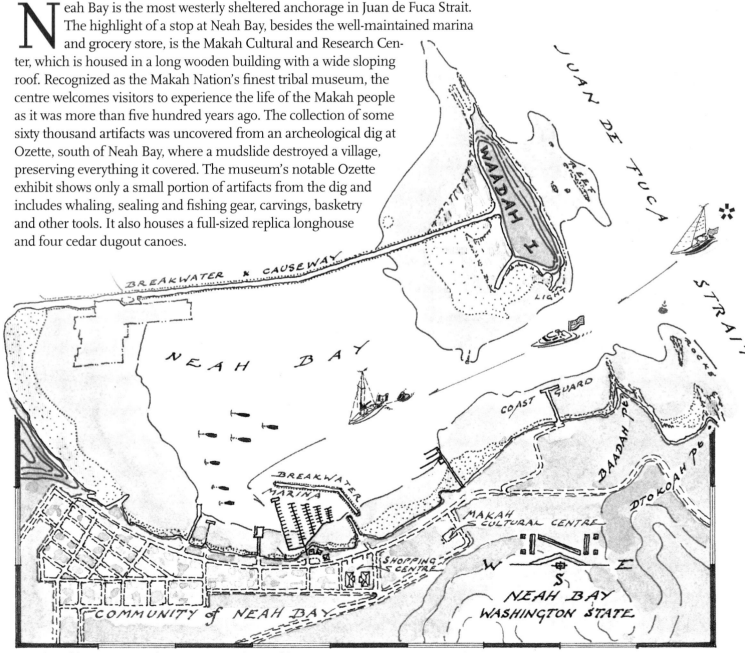

Not to be used for navigation. Depth contours are approximate and in metres.

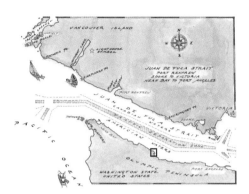

✵ 48°12.93'N 124°05.64'W

CHARTS 3606.

APPROACH From the NE with a sharp eye on the depth sounder. Round up off the sand spit or E of "The Pillars."

ANCHOR As close behind the pillars as possible to escape wind and swell. Holding is good in sticky mud and sand. Protected from the heavy W swell and winds, but exposed to E-NE winds, which are rare in summer months.

Note: The Pysht River delta silt shifts continuously.

Dramatic sandstone pillars mark a safe and convenient anchorage. Elsie Hulsizer photo.

Those who question this spot as a good anchorage, then try it, are converted. This overnight stop east of Port Angeles is a safe and convenient anchorage for boaters travelling to the West Coast of Vancouver Island from points south; from Seattle you can reach Barkley Sound in two days.

Tucked into a protected hook, this delightful spot is sheltered from W winds and ocean swells. Views range from the dramatic twin sandstone pillars across the tidal flats and marshland to the Pysht River. When the tide permits, a dinghy trip up the calm river is worthwhile. At LW walk barefoot along the driftwood-strewn sand spit and tidal flats—it's a beachcomber's delight.

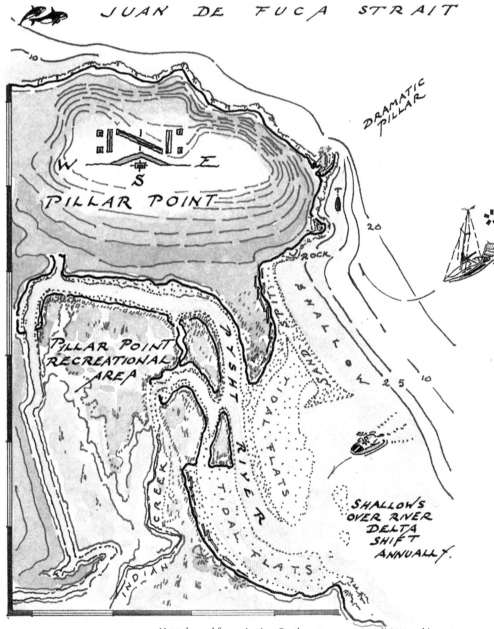

Not to be used for navigation. Depth contours are approximate and in metres.

Port Angeles, tucked south of Ediz Hook, is a natural deepwater port and a substantial small city. It is also the US Customs Port of Entry on Juan De Fuca Strait. Customs officers, upon prior arrangement (360-457-4311) will meet boats at the downtown City Pier or at Port Angeles Boat Haven.

Downtown Port Angeles, with its funky sixties feel, is well worth a visit. It is a good rendezvous spot, with the terminus for the *Coho* car and passenger ferry. Victoria Express Ferries also has daily sailings (passengers only) to Victoria and Friday Harbor.

The best way to visit the downtown shops, cafés and restaurants is to tie up at the City Pier and stroll into town. Or if you moor at the Boat Haven and provisioning is on your to-do list, consider taking a taxi to the downtown shopping centre which has a great supermarket and wine store.

CHARTS 3606. 18468 US (detail).
APPROACH From the NE close to the starboard-hand (red) buoy off the tip of Ediz Hook. The tower roof at the tip of the City Pier tends to shine in the daylight and is conspicuous.
ANCHOR E of the City Pier. The anchorage is quite rolly in strong westerly winds and is exposed to the E. A better anchorage can be found off the City Park, west of the ferry dock. Depth and holding not recorded.
CITY PIER The two outside floats have good depths but the two inner floats are more suitable for shallow-draft boats. Boats to 12 m (40 ft) only.
MARINA Port Angeles Boat Haven is open all year (360-457-4505) and has visitor moorage on the N side of F dock—rafting is permitted. Power and water on the docks. Sewage pump-out, marine repairs and haul out available.

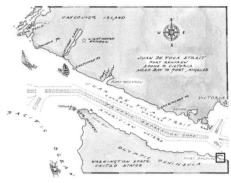

✼48°08.53'N 123°23.45'W

FUEL Gas and diesel at the Boat Haven fuel dock.
CUSTOMS Port Angeles is the only US Customs port of entry on the Juan de Fuca Washington shore. Call 360-457-4311.

Note: Port Angeles is a substantial port with large ships at anchor or manoeuvring. The harbour serves as a coast guard and pilot station. Keep clear of military and commercial shipping.

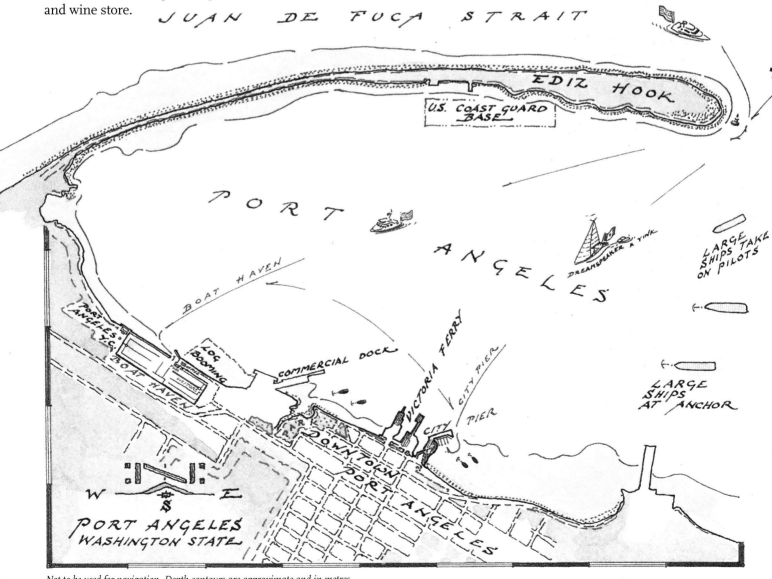

Not to be used for navigation. Depth contours are approximate and in metres.

SELECTED READINGS

Andersen, Marnie. *Women of the West Coast. Then and Now.* Sidney BC: Sand Dollar Press, 1993

Baron, Nancy and John Acorn. *Birds of Coastal British Columbia.* Edmonton AB: Lone Pine Publishing, 1997

Clark, Lewis. *Wild Flowers of the Sea Coast in the Pacific Northwest.* Madeira Park, BC: Harbour Publishing, 2004

Douglass, Don and Reanne Hemingway-Douglass. *Exploring Vancouver Island's West Coast.* Anacortes, WA: Fine Edge Productions, 1999

Gazetas, Mary. *Around One More Point.* Surrey BC: TouchWood Editions, 2006

Hale, Robert. *Waggoner Cruising Guide.* Bellevue, WA: Weatherly Press. Updated and Published Annually

Hill, Beth. *The Remarkable World of Frances Barkley, 1769-1845.* Sidney BC: Gray's Publishing, 2006

Horsfield, Margaret. *Cougar Annie's Garden.* Nanaimo BC: Salal Books, 2000

Hulsizer, Elsie. *Voyages to Windward. Sailing Adventures on Vancouver Island's West Coast.* Madeira Park, BC: Harbour Publishing, 2005

Jones, Laurie. *Nootka Sound Explored. A Westcoast History.* Campbell River, BC: Ptarmigan Press, 1991

Kimantus, John. *The Wild Coast. A Kayaking, Hiking and Recreation Guide for North and West Vancouver Island.* Whitecap Books, 2005

Pacific Yachting's Marina Guide and Boaters Blue Pages: Complimentary Guide to BC Marinas and Marine Services updated and published annually by Pacific Yachting Magazine.

Sept, Duane J. *The Beachcomber's Guide to Seashore Life in the Pacific Northwest.* Madeira Park, BC: Harbour Publishing, 2008.

Spalding, David A.E. *Whales of the West Coast.* Madeira Park, BC: Harbour Publishing, 1999

Turner, Nancy J. *Food Plants of Coastal First Peoples.* Vancouver BC: UBC Press, 1995

Walbran, John T. *British Columbia Coast Names, 1592-1902.* Vancouver BC: Douglas & McIntyre, 1971

Watmough, Don. *Cruising Guide to the West Coast of Vancouver Island. Cape Scott to Sooke including Barkley Sound.* Shoreline WA: Evergreen Pacific Publishing Ltd, 1998

INDEX

THE DREAMSPEAKER SERIES

BY ANNE & LAURENCE YEADON-JONES

A COMPREHENSIVE SET OF
CRUISING GUIDES TO
THE COASTAL WATERS
OF THE PACIFIC NORTHWEST

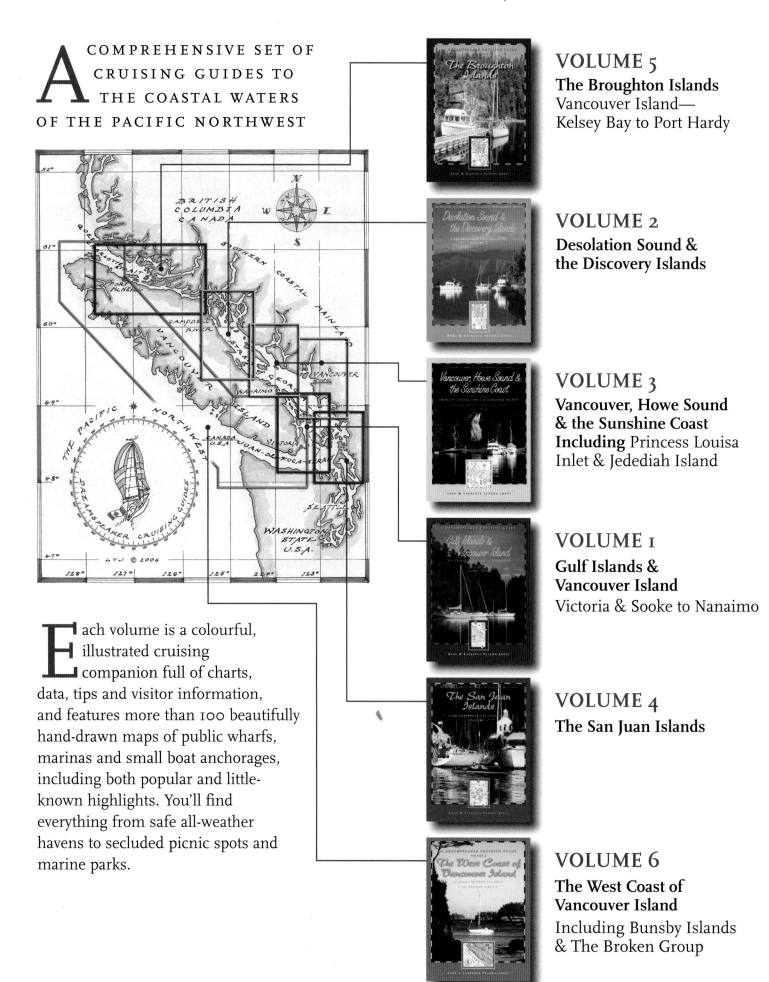

VOLUME 5
The Broughton Islands
Vancouver Island—
Kelsey Bay to Port Hardy

VOLUME 2
**Desolation Sound &
the Discovery Islands**

VOLUME 3
**Vancouver, Howe Sound
& the Sunshine Coast
Including** Princess Louisa
Inlet & Jedediah Island

VOLUME 1
**Gulf Islands &
Vancouver Island**
Victoria & Sooke to Nanaimo

VOLUME 4
The San Juan Islands

VOLUME 6
**The West Coast of
Vancouver Island**
Including Bunsby Islands
& The Broken Group

Each volume is a colourful,
illustrated cruising
companion full of charts,
data, tips and visitor information,
and features more than 100 beautifully
hand-drawn maps of public wharfs,
marinas and small boat anchorages,
including both popular and little-
known highlights. You'll find
everything from safe all-weather
havens to secluded picnic spots and
marine parks.